THE POWER OF
Latino
Leadership

*The future is
Latino/a*

Juana Bordas

SECOND EDITION
REVISED AND EXPANDED

THE POWER OF
Latino Leadership

CULTURE, INCLUSION, AND CONTRIBUTION

¡Ahora!

JUANA BORDAS

Berrett–Koehler Publishers, Inc.

Berrett-Koehler Publishers, Inc.
1333 Broadway, Suite 1000
Oakland, CA 94612-1921
Tel: (510) 817-2277
Fax: (510) 817-2278
www.bkconnection.com

ORDERING INFORMATION
Quantity sales. Special discounts are available on quantity purchases by corporations, associations, and others. For details, contact the "Special Sales Department" at the Berrett-Koehler address above.

Individual sales. Berrett-Koehler publications are available through most bookstores. They can also be ordered directly from Berrett-Koehler: Tel: (800) 929-2929; Fax: (802) 864-7626; www.bkconnection.com.

Orders for college textbook / course adoption use. Please contact Berrett-Koehler: Tel: (800) 929-2929; Fax: (802) 864-7626.

Distributed to the U.S. trade and internationally by Penguin Random House Publisher Services.

Berrett-Koehler and the BK logo are registered trademarks of Berrett-Koehler Publishers, Inc.

Printed in the United States of America

Berrett-Koehler books are printed on long-lasting acid-free paper. When it is available, we choose paper that has been manufactured by environmentally responsible processes. These may include using trees grown in sustainable forests, incorporating recycled paper, minimizing chlorine in bleaching, or recycling the energy produced at the paper mill.

Library of Congress Cataloging-in-Publication Data

Names: Bordas, Juana, author.
Title: The power of Latino leadership : culture, inclusion, and
  contribution / Juana Bordas.
Description: Second edition, revised and updated. | Oakland, CA :
  Berrett-Koehler Publishers, [2023] | Includes bibliographical references
  and index.
Identifiers: LCCN 2022041887 (print) | LCCN 2022041888 (ebook) | ISBN
  9781523004089 (paperback ; alk. paper) | ISBN 9781523004096 (pdf) | ISBN
  9781523004102 (epub) | ISBN 9781523004119 (audio)
Subjects: LCSH: Hispanic Americans. | Leadership.
Classification: LCC E184.S75 B6724 2023 (print) | LCC E184.S75 (ebook) |
  DDC 973/.0468—dc23/eng/20220902
LC record available at https://lccn.loc.gov/2022041887
LC ebook record available at https://lccn.loc.gov/2022041888

Second Edition
30 29 28 27 26 25 24 23   10 9 8 7 6 5 4 3 2 1

Cover designer: David Ter-Avanesyan
Interior illustration: Jorge Enciso: Design Motifs of Ancient Mexico (Dover).
Interior design and composition: Seventeenth Street Studios
Author photo: Judy Miranda

For the hundreds of thousands of Latino leaders who are uplifting their communities and building an inclusive society that cares for its people

For our young and emerging leaders who will fulfill the vision of Latino destino

And for the first US Latino/a president, who has already been born

Contents

Preface

MANY PEOPLE BELIEVE THAT the rising Latino influence is a recent phenomenon fueled by our growing demographics. It's true that the Latino population in the United States accounted for more than half of the population gain in the last decade. Today, 1 in 5 people in the United States is Latino. Our numbers are 62 million strong.[1] And tomorrow? By 2045, 1 in 4 Americans will be Latino.[2]

Most Latinos, however, understand that our advancement is not a recent occurrence. It has taken centuries. Our roots go back to before the United States was a nation. Hispanics were born of conquest and colonization. We are a fusion people—mainly the offspring of the Spanish conquistadores and the Indigenous people of this hemisphere. But many Latinos have African as well as European ancestors, such as from Germany or France, who also settled the Americas. Hispanics are a medley of cultures, languages, races, and nationalities. (In this book we will be using both *Hispanic* and *Latino*—keep reading to understand the distinction.)

In the past decade, since the first edition of this book was published, Latino impact in the United States has exploded! Today, we are emerging with a collective identity, embracing our culture and language, gaining economic and political clout, and expanding our global connections. These gains have only been possible because of the vision, contribution, and relentless activism of our leaders. They have built a legacy of inclusive community leadership, based on cultural values and traditions, that has as its purpose to uplift people. And yet the story of how Latino leaders have guided their people has not been fully told.

I aspire to make that contribution. *The Power of Latino Leadership* is the first book squarely focused on describing the principles and practices of how Latinos lead. It will support Latinos in being effective and powerful by leading from their cultural core and will infuse mainstream leadership with an inclusive community spirit that fosters contribution and service.

The concept of Latino power, however, warrants a new definition. Historically, power was hierarchical, the domain of the influential few, and associated with control and dominance. Most often, power has been found in the hands of White males. Latino power, on the other hand, has evolved from the community—it is the power of *We*—the power that people have to change their lives for the better.

Latino power is accessible to many people. Diffused power means leadership is not concentrated in only the hands of a few. Instead, Latino power is *leadership by the many*—the thousands of Latino leaders working every day in communities across the country. Julián Castro, the former mayor of San Antonio and a 2020 presidential candidate, follows this tradition: "I think that what our young people should understand is that they can be leaders in their own right in their own community—in their neighborhood, church, college, job, or career, wherever it is. That is more empowering than looking up to one person as the Latino leader."[3]

Latino power is rooted in history and tradition, an understanding that the past is the rich soil that nourishes tomorrow. Latinos owe a great debt to the leaders who have paved the way for our community to blossom. *The Power of Latino Leadership* acknowledges their contributions and delineates a path for continued advancement.

Latino power is now! In the 2020 presidential elections, 13 percent of eligible voters were Latinos, with a record 16.6 million voting—an increase of 31 percent over the 2016 presidential election. Additionally, Latinos live in several battleground states, including Arizona, Florida, Georgia, Pennsylvania, and Wisconsin, where their vote is a decisive factor.[4] Latino congressional representation has grown from nineteen members in 2001 to fifty-one after the 2022 midterm elections—an increase of 168 percent.[5]

And *Latino power is our futuro*, the promise and potential of youth. Today we are experiencing vast generational shifts as ten thousand Baby Boomers retire every day.[6] At the same time, in the general youth population millennials and Gen Zs are the most numerous in history. Projections show that by 2036, they will make up more than half of all eligible voters.[7] Latinos are the harbingers of this change; nearly 6 in 10 are millennials or younger.[8] Never before has an ethnic group made up so large a share of young Americans. This makes preparing the next generations to take the helm of leadership an imperative!

Moreover, *Latinos are diversity*—they are a cultural and ethnic group, not a race. Latinos are Brown, Black, White, Yellow, and all the beautiful hues in between. Some Latinos have ancestors who were here before this country was the United States. Others have recently immigrated. Our extended families are composed of multiple generations. These differences drive inclusive and intergenerational leadership rooted in the culture's expansive diversity. Latino leadership is one of coalition building, bringing people together, working across sectors, and embracing partnership. Latino leaders leverage the power of inclusion.

Latinos are international and maintain close ties to their twenty-six nations of origin.[9] They are culturally linked with people in North, Central, and South America. Over one-third of the continental United States was historically part of México, and these roots remain strong. Latinos' power, therefore, is global in scope. Furthermore, from 2010 to 2020 more than 33 percent of Latino growth was fueled by immigrants, who bring hope and determination, and *replenish the cultural core*.[10] Unlike previous waves of immigrants, who assimilated, Latinos are acculturating, and infusing the United States with a rich Latino flavor.

Sustained by a culture of celebration, faith, and hope, *Latino power is destino* (destiny). It is the collective contribution Latinos will make to America. Based on their people-centered values, inclusiveness, and *bienvenido* (welcoming) spirit, Latino leaders are building a diverse and humanistic society. As Janet Murguía, the president of UnidosUS—the largest Latino civil rights coalition, urges, "I have every confidence that with hard work and perseverance, we will succeed. We are America. And it's time. Our voice will be heard." Murguía is expressing that for Latinos this is our defining moment. For this reason, *ahora*, which means "right now" or "do it now," was added to the title of this new edition. Ahora implies an urgency—a call to action!

And for those who are not Latino, a special bienvenido (welcome).

Bienvenido—A Model for an Inclusive America

M Y FAMILY IS A sundry variety of Latinos, like a delicious box of assorted chocolates. My seven brothers, sisters, and I emigrated from Nicaragua, and those older than I speak with a Spanish accent. Our children were born and raised in the United States and have a more blended Latino experience. Many of them married into different cultural groups, so now we have Latinos by marriage. My brother-in-law Karl, who is of German descent, and my niece Lorrie's Anglo husband can both attest that if you hang around Latinos long enough, the rhythm is going to get you. Then there are the wonderful amigos who have been part of our extended family for so long that they are now Latinos by affinity, or *corazón* (heart).

This tradition of welcoming people into the tribe or culture has ancient roots. Native Americans acknowledge that a person can have an Indian heart or spirit. African tribes have ceremonies to initiate people who have become one of them. African Americans have honorary aunties and uncles and "other mothers." Likewise, Latinos have elastic and expansive extended familias. People who have a special affinity are invited to become *comadres, compadres, madrinas, padrinos, tías* or *tíos, primos* and *primas.* (Much more on this as we continue.)

If you are not a Latino by birth, this book is an invitation to do likewise, to become part of the *familia.* To experience our dynamic culture and learn about the powerful ways Latinos have led their people. To tap your feet to the salsa beat and become a Latino by corazón! To reach out with respect and anticipation to people of all ages. To join us in creating an inclusive America and heal the divisions that have separated us.

This immense capacity for inclusion and welcoming people is rooted in the Latino bienvenido (welcoming) spirit. Because Latinos are a multicultural people and are themselves the product of cultural fusion, there is an openness, acceptance, and love of diversity.

Today there is racial reckoning taking place—a growing concern with race, equity, and inclusion. People from many backgrounds understand the historic divisions and continued inequities that exists. At a fundamental level, these inequities will only be ameliorated when there is new leadership in America—leadership that addresses the barriers perpetuating social and economic disparity and aligns us with our founding values of democracy, the common good, justice, pluralism, and equality.

The leadership practices that have sustained Latinos offer such a model. Latino leadership promotes participation that focuses on mutual advancement, people's well-being, and inclusion. Latino leadership can revitalize the American dream and bring us home to our founding values.

Latinos are becoming an influential cultural group in the United States and are already the predominant population in the Western Hemisphere. *The Power of Latino Leadership* will clarify and claim Latino advancement as the next positive wave of American evolution. It proposes a leadership model uniquely suited to the multicultural, Latino-flavored century that is rising.

Management guru Tom Peters, addressing the National Association of American Architects, was right on when he said, "Hispanics are just wonderful. They are the next wave of people who will revitalize America . . . If you took away Texas, Florida, Arizona, and California, we'd lose 85 percent of our national vitality."[11] *You heard it from the man!* Latino *destino* will reinvigorate the American spirit. We are living proof of how embracing culture, relishing diversity, and contributing to others enlivens the human spirit and enriches life. This is the essence of the growing Latino power today!

Welcome to the Latinization of the Americas.

We are all going to have a very good time!

¡Que Viva el Español!

Now, about the Spanish words sprinkled throughout this *libro* (book) . . . Spanish is used when the meaning of a word is obvious or when it adds flavor and cultural zest. The first use of a Spanish word in a chapter is italicized and translated in the glossary. If the context cannot be understood without translation, the *palabras* (words) will be in parentheses or set off by a dash. The intent is to have readers get into the rhythm of *español* and to learn new ways of communicating. For Spanish speakers, this makes the libro closer to their hearts.

But a little *español* is a good skill for leaders across the board. Knowing a few Spanish words facilitates positive work relations with the fastest-growing segment of the workforce. Spanish fosters a business's ability to tap into the lucrative and expanding Latino market. Teachers can connect with a growing percentage of their students. Spanish words are appearing in the mainstream. Evidence of this is Taco Bell's slogan "Live Más," or Disney's smash hit *Encanto*, which is set in Colombia.

Because of immigration and migration, we interact with people from many countries. The internet is connecting people from across the world like next-door neighbors. A great global passport is being able to communicate with people by saying a few words in their language. Spanish is a good start since it is spoken in twenty-six countries and spoken by the most people in the Western Hemisphere. And the United States is the fastest-growing Spanish-speaking country in the world.[12]

Leading Latino Style

M Y GREAT-GRANDMOTHER DOLORES WAS born on the remote northwest coast of Peru. Her straight hair, as black as charcoal, fell to her waist; she stood tall and proud like the algarrobo tree that grows in the Peruvian forests. Her mother knew the only future for her strong-willed daughter was submission to one of the arrogant men that left Spain *solitos* (alone). So she searched for a better life for her daughter. Dolores would go by boat to the Nicaragua coast, which was alive and thriving. She had cousins there who sold goods to the pueblos and haciendas.

In the 1840s, freight boats exported coffee, bananas, and sugar, and precious wood from the Nicaraguan jungle. A creative and inventive woman, Dolita became a talented baker—the bread she made was like manna from heaven for the Spanish.

He was taking a morning walk when the wondrous aroma engulfed him. Manuel Bordas was taller than any man Dolores had ever seen, with pale skin and steel-blue eyes. But he had a respectful spirit that was rare in those who had ventured across the great ocean. He married the bright and spirited Indian woman. This union—of the Spanish man and the

Indigenous woman—became my great-grandparents, reflecting the massive merger between two races that ushered in a new humanity in what was called the "new" world.

My ancestors remained on the Caribbean coast of Nicaragua, where I was born, until the 1940s, when my familia, due to a devastating tsunami, immigrated to Tampa, Florida. Tampa, where I grew up, is a cauldron of Latino culture, and in the tradition of Latinos we began to "mix it up"! Today, my extended familia includes Mexicans, Colombians, Spanish, Peruvians, Filipinos, and Cubans.

My own life path follows this tradition: I trained for the Peace Corps in Puerto Rico and love the rhythms and cultural vibrancy of *la isla* (the island). I served in Chile, so I consider myself Chilean by *corazón* (affinity). And I have lived in Colorado among my cherished Mexican American *hermanos* (brothers) for fifty years, which has instilled a deep love for these political, ranchera-dancing, and mariachi-loving people.

My ancestry and life experiences opened the doors for me to experience the kaleidoscope culture of my extended Latina familia. This allows me to put forth a comprehensive leadership model that brings together the nuances of the culture yet at the same time reflects our rich diversity.

I am also immeasurably fortunate to have worked with thousands of Latinos who have advanced our community and nation. Today, as an elder, I wish to integrate their knowledge into a viable theory of leadership based on our practical and collective experiences and woven from the beautiful culture that connects us. My *abuela* (grandmother) would simply have said, "Es tu destino" (It's your destiny).

And speaking of destino, what luck that you are reading this book! Ah, perhaps it is not luck; perhaps it is your destino that your past and present have led you to this point of learning about the powerful leadership in the Latino community. Latinos can take pride in the immense contributions our leaders have made. Non-Latinos can become more culturally adaptive and start using the principles in this book to lead with a more inclusive and generous spirit. People of all ages can form partnerships and work together to build a more viable and inclusive future. And we can all infuse our leadership journeys with a renewed sense of purpose and a vibrant Latino flavor.

Oh yes!—claro que sí!—if you are wondering about this Latino destino thing, chapter 5 will highlight five steps that will align you with your personal purpose and life vision, which Latinos call destino.

This second edition includes a new chapter, "*El Círculo*: Inclusiveness Across Generations," which features the voices, perspectives, and leadership practices of young Latinos and fashions an intergenerational leadership model. These practices are applicable to leadership development across all ages, communities, and sectors. Additionally, the book has been updated to include data from the 2020 census and information about the advancements Latinos have made in the past decade.

At the end of each chapter, I have added reflection and application exercise to expand your leadership practices. I recommend that you use a special notebook, or Latino Leadership Journal, to answer questions, consider what you are learning, and find connecting points or areas to practice. You also can share your perspectives and learning with others, and if the book is used in a class or book club, the exercises can be a catalyst for mutual learning and sharing.

Now let's look at the dynamics that make leading Latino style a viable model for our rising global community and multicultural world.

The Future Is Latino

BEYOND OUR CULTURAL INFLUENCE, Latinos will drive the American economic engine in this century. Hispanics are projected to account for 78 percent of net new workers between 2020 and 2030.[1] The US labor force growth rate has slowed over the past couple of decades and was heavily impacted by the COVID epidemic. The growth that has occurred is largely due to the increasing number of Hispanic workers. Given the group's strong entrepreneurial spirit, 80 percent of small business growth in the last decade was due to Latinos.[2] And US Latino spending power represents a $2.3 trillion market and the eighth-largest gross national product in the world, larger than Canada, Italy, or Brazil.[3]

On a more practical level, by the middle of this century, when Latinos become the majority workforce, organizations will do well to cultivate Latino talent and thus benefit from their dynamic work ethic. Companies who are part of the bilingual market economy will grow and prosper. *The Power of Latino Leadership* offers a hands-on, test-driven way to connect with and leverage Latino assets, energy, and values. It puts forth culturally specific leadership principles rooted in Latino history and tradition.

Another consideration is that, just as women left their imprint in the last century and changed every institution, Latinos will have a similar impact in the twenty-first century. Women began the 1900s as 18 percent of the workforce. Today, they are the majority of workers and 40 percent of managers. There are more women than men studying in colleges and universities, including law and medical schools.[4] Women have made leadership more collaborative and relationship oriented.

The Power of Latino Leadership describes how Latinos will have a similar impact in this century and validates the leadership practices that have held Latinos together through the tribulations of being conquered, colonized, and deemed a minority. Their resilience, contributions, and cultural vibrancy are a testament to the wisdom and perseverance of their leaders.

During the twenty-first century, the Eurocentric cultural imposition and colonization of the past five hundred years will be transformed into a diverse multicultural form. Jorge Ramos, an award-winning Univision news anchor, notes that the Latinization of America is the fundamental influence that will change the monocultural nature of our society and replace ethnocentric dominance with a multiethnic, multiracial, and multicultural nation.[5] Ramos observes that the melting pot is being converted into a delicious paella and that Latinos are adding color and flavor to our emerging rainbow nation. Now let's look at an overview of our exciting Latino leadership journey!

The Latinization of America is the fundamental influence that will change the monocultural nature of our society and replace ethnocentric dominance with a multiethnic, multiracial, and multicultural nation.

Part I. *La Historia*: Latino Fusion and Hybrid Vigor

THE POWER OF LATINO LEADERSHIP begins with the complex history that birthed the Latino phenomenon. Be prepared for an exciting roller coaster ride that starts in ancient Rome, traverses the conquest of the Americas, and examines Manifest Destiny in the nineteenth century.

Part I starts with the Romans' occupation of Spain and then traverses to the footprints of the Spanish conquistadores—both precursors of today's Latinos.

Chapter 1, "Ancient Roots and Mestizo Ancestry," surveys the Spanish racial and cultural dominion of the "new world"—a very different encounter from that which occurred in North America. Mestizos—the mixed-blood offspring of the Spanish and the Indigenous people of this hemisphere—became the prevailing population and are the ancestors of today's Latinos. We will explore a "creation" story of the Mestizo birth almost five centuries ago that foretold the appearance of this cultural fusion.

Chapter 2, "The Latino Legacy in the United States," describes the annexation of the US Southwest from México and the designation of Latinos as minorities. This was abetted by Manifest Destiny, which pro-claimed that Indigenous/Native tribes, Blacks, and the ancestors of today's Latinos needed to accept White civilization. Manifest Destiny swept in a belief in cultural superiority and laid the groundwork for the segregated society that continues until today.

Part II. Preparing to Lead: A Latino Perspective

ECOMING A LEADER IN the Latino community requires pondering questions such as Why do I desire to lead? What will be my unique contribution? How will I stay the course? Part II offers three culturally based principles that prepare a person for leadership.

Chapter 3, "*Personalismo*: The Character of the Leader," explores the belief that every person has inherent value and must be treated with respect. *Personalismo* is the leader's character—her persona—and prescribes that the leader establish genuine and caring relationships.

To become this type of person requires a leader's deep connection with their inner self. "*Conciencia*: Knowing Oneself and Cultivating Personal Awareness," chapter 4, highlights understanding one's history, heritage, and culture. A leader also must deal with the aftermath of exclusion and discrimination, personally and in relation to Latinos as a whole.

The belief that every person has a distinct life path is considered in chapter 5, "*Destino*: Personal and Collective Purpose." Individualistic cultures believe that a person determines their own future. Many Latinos believe it is impossible to control chance, fate, or unplanned events. (Having to deal with discrimination is a case in point.) Life presents certain opportunities, experiences, and challenges. *Destino is a dance with the currents of life.*

Part III. The Cultural Foundations of Leadership

ATINO INCLUSIVENESS IS EVIDENT in Latinos' *bienvenido*—welcoming—spirit. As members of a blended culture, their inherent diversity presented a conundrum for the Census Bureau, which since 1790 has counted, delineated, and described the US population. We will learn about the evolution of Latino identity, and how the inclusion of thirty Hispanic subgroups, transformed the census.[6]

Chapter 6, "*De Colores*: Culturally Centered Leadership," looks at shared values such as respect, honesty, and service, from which leadership flows. In most cultures, values are imparted through proverbs or adages, which for Latinos are called *dichos*. "Mi casa es su casa" (My house is your house), for instance, encourages generosity, sharing, and taking care of people. Dichos allow Latinos to tap into the wisdom of their *abuelos* (grandparents). For non-Latinos, dichos increase cultural adaptability and open the door to become Latinos by corazón. (More on this as we continue.)

"*Fe y Esperanza*: Sustained by Faith and Hope," chapter 7, explores the spiritual values and the abiding faith that grounds leadership. How else could Latinos have survived five hundred years since the conquest of this hemisphere? Faith, or *fe*, is a living current prescribing that people take care of one another and work together to improve their lives. César Chávez upheld spirituality as part of the activist nature of leadership. "I don't think I could base my will to struggle on cold economics or on some political doctrine," he said. "I don't think there would be enough to sustain me. For the basis must be faith."[7]

Part IV. Putting Leadership into Action

LATINOS ARE A *WE*, a collective culture in which the familia and community take precedence over the individual. Leadership, therefore, is not driven by individual success or credit but by contributing to the group welfare. The culture's humanistic core propels people-oriented collective leadership.

Leaders are community stewards who encourage dispersed, shared, and reciprocal power and cultivate the *leader as equal*—where everyone contributes. People power has primed many to work for change. This critical mass theory of leadership is described in chapter 8, "*Juntos:* Leadership by the Many."

Chapter 9, "*¡Adelante!* Immigrant Spirit, Global Vision, Multiracial Identity," depicts how Latinos are international, and the integrating force of the Western Hemisphere. Moreover, there are three dominant subgroups in the United States—Mexican, Puerto Rican, and Cuban—but the past twenty years have also seen the appearance of substantial populations of Dominicans, Guatemalans, Nicaraguans, and Colombians.[8]

These international connections make Latinos a prototype for global leadership.

Forty percent of Latino growth in the past century has been through immigration.[9] Any organization or business experiencing 40 percent growth must scramble to find the resources to integrate this type of expansion. Furthermore, leaders must constantly help the newly arrived with education, English classes, and basic services. Fighting for immigration reform remains a cornerstone of leadership and a testament to the social responsibility and activism of Latinos.

According to the 2020 census, more than half of the nation's population under age sixteen identifies as a member of a racial or ethnic "minority." Their fastest-growing identity is multicultural.[10] Additionally, the number of Latinos reporting more than one race increased 567 percent.[11] Because of their mixed heritage, this chapter affirms how Latinos will guide our transformation to a multicultural nation.

Chapter 10, "*Sí Se Puede*: Social Activism and Coalition Leadership," defines a leadership form that challenges inequities. *Sí se puede!* (Yes, we can!) was a rallying cry for the farm workers and coined by Dolores Huerta, the vice president of the United Farm Workers, who marched with César Chávez in the 1960s. Farm workers advocated for fair pay, decent working conditions, and adequate housing. Dealing with immediate issues while providing the skills and knowledge to address the institutional barriers that perpetuate injustice is core to leadership today.

The struggle for social and economic equality has endured because of *consistencia*—fierce determination and a lifelong commitment. Consistencia predicates that social change will take generations and multitudes of people. The most powerful Latino organizations are coalitions that bring the diverse Latino groups together. Coalition leadership is sorely needed today in a divided America.

As one generation departs and a new one ascends to power, there is an urgency to transfer leadership to younger people. Chapter 11, "*El Círculo*: Inclusiveness Across Generations," recognizes the intergeneration nature of Latinos, where age is venerated and young people are the promise of tomorrow. This new chapter integrates the voices and experiences of young Latinos into an intergenerational leadership model. Young Latinos are building on the activism of the past and are crafting a new social identity that is multicultural, global, and gender nonbinary.

In chapter 12, "*Gozar la Vida*: Leadership That Celebrates Life!," we discover that leadership has a social, family-oriented, and celebratory quality. Check out most Latino events and you will see music, dancing, good food, and socializing. *Gozar la vida* means "to enjoy life." For the 70 percent of Latinos who are working class or have dealt with discrimination, celebrating life replenishes their spirit and strengthens their resolve.

Part V. Latino *Destino*

IN 2045, LATINOS WILL be one-quarter of the people in the United States—certainly a critical mass that will influence the twenty-first century.[12] What lasting contributions will Latinos make to our nation? How will they achieve this? What actions are needed to coalesce their growing numbers, work with other groups, and actualize Latino power and contributions?

Chapter 13, Latino *Destino:* Building a Diverse and Humane Society," discusses how Latino values can create a compassionate society—where people and community come before material wealth or individual achievement. Second, as a mixed people, Latinos are *cultural adaptives* who connect across differences.

I propose that Latinos put forth an expanded definition of inclusiveness—one with an open door policy. This final chapter invites non-Latinos to join the familia and become Latinos by affinity, or corazón. And more good news: becoming a Latino by corazón is a springboard to experiencing other cultures, to becoming a cultural adaptive—a person who respectfully adopts and acknowledges beneficial behaviors, values, and reference points from a variety of cultures. The final section summarizes ten steps to actualize Latino power, increase collaboration among Latino organizations, and build bridges with mainstream groups.

La *Bendición*

O UR VENTURE INTO LATINO history, culture, and leadership ends with an ancient spiritual tradition. When people embarked on a journey or a new stage of life, during times of change or challenge, they would ask for a bendición, or blessing, from their abuela or another respected person, to protect them and prepare them for a good outcome. In that light, may this book inspire you to embrace and appreciate the contributions and promise of Latino people and join with us in bringing our generous, bienvenido, and people-centered values to our country.

The ending of this book heralds a new beginning: Latinos are ready to integrate their assets and unique leadership into the US mainstream and to create a diverse and humanistic society. As we embark on the good work of creating this noble future, we will contemplate a vision about today's increasing multicultural people and the contribution Latinos are making to this evolution.

Ten Latino Leadership Principles

Principle	Overview	Leadership Application
1. Personalismo The Character of the Leader (pages 61–70)	• Every person has inherent worth and essential value. • The leader's character earns trust and respect. • Personalismo secures the relational aspects of leadership. • Leaders nurture others and build community capacity.	• Treat each person with respect, regardless of status or position. • Never forget where you come from. • Connect to people on a personal level first. • Always keep your word. • Leadership is conferred by the community.
2. Conciencia Knowing Oneself and Cultivating Personal Awareness (pages 71–82)	• A leader must engage in in-depth reflection and self-examination. • Integrity requires paying close attention to one's intuition, motives, and inner voice. • The psychology of oppression and "White privilege" are barriers to inclusion.	• Examine your personal intention: Why do you do what you do? • Listen to your intuition and "inner voice." • Resolve discrimination and exclusion issues. • Develop a secure cultural identity and know your cultural assets.

Principle	Overview	Leadership Application
3. Destino Personal and Collective Purpose (pages 83–100)	• Every person has a distinct life path, purpose, and life pattern. • Destino is not fatalism. • Tapping into one's destino brings clarity, alignment, and direction. • Powerful leaders are in sync with their destino and personal vision.	• Know your family history and traditions. • Explore your heart's desire. • Identify your special skills and talents. • Reflect on your life purpose and legacy. • Open the door when opportunity knocks.
4. De Colores Culturally Centered Leadership (pages 105–122)	• *Hispanic* was added to the 1980 US census and is the only group that self-identifies. • Latinos are a culture and ethnic group, not a race. • Seven key values integrate the Latino cultura. • A *We* orientation and bienvenido spirit are cultural mainstays. • Latinos are de colores—a diverse, inclusive, multicultural people.	• Respect and learn about the many dimensions of Latino identity. • Lead with a *We*, collective orientation—center on group welfare, interdependency, and cooperation. • Establish personal ties with people—be inclusive and generous, and serve others. • Work side by side with people—do not ask them to do something you would not do.
5. Fe y Esperanza Sustained by Faith and Hope (pages 123–136)	• Optimism is esperanza, or hope—an essential Latino value. • Gratitude inspires optimism. • *Gracias* (gratitude) allows people to be generous and give back. • Latino spirituality centers on relationships and responsibility. • Spirituality is a moral obligation to ensure others' well-being. • Faith is central to leadership and fosters moral and ethical values.	• Have the faith and courage to make unpopular decisions. • Practice humility, modesty, and courtesy—foundational for the leader as equal. • Put an issue or a cause first; serve something greater. This lessens self-importance. • Tap into optimism, gratitude, and faith to inspire and motivate people.

(continued on next page)

Ten Latino Leadership Principles (continued)

Principle	Overview	Leadership Application
6. Juntos Leadership by the Many (pages 141–158)	• Juntos means "union, being close, joining, being together." • Latinos are servant leaders and community stewards. • Leadership is conferred by the community. • Leaders build a community of leaders and community capacity.	• Be part of the group; work side by side with people. • Follow the rules. • Be a leader among equals. • Include four practices: a collective vision; history and cultural traditions; mutual responsibility; and working *paso a paso*.
7. ¡Adelante! Immigrant Spirit, Global Vision, Multicultural Identity (pages 159–177)	• The United States is a nation of immigrants who bring initiative, hard work, optimism, and faith. • Latino growth has been fueled by immigration. • Latinos are acculturating, not assimilating. A cultural revitalization is occurring. • With ties to twenty-six countries, Latinos are a prototype for global leadership.	• Integrate the newly arrived and provide multiple services. • Be aware that 51 percent of Latinos identify with their nations of origin. • Address immigration as a civil rights and advocacy issue. • Strengthen cultural self-awareness and build relationships. • Tap into Latino global connections, assets, and knowledge
8. Sí Se Puede Social Activism and Coalition Leadership (pages 179–194)	• Economic discrepancies and social inequalities drive a social activist agenda. • Sí se puede is a community-organizing, coalition-building, and advocacy form of leadership. • The Latino model is leadership by the many. • An inclusive agenda speaks to the welfare of all Americans.	• Build people's faith that they can take action and get results. • Practice *consistencia*—perseverance and commitment. • Be a cultural broker and build partnerships with other groups. • Cultivate networks, be inclusive, and forge coalitions. • Have the courage to stand up and speak out about discrimination.

Principle	Overview	Leadership Application
9. El Círculo Inclusiveness Across Generations (pages 195–218)	• Latinos embrace an intergenerational *bienvenido* spirit. • Massive generational shifts require young Latinos to be ready to lead. • Fifty percent of children under eighteen are Latino—an emerging power. • They identify as multicultural, global, and nonbinary, and they are transforming our social identity. • Young Latinos are change makers using technology to lead with an intersectional approach.	• Create allies and partnerships and mutual respect across generations. • Learn generational differences, distinct ways of leading, pertinent issues. • Advocate for meaningful youth participation at all levels. • Recognize that young Latinos are fighting to change systemic inequities. • Respect young Latinos' urgent push for change and equity. • Provide young Latinos the tools, support, and resources to be ready to lead.
10. Gozar la Vida Leadership That Celebrates Life! (pages 219–233)	• Latinos have a celebratory, expressive, optimistic, and festive culture. • Celebration strengthens bonds, collective identity, and resolve. • Latinos are stirring the salsa and gusto into leadership. • Communication is key for getting things done through people.	• Allow time to socialize. • Communicate with charisma, *cariño* (affection), and *corazón*. • Speak the "people's language" and be a "translator" to the mainstream culture. • Always serve food. • Keep a "cultural balance" while utilizing strategic thinking and problem solving.

Special Contributions: Latino Legacy Leaders

THE ROOTS OF LATINO leadership run deep. Our leaders have transformed the tribulations of being deemed minorities into the incredible influence Latinos have today. Leaders are building on a tradition of people-centered, socially responsible, and community-based leadership exemplified in the 1960s, when César Chávez and Dolores Huerta led the United Farm Workers and marched for fair pay and decent working conditions.

The first edition included the voices and good counsel of nine outstanding leaders who follow this tradition and left a legacy to guide the Latino community. You will be inspired by their stories and life contributions. (Unless otherwise noted, all the quotations from these special contributors in this book come from personal interviews conducted with them, which were transcribed verbatim and then coded for common themes and patterns.) These leaders have brought the Latino community to where we are today. One of the book's purposes is to secure that legacy by describing the powerful ways these leaders served their communities.

I want to underscore that the intent of Latino leadership is to grow as many leaders as possible—to create a critical mass or *leadership by the many*. We believe this is the way Latino influence, values, and power will transform the mainstream. For this reason, many people, including Latinos, do not know who our leaders are—but the good news is that there are simply too many of them! My hope is that by getting to know the renowned leaders profiled here, you will understand the power, contributions, and generous spirit Latinos are bringing to leadership across this nation every day.

The second edition includes the voices of four young Latinos and recognizes the urgency to prepare young people to lead. *La cultura Latina* is intergenerational, and our leadership practices reflect this tradition. May this book reinforce the circle of leadership that has brought Latinos to where we are today, inspire the next generations to never forget where they came from, and infuse the American mainstream with a vibrant multicultural Latino flavor.

Legacy Leaders

I have termed these leaders "legacy leaders" because of the ongoing contribution they have made.

Honorable Anna Escobedo Cabral was US treasurer under President George W. Bush. From 1993 to 1999, she was deputy staff director for the US Senate Judiciary Committee and executive staff director of the Senate Republican Task Force on Hispanic Affairs.

Honorable Julián Castro was elected the youngest mayor of a top 50 US city in 2009. He was tapped as President Barack Obama's secretary of Housing and Urban Development in 2014 and was a 2020 presidential candidate.

Janet Murguía was named one of *USA Today*'s 2022 Women of the Year. She serves as president and CEO of UnidosUS, the largest Hispanic advocacy organization in the United States. Murguía served as senior White House liaison to Congress under President Bill Clinton.

Carlos Orta was president of the Hispanic Association on Corporate Responsibility, where he launched the Young Hispanic Corporate Achievers program. He worked in corporate philanthropy and government affairs at Anheuser-Busch, Ford, and Carnival Corporation.

Dr. Antonia Pantoja was an institution builder. Her legacy continues through ASPIRA (to aspire), a leadership program for Puerto Rican youth and Boricua College. Pantoja was the first Latina to receive the Presidential Medal of Freedom—the highest US civilian honor.

Honorable Federico Peña served as cochair of the Obama campaign in 2008 and 2012. He was elected mayor of Denver in 1983 and 1987, the first Latino mayor of a city with a minority Hispanic population. Peña was US Secretary of Transportation and US Secretary of Energy in the Clinton administration.

Honorable Hilda Solis was the first Latina elected to the California state senate and the twenty-fifth US Secretary of Labor—the first Latina to sit on a president's cabinet. She was a California congresswoman from 2001 to 2009 and won a seat on the Los Angeles County Board of Supervisors in 2014.

Arturo Vargas is executive director of the National Association of Latino Elected and Appointed Officials (NALEO) Educational Fund. Previously he was vice president for the Mexican American Legal Defense and Educational Fund. For five years he was named one of the most influential Latinos by *Hispanic* magazine.

Raul Yzaguirre was cochair of Hillary Clinton's 2008 presidency bid. As president of the National Council of La Raza for thirty years, he built it into the largest US Hispanic advocacy organization. Raul was ambassador to the Dominican Republic. He received the Order of the Aztec Eagle, the highest Mexican honor awarded to a citizen of another nation, and the US Presidential Medal of Freedom.

Young Latino Leaders

Honorable Ruben Gallego became chair of the Arizona Democratic Party at thirty and was elected to the Arizona house of representatives at thirty-four. Two years later, he ran successfully for the US Congress. He attended Harvard and served in the Marine Corps in Iraq.

Cristina Jiménez Moreta cofounded United We Dream, the largest immigrant youth–led network in the country. She influenced the enactment of the Deferred Action for Childhood Arrivals (DACA) program in 2012. Jiménez was named one of *Time* magazine's 100 Most Influential People in 2018.

Jamie Margolin is an activist, organizer, and author of *Youth to Power: Your Voice and How to Use It*—a road map for a new generation of social activists. She cofounded Zero Hour, which led the official 2018 Youth Climate March in Washington, DC, and more than twenty-five sister cities around the world. Her contributions are predominately drawn from her outstanding book.

Honorable Ritchie Torres grew up in a housing project in the Bronx. At age twenty-five, he was the first Afro-Latino and openly gay person to serve on the New York City Council. In 2019, he was elected to New York's Fifteenth Congressional District—the nation's poorest in terms of median income—with 91 percent of the vote.

Latino Diversity

THE LEADERS WHOSE VOICES grace this book have ancestry from Nicaragua, Cuba, Puerto Rico, México, Ecuador, and Colombia. Three were born outside the United States and one in Puerto Rico. Dr. Antonia Pantoja, who passed away in 2002, would be more than one hundred years old, Congressman Ritchie Torres is thirty-four years old, and Jamie Margolin, our youngest leader, is twenty-two. This reflects the intergenerational, intercultural, and international perspectives of Latinos in the United States.

Hispanic, Latino, Latinx, and Latine

Almost four decades have passed since the US government mandated the use of the term *Hispanic*. *Latino* was not added as a choice until the 2000 census.[13] Both *Hispanic* and *Latino* are used interchangeably this book. A study by the Pew Research Center, *When Labels Don't Fit: Hispanics and Their View of Identity*, noted that 51 percent of Latinos have no preference between *Hispanic* and *Latino*.[14]

Yet it is important to note the distinction. *Hispanic* derives from Hispania, the ancient name given to the Iberian Peninsula by the Romans. Today it signifies a person with a historical or cultural connection to Spain. The ancestry of the Indigenous people of the Americas is lost in this term. *Latino*, on the other hand, describes a person of Latin American origin or descent and includes Brazil, where Portuguese is the primary language. *Latino* connects people across this hemisphere.

Since 2004, *Latinx* has surfaced as a gender-neutral, nonbinary term. However, according to the Pew Research Center, only 3 percent of Latinos prefer this term.[15] I am respectful of those who prefer the *x*, and if a cited source uses *Latinx*, we will honor this perspective.

Ahora mas—*Latine* (pronounced la-ēn) was created by LGBTQ, gender nonbinary, and feminist communities in Spanish-speaking countries. *Latine* introduces the gender-neutral Spanish letter e. This is native to the Spanish language in gender-neutral words like *estudiante* (a student of any gender) or *gerente* (a manager of any gender). We will not be using *Latine* as it is still not a common term in the United States.

PART I

La Historia: Latino Fusion and Hybrid Vigor

LATINOS WHO LIVE IN the Southwest are keenly aware that less than 175 years ago—a historical hiccup—one-third of the continental United States was México. Other people sense this when they traverse *New* Mexico, or states with Spanish names like Arizona (arid zone), Montana (the land of mountains), or Nevada (the place where it snows). Cruising the California freeways, passing city after city named in the Spanish tradition for patron saints (San Diego, Santa Ana, Santa Monica, Santa Barbara, San Jose, San Ramon, San Francisco, and San Rafael), any driver might find it almost impossible to ignore their Hispanic roots—not to mention the *bendición* that comes from having so many *santos* presiding over cities or watching over us as we drive.

It is perhaps in El Pueblo de Nuestra Señora la Reina de Los Ángeles del Río de Porciúncula (the village of Our Lady, the Queen of the Angels of the River Porziuncola), now known as Los Angeles, that the United States' Spanish Mexican heritage is most apparent. Surfacing like fog lifting off the California coast, the past is etched into street names, historical monuments, the profuse mission architecture, the faces of the brown-skinned children, the Spanish exchanged on street corners, and the whiff of warm tortillas. The only city with more residents of Mexican descent is Mexico City.[1]

The truth of the matter, however, is that most Americans don't acknowledge these historical roots. Even with these antecedents splattered like graffiti on freeway bridges, city walls, and street corners, the past is tucked away, forgotten.

The people of Spanish, Mexican, and Indigenous descent, whose progeny are the modern-day Hispanics, herded the cattle and ran the ranchos, planted the corn, beans, and squash, carved out the mines, laid the railroad tracks, and provided economic muscle. The whitewashed history of the United States makes scant reference to these contributions. *Yet to integrate their power, Latinos must know their history.*

Contemporary America is speeding into the future and not looking in the rearview mirror. Like the great cottonwood trees that grow in the arid Southwest, however, people and societies have roots that anchor them. Roots ground us, holding us firm when the winds of change howl, offering perspective about what is lasting and significant, and nourishing growth and future discovery. The past safeguards the values, traditions, and wisdom of previous generations. History gives birth to the present and is the foundation for the future. If Latinos are integral to America's past, then surely they will be a powerful force influencing our future.

Mucho Gusto: An Introduction to Latino Origins

THE STORY OF HISPANIC origins begins centuries before the founding of the United States, and even before the conquistadores made their tumultuous journey across the vast Atlantic. Spain, considered the motherland of Hispanics, etched a unique landscape that blended many races, cultures, and nations. This cultural permeability is a distinctly Spanish characteristic and flourishes today in the expansive diversity of Hispanic people.

We begin with Columbus landing in Hispaniola and the conquistadores penetrating the Americas. The Spanish conquest could have washed away the footprints of the Indigenous people. Instead, racial blending produced a resilient progeny, the genetic origins of today's Latinos. The first chapter reveals a beautiful creation story prophesying the birth of Latino people and the advent of the Mestizos, or multicultural people.

It is important to note that Latinos are not just a US phenomenon; like the resilient sparrow that flies across many lands to find a home, Latinos are scattered across this hemisphere and many other parts of the world. The evolution of US Latinos is intertwined with the history of their Indigenous and Spanish ancestors.

In chapter 2, we see how Spanish influence profoundly affected our nation's development. This is followed by a slice of US history, including Manifest Destiny, which proposed that Latinos and other people of color had to learn the superior ways of White civilization. While today this may seem like a historical anomaly, it raises the concept of *destino*—the belief that a country or a people may have a distinct contribution to make.

The current state of US Latinos and the cultural explosion that heralds the Latinization of America foretells a transformation of our country. Latino destino, explored in the final section, presents an intriguing concept about the distinctive contribution and tremendous influence US Latinos have today and their potential for shaping a new American future.

CHAPTER 1

Ancient Roots and Mestizo Ancestry

MOST PEOPLE TODAY ARE genetically mixed—our blood intertwined through ongoing migrations, our genetic streams run together from unknown sources. The difference for Latinos is that the fusion of races, nationalities, and cultures was so pervasive that it spread across our entire hemisphere, producing a people traditionally known in Central and South America as *Mestizos*, the offspring of the Indigenous people of the Americas and Europeans, primarily the Spanish.

The *mestizaje*, as the process was termed, is not a concept commonly embraced by US Latinos. There are advantages, however, to including it as part of the complex Latino identity. What is important to note is that the Mestizo experience is a precursor to the Latino culture and the bedrock of its inherent diversity.[1] (Although México is technically part of North America, in this book it is considered part of Central America, due to cultural and historical antecedents.)

The lineage of many Hispanics comes from Indigenous mothers and Spanish fathers. Mothers traditionally preserve—and transmit—tradition, values, spiritual practices, and customs. Much of the culture, consequently, reflects this Indigenous background. The integration of the Spanish and

Native cultures is evident right at the family dinner table. Rice and beans is a primary dish for all Latino subgroups. The Spanish introduced rice, while beans are indigenous, a food of American Indians. Corn tortillas come from Native cultures, but flour for white tortillas comes from Europe. The many varieties of potatoes, chilies, squash, and salsas are from the Americas. The Spanish diet included pork: jamón, chorizo, carnitas, and lechon, which are now Latino favorites.

Whether the term *Mestizo* is used or not, much of the Latino culture reflects this blended ancestry. Since US Latinos were only identified as a group from the 1980 US census on, and their roots go back more than five hundred years, Mestizo is a more accurate historical reference. Looking at the mixing of culture and races in Spanish history will shed light on why the mestizaje occurred in this hemisphere.

The Spanish Are the Mestizos of Europe

L ET'S BEGIN IN 200 BC, when the Romans commenced their seven-hundred-year occupation of Spain. Roman influence is visible today in the aqueducts that stand like centurions across the Spanish plains. The term *Latino* comes from *Latin*, the language spoken in the Roman Empire (and painfully studied in the Catholic high school I attended). The major Latin-based languages are Spanish, French, Portuguese, Romanian, and Italian.[2] *Latin* also refers to Latin America.[3]

In the fifth century, after the decline of the Roman Empire, the Visigoths, or modern-day Germans, began invading Spain. German rulers converted to Christianity and maintained much of the legal system and institutions developed by the Romans.[4] The melding of cultures rather than just the imposing of one over the other was a trademark of Roman occupation and would carry over when the Spanish came to the Western Hemisphere in 1492. (This was very distinct from what happened in North America, as the Anglo-Saxons did not mix their culture with that of the Native people.) This is not to say that Indigenous populations were not systematically oppressed and eliminated, but the melding of cultures also occurred, and is still integral to Latinos today.

Geographically, Spain is the southernmost part of Europe and the crossroads between Europe, Africa, and the Middle East. In the eighth century, the Moors invaded Spain and remained for eight hundred years. (*Moors* has been used to describe the Muslims in Spain, Europeans of African descent, or Muslims living in Europe.)[5] During this period the Spanish became the most culturally blended people in Europe. The Jews, Christians, and Moors ushered in a golden age of learning while the rest of Europe grappled with the Dark Ages. More than eight thousand Spanish words are derived from Arabic, and more than a thousand villages with Moorish names dot the Spanish countryside.[6]

In 1469, when Isabella of Castile and Ferdinand of Aragon married, they set out to unify Spain and spread Catholicism as the official religion. Thus began a period in history during which Jews and Muslims were forced to convert or leave the country. Many Jews were subjected to the Inquisition, which purged Spain of so-called infidels. It is estimated that at this time one-third of Spain was Jewish. Thus, the Jewish exodus to the "new world" began, and therefore many Latinos have Jewish ancestry. Thus, similarities of Latinos as an ethnic group to the Jewish community have cultural, historical, and genetic antecedents.[7]

When delving into Latino diversity, it is useful to consider that the Spanish heritage comprises Moorish, Arab, and Jewish lineages. The blood of Romans, Germans, and Celts had already mingled in Spanish veins. Thus, the Spanish were the Mestizos of Europe when Queen Isabella authorized the expedition of Christopher Columbus. Paradoxically, as Spain was becoming a more homogeneous and a united Catholic country, the fusion of cultures was being transported to the new world. Diversity was already integral to the budding Latino soul.

The melding of cultures was a trademark of Roman occupation and would carry over when the Spanish came to the Western Hemisphere in 1492.... This tendency to meld cultures is still integral to Latinos today.

The Prophesy and the Promise

As IN MANY CULTURES still connected to their ancestry, there is a Mestizo creation story. Creation myths speak to a group's essence and foreshadow the special contribution they will make. The US story, for instance, includes the resilience of the immigrant spirit, the settling of the West, and the emergence of a new nation. The fight for independence and freedom frames our national identity.

The Mestizo creation story begins with a painful birth. When Hernán Cortés set foot on the expansive land that is now México, Tenochtitlan, which today is Mexico City, was larger than any city in Europe, with more inhabitants than London or Seville. The conquistadores found a radiant island metropolis laced with canals, opulent marketplaces, exquisite palaces, and mountains of gold and silver.[8] Starting in northern México, maneuvering across the tiny isthmus to South America, over the high Andes, and into Peru, Indigenous people built magnificent cities, and spectacular temples rose to the sky like the great condor. The conquistadores traversed these lands and made them their own.

It took only fourteen years for the armies of the Spanish conquerors—mounted on horses, protected with steel breast plates and armor, and using firearms as formidable weapons—to reach across Central and South America. Francisco Pizarro marched into Peru, and the great Inca Empire fell in 1532. The extent, speed, and permanence of this military adventure was as devastating as the great plagues and diseases the foreigners brought.[9]

Unlike the Anglo-Saxons to the north, who were fleeing religious persecution, the Spaniards were overwhelmingly Catholic and united in the belief of the "one true faith." The Church issued an edict declaring that Indians and Black people had souls and should not be enslaved. To be sure, the Spanish oppressed the Indigenous people, but they wrapped their mission around a holy grain. The Spanish would baptize the Indians and bring them into the "everlasting faith."

Life for the Indigenous people conquered by the Spanish, however, was not otherwise guided by a Christian conversion experience. An oppressive cloak was thrown over them. They lost their land, wealth, and gold. Dominance and colonization resulted in desecration, particularly of the Indigenous women. Their gods were stripped and their temples were in ruins. The Indigenous immune systems could not repel the invaders— 85 percent died from diseases.[10] The rest were shackled in mines, sweating in *fincas* (farms) and haciendas, or building the missions where the Spanish lived.

The Indigenous people were losing their will to live, and they contemplated racial suicide. "If it is true that our gods don't exist and have abandoned us, then let us die."[11] Though this desolation began in México, this is not a story about the Spanish conquest of México but of the plight of the Indigenous people across the Americas. During this time, the Indians needed a spiritual infusion, a reason to live and to hope for the future. They needed *un milagro*—a miracle.

When Hernán Cortés set foot on the expansive land that is now México, Tenochtitlan, which today is Mexico City, was larger than any city in Europe, with more inhabitants than London or Seville.

El Milagro at Tepeyac

O N A COOL DECEMBER sunrise in 1531, an Indigenous elder wrapped in a traditional *tilma* (poncho) and wearing a straw hat was walking in the foothills of what is now Mexico City. Juan Diego, on his way to church, suddenly hears celestial music and wonders, *Am I dreaming? Am I in heaven?* Looking up, he sees a radiant brown woman with distinct Indian features arrayed as the Madonna. Stars circle her mantle and a crescent moon lies at her feet. An angel lifts the folds of her azure dress. The mesquite bushes, thistles, and nopal cactus sparkle like fine turquoise.

"Where are you going, the smallest of my children?" she sings in the Nahuatl Indian language. "I am the perfect and perpetual Virgin Mary,

mother of the true God, through whom everything lives. I am your merciful mother, yours and all the people who live united in this land and all
the other people of different ancestries. I want very much to have a church
built for me. Here I will hear their weeping and heal all their sorrows
and hardships and suffering."[12] She acknowledges that the different races
have clashed, but despite the horrendous upheaval this has cost, they now
inhabit this land together.

The radiant lady asks Juan Diego to go talk to Bishop Juan de
Zumárraga about building her church. Well, that is like asking a peasant
to speak to a king; to the Spanish, the bishop is the most important man
in México. Juan Diego goes to the bishop's house and waits patiently. The
bishop finally listens but does not believe him.

Juan Diego returns to the hill at Tepeyac to find the Madonna waiting.
He laments, "Forgive me, but send a nobleman who would be held in high
esteem. I am not important, and you are sending me to a place I do not
belong." Insisting that he is the one she has chosen, she asks him to return.
Dutifully, after many difficulties, Juan Diego prostrates before the bishop,
who asks for a sign to prove the story is true. Juan Diego returns and
recounts this to the Madonna, who says she will give him a sign.

The next morning, she appears as if floating on a cloud. "My dearest
and youngest of my sons," she says. "Let nothing trouble you or in any way
disturb your countenance, your heart. For I am here—your mother—your
foundation of life. You are in the cool of my shadow. I am your source of
contentment. You are cradled in my arms. Is there anything else for you
to need? Now, go to the top of the hill, cut the flowers growing there, and
bring them to me."[13]

The hill is stony, full of thistles, thorns, and mesquite. It is December,
the time of frost and brown grasses. Yet exquisite flowers bloom, sparkling
with morning dew. Gathering them in his tilma, he brings them to the
Madonna who arranges the flowers and sends him to the bishop, saying,
"Trust in me. Am I not your merciful mother?"

It is still twilight at the bishop's house. The servants ignore Juan Diego.
And so, he waits for a long, long time, patient and steadfast, his head
lowered, as silent as stone. The sweet fragrance inspires their curiosity.

Looking inside his tilma, they see exotic flowers that do not grow on the cactus hillside. Amazed, they hurry to find the bishop.

Prostrating before the bishop, Juan Diego opens his tilma. Beautiful crimson Castilian roses that grow only in Spain tumble to the floor. The bishop falls to his knees, making the sign of the cross and praising heaven. For there, embedded in the simple tilma worn by all the Indians across the southern continent, is the brown-faced image of the Holy Mother of Creation, known today as Our Lady of Guadalupe. She is not a Spaniard; she is a Mestiza. Her image is preserved five hundred years later in the church that was built at Tepeyac—one of the most venerated and visited religious shrines in the entire world.

 "I am your merciful mother, yours and all the people who live united in this land and all the other people of different ancestries."

—Our Lady of Guadalupe

Our Lady of Guadalupe

OUR LADY OF GUADALUPE is perhaps the most influential and prophetic spiritual voice of the Americas and a revered religious symbol of Indigenous people. Since the conquest of our hemisphere, her iconic image can be found on wall hangings, paintings, key chains, jackets, baseball caps, and T-shirts. She was named empress of the Americas and patroness of the Western Hemisphere by a papal proclamation in 1998.[14]

The significance of her apparition in December 1531, even if understood as a myth, must be seen in the context of the times and in the message she brought to the Indian people. At this time, México was a huge landmass that extended north to the Colorado Rockies and across to the Pacific Northwest. Furthermore, the Spanish conquest commenced in

México but quickly engulfed the entire Southern Hemisphere. The legend of Guadalupe, therefore, is pertinent to the Indian holocaust occurring across these lands. Appearing just twelve short years after the Spanish set foot in México, she says she hears weeping and sorrows and wants to alleviate suffering.

For the Indigenous people who worshiped the sun, there was great symbolism in her image. The sunrays circling her meant she came from their god. Her name in Nahuatl, the indigenous language of the Aztec people, is Tlecuautlapcupeuh, which means "the one who comes from the region of light on the wings of an eagle."[15] The eagle represents vision and the future. Her hands are in the Indigenous style of offering—she was bringing hope, protection, and acceptance at a time of desolation. The eyes are cast down in quiet composure, a stance many Indians would take to survive.

Her exquisite mantle was turquoise, a color sacred to the Indigenous people. On her dress were gold flowers in the cross shape of Nahuatl glyphs symbolizing the four sacred directions and indicating a new life was coming.[16] The Maya, Aztec, and Inca were great astronomers who looked to the sky for guidance and divination of the future. Her mantle was sprinkled with sparkling silver stars.

Juan Diego was not a lofty Spanish official but a humble Indian. As the story is told over and over, the Indigenous people recognize that by choosing one of their own and by speaking in their language, the Madonna affirms their worth and goodness. She looks like a Mestiza, like many children after the conquest. The Indigenous people embrace her: "She is one of us." As a conquered people, they were losing pride in their great civilizations and being made ashamed of their ancestry. She was restoring their dignity and belief in themselves.

Our Lady of Guadalupe symbolizes the integration of the indigenous faith with the Catholic Church; this would be the spiritual fount from which the cultural mixing would flow. The place where she wanted her church was a site sacred to the Indigenous people. Unlike Protestant religions, which do not have a litany of saints or a strong devotion to the mother of Jesus, the Catholic Church had a strong dedication to Mary. In fact, Columbus's largest ship was named the *Santa María* (Holy Mary).

This followed the traditions of the Nahuatl, Mayan, Inca, and Aztec religions, which honored the female aspects of God. As a result of Guadalupe's apparition, the Church began incorporating Native symbolism and rituals. The power of this integration is evident—8 million Indians were baptized into the Catholic faith in the next seven years.[17]

On December 12, the feast day of Guadalupe, Catholic churches across the hemisphere are littered with red roses. For the Aztec, flowers symbolize truth, beauty, authenticity, and divinity. Guadalupe's message told the Indigenous people that, as perennial as the flowers, they would survive. Why? Because the black sash she wore was the Aztec symbol of a pregnant woman.[18] The Catholic Church always referred to Mary, the mother of Jesus, as a virgin. To the Indians, their spiritual mother was of the earth, the giver of life, and had children. This was a message tailor-made for them.

Our Lady of Guadalupe symbolizes the integration of the indigenous faith with the Catholic Church; this would be the spiritual fount from which the cultural mixing would flow.

But who was the child she was carrying? To understand this, we must take a short detour. Rest assured that the inception of the Mestizo people began on that small rocky hill at Tepeyac. Everything that has emerged since the apparition—the culture, the leadership traditions, the prominence of today's Mestizo and Latino people—rests on the black sash of Our Lady of Guadalupe, first known almost five hundred years ago.

La Madonna in Las Americas

ACROSS CENTRAL AND LATIN American countries, there are special Madonnas who are revered as protectors and patron saints and form part of national identities. Because the Spanish conquest began in México, Our Lady of Guadalupe was the first of these. Many

Madonnas are racially mixed, representing the cultural integration that would occur. Another characteristic is that they appear to oppressed and colonized people, not to the Church clergy, the rich, or those of high Spanish birth.

In Cuba, for instance, the Virgin of Charity appeared to two Indians and a Black slave and became the symbol of people's triumph over oppression. She is a Black Madonna, embraced by African slaves brought to Cuba as early as 1531. The slaves beseeched her for their emancipation.[19]

The patroness and protector of Brazil is Our Lady of Aparecida (the one who appeared). Her statue was found by three humble fishermen, and many miracles have been attributed to her. She is a Black Madonna and was called on for protection during the hundred years it took for people to win independence from Portugal. Our Lady of Aparecida stood as an icon of the emerging Brazilian identity, giving people hope, strength, and solace.[20]

Just as Guadalupe personified the Indigenous ancestry of México, so do the Cuban and Brazilian Madonnas reflect the Afro-Cuban and Afro-Iberian heritage of these countries. All three represent the mixed racial heritage that would become a defining characteristic of Central and South America. Likewise, these Madonnas embodied cultural and religious integration. They gave hope to colonized people and were embraced as symbols of emancipation and liberation.

The characteristics embodied by these Madonnas are still evident in the expansive diversity, spirituality, social activism, and hopeful spirit of US Hispanics. The marches of César Chávez and the United Farm Workers drew people from many cultural backgrounds and were always led by a huge tapestry of Our Lady of Guadalupe, symbolizing this integration.

The Mothers of the Mestizo Race

I NEVER MET MY MATERNAL grandfather. As a child, it never occurred to me to ask why my mother's last name was the same as *mi abuela's*— my grandmother's. My abuela had long raven braids that hung to her waist, and she had my mother when she was a very young girl. Often they seemed more like *hermanas* (sisters) than mother and daughter. No one ever mentioned my mother's father. These ancestral roots withered away and remain in the family closet, which shut tight when my parents died. Recently, I was sharing this story with a Hispanic leader who said, "My wife just figured out the same thing, but it was never talked about."

The Spanish commonly used Indigenous women as concubines or as common-law wives. The Anglo settlers did not procreate on a mass scale with the Indigenous people. Western European concepts of racial separation and superiority, as well as religious beliefs, prevented this. But, as noted, the Spanish were already the Mestizos of Europe, with Roman, African, Arab, Anglo, and Celtic blood. From the Sierra Nevada to the tip of Tierra del Fuego, the mixing of Indigenous people with the Spanish conquistadores was so widespread that today Mestizos, or mixed-race people, are the majority population in Central and South America and the antecedents of many of today's Hispanics.

There was also intermarriage, as was the case with my great-grandparents Dolores and Manuel Bordas, but this was not the common practice.

The progeny of these forced unions were ashamed of their Indigenous selves—for integral to any conquest is the denigration and subjugation of the culture of the conquered. Their Spanish fathers often did not recognize them as legitimate offspring, which denied the very talents and attributes they inherited from their European ancestors. This trauma carved a deep psychological scar. The resolution of the internal battle between their Indigenous selves and their Spanish heritage would take generations to mend.[21] (The emergence of the complex Latino identity is discussed in chapter 6.)

Just as roses unfold in their time, so too did Indian grandmothers transform the pain of the conquest through loving and nurturing their Mestizo children. The anchor and salvation of the Mestizos were the Indigenous culture, values, and hope passed on by their mothers and grandmothers. They could taste it in the tortillas, the black beans, and fried plantains they ate. Year after year they were told to hope for the future. Hard work and faith would bring a better life.

The flourishing of the Mestizo people would be a miracle, one prophesied by Our Lady of Guadalupe. The black belt foretold a nativity, a new race of mixed-blood people, the proud descendants of many nations.

During the conquest, thousands of Indian women had been desecrated. Many felt ashamed and in great pain. Yet here was the mother of God saying, "I am pregnant, and I am holy." This was a great benediction to the Indian women who carried the seed of the oppressor. It gave them a sense of destiny, of divine intervention, and most of all of *esperanza*, or hope, for their children.

Yet Our Lady of Guadalupe's message was also for all of us who live in these times, because she said, "I am truly your merciful mother, yours and all the inhabitants of this land."[22] She appears as a woman of mixed race, the face of the future, who speaks of universal acceptance and portrays humanity as brothers and sisters. Guadalupe is not just the mother of Indigenous Mestizos but also the mother of diversity—of the European and other immigrants who are part of this land. Perhaps because of this, people of all ages, races, and nationalities have embraced her message and honor her today.

The Birth of la Raza

IT WOULD TAKE GENERATIONS, but the Mestizos from South and Central America and the continental United States would evolve into today's Hispanics and Latinos. They are connected by their heritage and ancestry as a mixed-race people, the Spanish language, a common spiritual tradition, colonization, and the struggle to free themselves from discrimination. Latino hybrids are the survivors of the conquest and racial conflict but also represent resolution, forgiveness, and cultural reconciliation. These traits, as we shall see, are present in Latino leadership today.

Latin Americans and Hispanic Americans today do not celebrate Columbus Day as the date of the "discovery" of America. After all, our Indigenous ancestors were already here! Latinos across the hemisphere celebrate the encounter of cultures and the birth of a new race on October 12—El Día de la Raza. The term *la Raza* can be best translated as "the new Latino people of the new world." A more inclusive definition of *la Raza* is a new family composed of the original inhabitants of the Americas and all the immigrants from throughout the world who since the time of Columbus have come to the new world in search of a new creation.[23]

But let's not get ahead of ourselves. To move toward this multicultural vision, we must first understand and resolve a number of additional historical dynamics. We will circle back to the concept of la Raza in our final section.

"Latinos across the hemisphere celebrate the encounter of cultures and the birth of a new race on October 12."

—El Día de la Raza

Now we will make a historical leap to the continental United States, where a different experience was brewing, one that would mold the modern-day US Latino experience. The Spanish penetration into what is now the US Southwest encompassed an area that was once half of territorial México. The United States forcibly acquired these lands in 1848 and subsequently began invading Central and South America. These acquisitions were sanctioned by a belief in Manifest Destiny and sealed the fate of US Latinos until the dawn of civil rights in the twentieth century. The next chapter outlines the growing cultural, social, political, and economic influence of Latinos today, despite these historical traumas, which is positioning Latinos to lead and transform the American mainstream.

¡Ahora! Reflection and Application

Spanish History

The Spanish were the most culturally mixed people in Europe, with Moorish, Arab, and Jewish lineages as well as many races and nationalities. How do you see these antecedents reflected in Latinos today?

Indigenous women, like my abuela, experienced massive abuse at the hands of the Spanish. Given this fact, is it surprising to you that many Latinos today are proud of their Spanish heritage?

What facilitated this reconciliation? (More about this important process in chapter 7.)

The Brown Madonna

Our Lady of Guadalupe appeared as a mixed-race woman and predicted that people from across the world would settle this hemisphere and create a "new humanity."

> What did you learn from her apparition story that foretold a multicultural or mixed future?

> Why is Guadalupe called the mother of the Mestizo people? And the mother of diversity?

> Can you think of ways Guadalupe can be a healing force today, as she was five hundred years ago?

There is a saying: "In 'Guad' we trust!" Many Mexicans and other Latinos affectionately call Guadalupe *Madrecita* (little mother) and believe in her compassion, power, and healing.

> Is this devotion something you understand or have followed? If yes, how have you experienced this?

> If no, how do you understand the devotion people have for her?

Honoring the Feminine

Indigenous people honor the female aspects of creation as Mother Earth. The Spanish revere Mary as the mother of Jesus. This connection fostered spiritual integration.

Jot down how this is distinct from the Protestant religion in the Northern Hemisphere. And why is this significant?

How would recognizing the spiritual power of women change and enhance the narrative about women's rights? Why is this critical to leadership today?

Adiós, Columbus Day!

What is the difference between Columbus Day and Día de la Raza?

Why is it important to look at the conquest of this hemisphere from the perspective of Indigenous people? How would this help us "heal the past"?

Why do you think that the Spanish are called conquistadores while the northern settlers are called colonists?

How might this indicate an inherent prejudice or White supremacy?

CHAPTER 2

~~~~

The Latino Legacy in the United States

I DISTINCTLY REMEMBER SITTING IN my second-grade classroom and learning about the "discovery" of America, chorusing with my classmates, "In fourteen hundred and ninety-two Columbus sailed the ocean blue." Next we learned that, in 1607, the first British colony was established at Jamestown, Virginia. None of us thought to ask, "What happened in the intervening 115 years? Did the earth stand still?"

In fact, the Spanish conquistadores were trudging the North and South American continents from the tip of Alaska to Argentina and from the Florida Keys to the Hudson River. Saint Augustine, Florida, was founded in 1565, forty-two years before the English colonized Jamestown and fifty-five years before the Pilgrims landed at Plymouth Rock. What an inconvenient truth! Our historical selection process discarded these facts.[1]

European civilization was first introduced to this hemisphere by the Spanish and then advanced by their mixed-race progeny, who are today's Hispanics. They established the bases for agriculture, commerce and trading, mining, and ranching that would eventually drive the engine of the US economy. In 1600, Spanish settlers introduced the plow and the ox to the Native Indians, as well as the first European-bred livestock. California,

Texas, and Florida continue to be among the largest producers of fruit and vegetables in the world today. Hispanics were *los vaqueros*—the original cowboys—and as late as the 1800s were prominent on the open range.

Many institutions that have become identified as "American"—schools, universities, libraries, and state, county, and municipal court systems— were first introduced to North America by the Spanish. The earliest schools in what would become the continental United States were started in 1600 in Florida, Georgia, and New Mexico.[2] The building of the first European-style towns, the first ports for commerce, the initial trade roads, and the first widespread irrigation systems can be traced to the Spanish and their mixed-race offspring.

Spanish was the first European language spoken in this hemisphere, the primary language in the Hispanic South and Southwest, which is today almost half of the continental United States. The earliest recording of the settlements in Florida was written by Juan Ponce de León in *español*. The written travel diaries of the Spanish expeditions laid the foundation for colonial governance, commercial exploration, and legal precedence and documented the official story of Hispanic life in these lands.

The war with México in 1848 and the annexation of the Southwest ter- ritories shaped the second phase of Hispanic history in the United States. Mexicans became colonized people in their own lands. Leadership as social activism is grounded in this tale of conquest, land confiscation, and colonization. During industrialization, many displaced Hispanics became field laborers or immigrated to the cities as factory workers. This eco- nomic upheaval resulted in Latinos playing a pivotal role in the evolution of the US labor movement.

Spanish was the first European language spoken in this hemisphere, the primary language in the Hispanic South and Southwest, which is today almost half of the continental United States.

As early as 1883, Juan Gómez led cowboys in a strike in the Texas Panhandle. Soon to follow were tobacco worker strikes in New York City; Tampa, Florida; and Puerto Rico. In the early twentieth century, Mexican Americans joined with Japanese farm workers to win the first strike against the California agricultural industry.[3] The farm labor movement in the 1960s persisted with the work of César Chávez and Dolores Huerta, who organized the largest union of agricultural workers, resulting in national boycotts and legislative action in California.

This history established a tradition of activist-oriented leadership with community organizing at its core. Latino leaders became a voice for people who lived in the margins. This continues today, as the median income for Latinos is 24 percent less than for White people and their median net worth is one-eighth that of White households.[4]

Powerful political and social forces justified the acquisition of the Southwest and set the stage for cultural dominance, exclusion, and a society where racism and discrimination remain today. Instead of embracing its culturally rich history, the territorial United States went from a land that was basically bicultural or multicultural (if we include Indigenous people, African Americans, the French territories, and the Louisiana Purchase) to a nation that constructed "American" history to be White, Anglo-Saxon, and Protestant. According to this narrative, the first chapter of American history began when the Pilgrims made their long, arduous journey to Plymouth Rock. One of the most powerful forces that sanctified historical whitewashing was the belief in Manifest Destiny.

 This history established a tradition of activist-oriented leadership with community organizing at its core. Latino leaders became a voice for people who lived in the margins.

Manifest Destiny

IN THE NINETEENTH CENTURY, the concept of Manifest Destiny proposed that the United States should extend democracy to coveted parts of the hemisphere. It was based on three rationales: the virtue of the Protestant ethic and of Anglo-Saxon people, the superiority of their institutions, and the God-given mission to redeem the world and remake it in the image of the United States. Manifest Destiny was further supported by the belief that American Indians, Mexicans, and other people of color were incapable of self-rule and would therefore benefit from being under the US mantle.[5] Manifest Destiny rationalized imperialism—the quest for expansion, land, wealth acquisition, and the domination of other races.

Like a historical rupture, Manifest Destiny shaped nineteenth-century history and sanctioned the US acquisition of former Spanish and Mexican lands. The most coveted were the Mexican territories, including Arizona, California, Colorado, Nevada, New Mexico, Texas, Utah, and Wyoming. In one fell swoop, Hispanics became de facto minorities. Bolstered by this victory, the United States expanded its intervention into Central and South America with the war with Spain in 1898. Cuba, Guam, the Philippines, and Puerto Rico were conquered, consolidating the United States as a world empire and fortifying its belief in Anglo-Saxon cultural superiority.[6]

Manifest Destiny also exported Black slavery into the Southwest. One of the major pushes by the southern states was for the annexation of Texas, then part of México. When settlers from the United States began arriving, they initially accepted Mexican authority. The *problema* was that slavery was illegal in México, and the settlers from the southern states had brought slaves with them. That the goal was to annex Texas to the United States as a slave state was understood from the start. Texas joined the Confederacy at the outbreak of the Civil War. Former Mexican inhabitants would soon join Black slaves in being subjugated by the newly arrived White settlers and ranchers.

The events that led to Texas becoming a state are an interesting machination of Manifest Destiny. Most Americans know the emotional battle cry "Remember the Alamo!" Depending on which side of the Tex-Mex border you were on and your position on the United States' right to occupy foreign land, this was either a Mexican victory or a Texas massacre. In 1893 the Alamo was a mission residing on Mexican land. Several months previously, the Americans had driven the Mexican army out of Texas. The battle of the Alamo was the Mexican army returning to defend its land. They reconquered the old Spanish mission in a bloody battle, where Davy Crockett and Jim Bowie died.[7] This was short lived, and México lost Texas. "Remember the Alamo!" became a raison d'être for annexing the Texas territories.

Today the Alamo is the most popular tourist site in Texas and was designated an official state shrine by the Texas legislature in the twentieth century.[8] It may be a grievous sin to recognize (or even mention) the irony of this historical Texas two-step, but the fact remains that White colonists invaded Mexican territory, the Texas Rangers became an arm of domination, and as a result Black slavery was safely secured in Texas.

Manifest Destiny rationalized the quest for expansion, land, wealth acquisition, and the domination of other races.

Continental expansion implicitly meant the occupation and annexation of Indigenous lands that were acquired by treaty and sale (usually under questionable circumstances—including a lack of voluntary and knowing consent by the Native signatories). Indigenous people were encouraged to sell their vast tribal lands and become "civilized." This meant abandoning hunting and their nomadic lifestyle, becoming farmers, and reorganizing their society around the family rather than the clan or tribe. "Indian civilization programs" greatly reduced the amount of land needed by the Indians, making more land available for homesteading by White settlers.[9]

One of the most distasteful tenets of Manifest Destiny was the idea of the "White man's burden." Popularized in an 1899 poem by the English poet Rudyard Kipling, colonization or slavery was said to benefit nonwhite ethnic and racial groups. Indeed, a noble enterprise! Whites would bear the yoke of educating and civilizing these lesser groups until they could evolve enough to adopt Western ways.[10]

Manifest Destiny established the foundation for many of the discriminatory practices that created an unequal, racist society. The history of people of color would be rewritten from a White point of view, and segregation and racism would spread their ugly hand across the United States.

Exploring Latino *Destino*

MORE THAN A HUNDRED years after Manifest Destiny, a new future began to emerge as the civil rights movement took hold. Martin Luther King Jr., who gave voice and power to this movement, believed that America had a different kind of destiny—to fulfill its founding values and to unfold a society that established equality and domestic tranquility for all. King also believed that African Americans who had held on to their spiritual values were destined to "save the soul of our nation."[11] America, at the time a deeply segregated and racist society, would begin the difficult journey to keep its promise—to embrace the common good, equality, and justice and thus fulfill its true destiny.

King's vision and the civil rights movement tore apart the seams of White supremacy and dominance inherent in Manifest Destiny. People of color began uncovering their history, embracing their identity and power, and making immense contributions. While much work is still called for, the United States took great leaps toward becoming an equitable and inclusive society where all people could realize their potential.

In the twenty-first century another force of destiny is rising that will further the civil rights movement and transform our country into a mosaic nation. By 2045, Hispanics will make up at least one-quarter of the population.[12] Latino *destino* will encompass a demographic and cultural revolution that will alter America's complexion from white to mocha.

As noted, Latinos are racial and cultural hybrids. In the plant and animal kingdom, hybrids have increased vigor and other exceptional qualities, including improved physical capacity, greater stamina, and higher yield. Hybrid vigor is apparent in the strong Latino workforce, prolific population growth, and physical beauty. Latinos are living proof that being a genetic hybrid, embracing diversity, and reveling in a multicultural mélange enriches and enlivens the human experience.

Five hundred years have passed since Columbus first docked the *Santa María* in Hispaniola. But Latinos today draw strength and resilience from our past and are ready to be a dominant influence in shaping our multicultural nation. Latino destino will infuse hybrid vigor into the American spirit—to stir salsa into the American melting pot. The time for Latino destino is now! Ahora!

Latino destino will infuse hybrid vigor into the American spirit—to stir salsa into the American melting pot.

The Latino Explosion

BUENO, LET US REVIEW the Latino dynamics—global connections, language, economic viability, cultural vitality, demographic growth, and political clout—that are transforming the American mainstream.

In this global age, Latinos are connected by language, culture, and kinship to twenty-six countries. Latino cultural roots can be found in Europe, throughout Spain, and through kinship with Portugal, Italy, and even Romania. In the East, the Philippines have mixed Spanish and Asian heritage. Even on the African continent Spanish remains the official language of Equatorial Guinea (formerly Spanish Guinea).[13] Latinos are the weft upon which our global culture will be woven.

Latinos are also an integrating economic force in the Western Hemisphere, the bridge linking North, South, and Central America. US exports to the Western Hemisphere accounted for 43.3 percent of overall US exports in 2019, while US imports *from* the Western Hemisphere accounted for 31.5 percent of overall US imports.[14] México is our largest trade partner.[15]

Call your banks, telephone companies, public service companies, and government agencies, and you will hear "Sí quieres hablar español—oprima el número." Many nations understand that speaking multiple languages is a coveted asset in our world community. The United States is becoming a bilingual nation and just passed Spain as the country with the second-highest number of Spanish speakers.[16] Eighty-five percent of US Latinos speak some español at home.[17] Español is the second-most-spoken language in the world. More people speak Mandarin, but it is mostly spoken in China.[18] The difference is that people speak español in twenty-six countries. It is the *lengua* of the world!

In this global age, Latinos are connected by language, culture, and kinship to twenty-six countries.

And talk about *dinero!* Hispanic purchasing power in the United States is more than $2.3 trillion annually. Buying power for those of Hispanic ethnicity grew by 87 percent between 2010 and 2020.[19] If US Latinos were a country, they would boast the eighth-largest gross domestic product in the world—larger than the GDP of Brazil, Italy, or South Korea.[20]

If you've taken a vacation to a Mexican beach and just wanted to soak up the sun like an iguana, you probably had numerous (I mean, *muchos!*) vendors trying to sell you jewelry, tacos, serapes, shrimp, pottery—*y más!* You are witnessing Latino entrepreneurship! In the United States, Latinos have the fastest-growing small business sector and accounted for 80 percent of new small business in the past decade.[21] Latino-owned businesses contributed approximately $500 billion to the economy in annual sales.[22]

Then there is political power. Latinos are the fastest-growing segment of the electorate. Nationwide, Latinos cast 16.6 million votes in 2020, an increase of 40 percent over the 2016 presidential election.[23] Leveraging their expanding numbers, a record number of Latinos were elected to

Congress during the 2022 midterm elections, making up 10 percent of the House of Representatives.[24] All of this points to this being Latino time in America today. Latinos are at the crossroads of power. Latino destino is calling. Ahora!

A Latino Cultural Infusion

WHILE THESE FACTS SUPPORT the growing Latino influence, the real *caramba* is in the rich *sabor* (flavor) of the Latino way of life. Spicy and delicious Mexican food is now America's favorite cuisine.[25] Tortilla sales are outpacing sales of bread.[26] Tortillas can be wrapped, eaten as burritos, made into tacos, fried for chimichangas or flautas, or broken up for chips. Talk about Latino diversity and versatility!

In the morning, people wake up and smell the *cáfe*—a renowned Latino tradition. At night they might enjoy America's favorite mixed drink—a margarita—with a little salsa and chips. For thirty years, salsa has been our favorite condiment, having passed the more homogenized ketchup in the early nineties.[27] And salsa has almost no calories—what a cultural bonanza! Today, people eat more nachos than hot dogs at baseball games, and one-third of players are Hispanic.[28] Not to mention the weekly celebration of Mexican food, *Taco Tuesday!*

Latinos are kinetic people and love to dance! All over America people are joining the salsa dance craze. They are swaying to a rumba, *cumbia*, merengue, or cha-cha-cha. For those who like a slower beat, there are the polka-sounding *rancheros* and the country sway of a *bachata*. Latino diversity is evident even on the dance floor. Latinization will really be in full swing when more people can move their feet to the Latin beat.

Latin music is blasting the airwaves with a renaissance of artists, mixes, sounds, and cultures that echo the international Latino world. Reggaeton, for instance, is a synthesis of hip-hop, reggae rhythms, Latin beats, rapping, and African percussion. The reggaeton music video for "Despacito" by Luis Fonsi and Daddy Yankee became the most streamed YouTube video of all time—heralding the beginning of a new Latin crossover era with worldwide success. Approximately 40 percent of Latin music fans do not identify as being of Latin, Hispanic, or Spanish origin.[29]

The international flavor of Latino culture is evident in Colombian-born Shakira combining her Middle Eastern ancestry with her Hispanic roots. The hot, hot rhythm and rap of Bad Bunny was born in Puerto Rico. Santana's fusion mixes Mexican, African drums, and rock and roll. Celia Cruz, considered the queen of salsa, was as Cuban as the maracas. Singer-songwriter Juan Luis Guerra hails from the Dominican Republic. Rosalia, the 2020 Grammy winner for best new artist, is Spanish. These singers are transnational, and their music blasts out from Buenos Aires to Barcelona, from New York City to Stockholm, in español and *inglés*.

Latinos are influencing the entertainment industry as well, particularly with younger audiences. The movie *Coco*, about Día de los Muertos (Day of the Dead), highlighted the tradition of connecting with ancestors, which is becoming a revered celebration across the United States. In 2021, Disney released the blockbuster *Encanto*, featuring a heroine from Colombia. *Dora the Explorer* connected young people with the Latino culture and español for almost twenty years. *Vivo*, the first animated musical by Sony Pictures, features songs by Lin-Manuel Miranda and is set in Cuba and Miami.

Lin-Manuel Miranda's musical and film *Hamilton*, about Founding Father Alexander Hamilton, was acclaimed as a cultural revolution. The musical combined hip-hop, R & B, pop, soul, and show tunes—a tribute to Latinos' love for mixing distinct elements into new forms. Though the Founding Fathers were White, *Hamilton* cast people of color as actors, bridging the past with the demographics of the present.

Latinos are making their mark in films as well. Spanish movie stars like Penelope Cruz and Javier Bardem have won Oscars. Mexican director Alejandro González Iñárritu saw his film *Babel* win many awards, and his countryman Guillermo del Toro's sensational *The Shape of Water* garnered four Oscars. For more than four decades internationally acclaimed Spanish director Pedro Almodóvar continues to wow movie aficionados with his edgy, complex films.[30]

The infusion of Latinos into music, entertainment, and food is the tip of the cultural iceberg. Rest assured that this blending of US and Latino cuisine has just begun to enrich our country's palate. More good times await us as we go full steam ahead into the Latino-flavored multicultural century.

Mexican food is now America's favorite cuisine. Tortilla sales are outpacing sales of bread.... In the morning, people wake up and smell the cáfe—a renowned Latino tradition.

Understanding the complex antecedents that shaped the Latino experience is key to appreciating Latino culture and unique leadership forms. The next section looks at the ways in which Latinos prepare for leadership and overviews three concepts: *personalismo*, *conciencia*, and *destino*.

Personalismo is the inner work leaders must do to become the kind of person that people will follow; it places high value on good character. Conciencia is conscious awareness, the mechanism by which a leader stays consistent and connected to her inner self, personal motivation, and culture. Destino speaks to an even deeper understanding of one's unique calling or life's work.

These concepts are a passport for young Latinos and others who aspire to become the type of person that people would respect and follow. They stem from the ancient practices of our Indigenous ancestors, with new approaches for these times.

¡Ahora! Reflection and Application

The Spanish Conquest

What did you learn about the history of Spanish conquest?

Note three ways in which the Spanish conquest was distinct from the Anglo "colonization" of the Northern Hemisphere. How does this historical difference affect racism and inclusion in the United States today?

Characteristic   Impact

1.

2.

3.

Manifest Destiny

What is your gut reaction to Manifest Destiny, especially in the light of our current day's racial reckoning and movements toward inclusion, diversity, and equity?

Group Activity/Discussion

Many Anglo-Saxons have a "historical blind spot" about acknowledging Manifest Destiny as a key determinant in shaping today's inequities. How is Manifest Destiny still evident in White privilege, supremacy, and structural racism? List these observations.

What hree things we can do to heal from the dark past of Manifest Destiny?

1.

2.

3.

The Latino Cultural Explosion

Before we delve into Latino culture and leadership, let's review ten amazing facts about Latinos today that will get us pumped up about their potential and contributions. Place a check mark after each of the following that you already knew.

1. Florida was the first European settlement, in 1565—fifty-five years before Plymouth Rock. _____

2. In addition to exploring the Southwest, the conquistadores trudged from Florida to Georgia to the Pacific Northwest, including the San Juan Islands, and all the way to Valdez, Alaska. _____

3. Spanish was the first European language spoken in the Western Hemisphere. _____

4. Hispanic Heritage Month began in 1989, but Hispanic heritage was present before the United States became a nation. _____

5. The US census notes thirty Latino subgroups, thus validating the extensive and mixed identity of Latinos today. _____

6. *It's Taco Tuesday!* Spicy-delicious Mexican food is now America's *numero uno* cuisine. _____

7. *Tap your feet to the Latino beat!* Approximately 40 percent of Latin music fans do not identify as being of Latino or Spanish origin. _____

8. *¿Habla español?* The United States ranks second in the world in Spanish-language use. Only México has more Spanish speakers. _____

9. *Business is business!* Eighty percent of small businesses in the past decade were started by Latino entrepreneurs. _____

10. *Remember your ancestors!* Día de los Muertos (Day of the Dead) connects people with the power and contributions of their ancestors. _____

How Did You Do?

Score 1–3: *Bienvenido!* You have come to the right place! Read on.

Score 4–6: *Muy bueno!* You are on your way to understanding the Latino experience.

Score 6–9: *Excelente!* You've got it going on.

Score 10: *Estrella!* (Star!) You are a Latino superstar.

PART II

Preparing to Lead: A Latino Perspective

MANY OF TODAY'S LEADERSHIP THEORIES build on the wisdom and experience of earlier times. As far back as the sixth century BCE, the great Chinese sage Lao Tzu counseled people, "Do you want to be a positive influence in the world? First get your own life in order." Lao Tzu divined that the leader's behavior—like a rock that ripples across water—would influence those around him. Thus, he stressed personal preparation and setting a good example.[1]

A number of contemporary leadership concepts follow Lao Tzu's advice and emphasize that leaders should first be concerned with their own behavior, ethics, and character. In their seminal work *The Leadership Challenge,* James Kouzes and Barry Posner challenge leaders to "model the way"—to become the type of person people would follow. This requires exploring your inner self.[2] Likewise, Stephen Covey's work on principle-centered leadership emphasized an "inside-out" approach: start first with the self—your character and motives.[3]

A similar concept in the Latino culture is *personalismo,* which speaks to a leader's character, reputation, and contributions. Personalismo places value on the authentic self and the preparation to lead. For Latinos, this implies having cultural integrity and staying connected to one's community.

Second, personalismo dictates that every person should be treated in a respectful and courteous manner. This strengthens relationships, recognizes everyone can contribute, and builds leadership by the many—a principle of Latino leadership we will delve into as we continue.

In *español* there are two words that signify "I am." *Soy* is permanent. It means "This is the way I am; it is my essence." *Estoy* is temporary and changeable. Estoy means "This is how I am feeling in my current circumstances, or what I am doing right now." The expression "*Soy como soy*" means "I am the way I am." Personalismo is a directive to be yourself. Be authentic and real! Tap in to the soy of your being.

Conciencia, the second aspect of leadership preparation, beckons the leader to know why she seeks to be a leader and what she wants to accomplish. Conciencia reflects a leader's clarity and congruence, an awareness or consciousness of personal motivation. This entails dealing with the effects of being marginalized and growing up as a "minority." Leaders must understand how this has affected them personally and the Latino community as a collective.

In *Leading with Soul*, Lee Bowman and Terrence Deal urge leaders to explore their inner self, to search for their special contribution, and to tap into their existential core. Leading others, they state, is not possible if a person does not know oneself at the deepest level.[4] Inner awareness is conciencia—the firm ground, the nucleus of the leader.

Latinos have an intriguing concept known as *destino*, which implies that everyone was born for a distinct reason at a precise time in history and has a unique life path. Destino is the existential core or "overarching purpose" that Robert Greenleaf notes in *The Servant as Leader*.[5]

Understanding one's destino is like the vision quest of many Indigenous people, where a person engages in a solitary pursuit to answer questions such as Who am I? What is my life's work, and what was I born to do? The vision unveiled speaks to the true purpose of a person's life and becomes a powerful aid in fulfilling one's life work.

For Latinos, the process is not as structured, but rest assured that leaders must have a clear sense of purpose and understand the unique contribution they will make. Unfolding one's destino is an ongoing, organic process that evolves as a person grows, matures, and cultivates conciencia.

CHAPTER 3

Personalismo: The Character of the Leader

I WAS A YOUNG LEADER working as the executive director of Mi Casa Women's Center when my mentor Bernie Valdez showed me, through his example and extraordinary life, how *personalismo* was a powerful determinant in leading people. Like many early Latino leaders, Bernie didn't read leadership books. He earned respect because of the kind of person he was and by the way he valued and validated everyone.

The first time I picked up Bernie for our monthly lunch, I expected his home to mirror his stature in the community. Much later, Bernie would have the Colorado Hispanic Heritage Center and a public library named after him. Yet he lived in a little house behind the stadium where the Broncos played football and where he and Dora raised their children. He lived simply and modestly, much like the people he led.

Bernie had worked in the sugar beet fields and had been a union organizer. By the time we were having lunch together, he had served as president of the Denver Board of Education, headed the Social Services Department, and started numerous community organizations. Bernie had impeccable follow-through, no matter how long it took or how difficult it would be. "You have to work hard and not give up," he would tell me. In the turbulent 1960s, when Latinos were just beginning to forge their public identity and to organize as a community, Bernie inspired others to do the same. The decades it took to desegregate the Denver Public Schools are a testament to his endurance and persistence.

Whenever Bernie faced a conflict or challenge, he was gracious and humorous. His "Don't take things so seriously" approach gave people perspective and made working together enjoyable. I later realized that humor and equanimity were smart strategies when strenuous, long-term work was asked of people. (Chapter 12 has more about how making leadership an enjoyable process ensures continuity.)

When I asked Bernie about leadership, he paused and then said, "Well, first, a leader has to be really secure. You have to know who you are and have respect for yourself." He radiated that sense of self. You could always count on Bernie being Bernie. "To get things done," he cautioned, "you have to be sensitive to what people need and have genuine feelings for them." He demonstrated this by being accessible, listening intently, and having a warm and humble manner.

Bernie and I would eat burritos or egg rolls and "just visit" during our lunches. But our relationship had a profound impact on my leadership. He would counsel, "Be yourself—no one can do that better than you can!" Bernie taught me the essence of personalismo:

1. First and foremost, a leader is an authentic person who fosters consistency and dependability.

2. Relationships are fashioned in a familial manner, like the one I had with Bernie.

3. A leader has genuine feelings for people, listens to them, and treats them with respect and courtesy.

4. A leader is *un hombre de palabra* (a man of his word). Actions align with words, which fosters congruence and engenders trust, or *confianza*.

"Well, first, a leader has to be really secure. You have to know who you are and have respect for yourself. To get things done, you have to be sensitive to what people need and have genuine feelings for them."

—Bernie Valdez

The Personalismo of the Leader

WHILE EVERYONE HAS INHERENT worth, respect is given to a leader based on his character, how he lives and treats others, and the contribution he makes to family and community. A leader's credibility depends on having a reputation for caring about others and treating everyone equally.

To act like one is better than or knows more than someone else, or to practice any kind of elitism, runs contrary to personalismo, where everyone has something to contribute and has inherent worth. Personalismo is the great equalizer driving a shared leadership process.

Leadership is evolving into a collaborative and participatory form in which people, relationships, and cooperation are central—these are pivotal traits of the Latino culture. Personalismo secures these relational aspects of leadership.

Since personalismo encourages authenticity, spending time with a group of Latino leaders will quickly make it evident that conformity is not a cultural mainstay. The Latino commandment to "be yourself" can be seen in a love of distinctiveness—bright colors, conspicuous jewelry, boisterous conversation—and the permission to express your true feelings. This makes for a whole assortment of leaders, a tolerance for different styles, and support for individuality!

I have been the beneficiary of this warm acceptance. My very outgoing, determined, sometimes "pushy" personality could have been rebuffed.

Instead, I have been told this allows me to accomplish things others might not attempt—and enables me to enlist others in coming along. The love I have felt from my *gente* (people) has encouraged me. Latinos will say, "That is just Juana," which for everyone means "Just be you. Nobody's perfect, and you can bring your unique talents into play."

When people are encouraged to be themselves and to take different roles based on their talents and attributes, everyone can contribute. Like embroidered flowers on a colorful serape, each person expresses their unique beauty. Thus, people do not have to compete and can share their talents. The concept of leader as equal, which we will explore, is based on personalismo and respect for the individual.

Personalismo is the great equalizer driving a shared leadership process....Personalismo secures the relational aspects of leadership.

Personalismo Builds Relationships

IN MORE MATERIALISTIC OR status-conscious societies, a person might be respected for monetary wealth, position, the neighborhood in which they live, car, clothes, or other trappings of "success." But this does not reference a person's inner values, morals, or social contribution.

In the Latino culture, people's value stems from who they are unto themselves and from their membership in a family group, rather than from their social status or professional accomplishments. Personalismo is the unconditional recognition of the essential value of every individual.[1] It springs from the culture's humanistic values. The warm, friendly, and personable way Latinos relate to one another, and the active interest they take in people's lives, reflects personalismo. By emphasizing good manners and congenial relationships where people validate and support each other, personalismo reinforces the *We*, or collective.

Miguel Corona, a faculty member at the University of Phoenix who speaks on the Latino workforce, explains in his blog *Intern Matters* how utilizing personalismo creates credibility:

> A few weeks ago, [I presented] to a Latino student organization . . . Before my presentation, I spent quite a long time talking with many of the students, asking them about their backgrounds and experiences, respective majors and classroom work, and expected plans after graduation. I also shared everything about my background, and how it mirrored many of their experiences.
>
> By the time I was introduced to speak, I had already established an initial relationship with most of the students in attendance . . . I could sense that the rapport I had developed with some in the group had already helped me generate credibility before speaking one word. This . . . highlights the special emphasis Hispanics put on relationship-building prior to engaging in business or developing professional relationships. It's based on the cultural idea that individuals are valued more than material belongings and is known as *personalismo*.[2]

Corona is modeling four qualities of personalismo: respect and regard for the individual, sharing one's own background and personal experiences, building personal relationships, and creating a "cultural bond" with people. These qualities facilitate people's identification with the leader and make it easier to follow and emulate him.

Cultural connectivity is the special tie Latinos have with one another. When establishing a relationship, a person usually shares where she is from, who her *familia* is, and tidbits about her background. Latinos come from intact communities where people feel like they belong; may have similar backgrounds, values, and experiences; and share a collective identity and history. For instance, Latinos might have similar childhood memories (like eating rice and beans, celebrating their first Holy Communion, or having extended familia live with them). They may know a member of someone's large extended family, have a mutual friend, or participate in the same community group or church.

An upward nod of the head and a pursing of lips is the physical signal that Latinos recognize each other as belonging to the same group. Today, their growing identity and special affinity, known as *la Raza*, is strengthening their preference for establishing personal relationships and connecting through culture.

Because leaders come from and derive their authority from their communities, practicing these qualities of personalismo establishes credibility. And it is the foundation for a valued leadership asset—being seen as a person of *confianza* (trustworthiness.)

Latinos come from intact communities where people feel like they belong; may have similar backgrounds, values, and experiences; and share a collective identity and history.

Personalismo Promotes Confianza

BERNIE ALWAYS KEPT HIS word. For Latino leaders, this often means never surrendering to the odds and being determined to go the long haul. He modeled dependability and stayed active in the community until the day he died. These traits made Bernie a trusted leader and a person *de confianza* to the thousands who followed him. Confianza means the leader has established trust based on his honesty, quality personal relationships, and demonstrated reliability.

The description "hombre de palabra" (man of his word) emphasizes that a person will do what they say they are going to do. Furthermore, since Latinos value cooperation, with everyone doing his or her part, a person who doesn't follow through is letting down the entire group. In a survey of more than three thousand Latinos, the National Community for Latino Leadership found that keeping one's word and delivering on one's promises was the most valued quality for Latino leaders.[3] Being de confianza underscores a leader's credibility.[4]

Historical antecedents underlie the significance of confianza. Because Latinos had to succeed in schools, jobs, and other social institutions where dominant-culture rules were sometimes murky and confusing, they had to rely on one another. Minorities often watched each other's backs and shared information on what was acceptable behavior or what might get them into trouble. Economic survival and advancement required nurturing long-term support and trust. (White privilege and the psychology of oppression are discussed in chapter 4.)

A people-based culture would unravel without confianza, which strengthens trust, loyalty, and dependability. The extended and elastic familia—which broadly refers to groups that have an affinity and have established mutual trust—reinforces confianza, especially since relationships are lifelong and reciprocal.

Carlos Orta, past president of the Hispanic Association on Corporate Responsibility, observes, "Traditionally, trust (confianza) was the basis for making agreements and conducting business. We don't do business with people we don't know—establishing a personal relationship always precedes any kind of transaction." Shaking hands and relying on the person's word, not lawyers or contractual agreements, was sufficient because neither party would let the other down. When a leader is de confianza, he is trusted as being part of the group or accepted as familia.

"Traditionally, trust (confianza) was the basis for making agreements and conducting business. We don't do business with people we don't know—establishing a personal relationship always precedes any kind of transaction."

—Carlos Orta

Personalismo as a Leadership Practice

ERSONALISMO AND CONFIANZA ARE threads weaving together the extended familia and sense of community that blesses Latino people. By establishing meaningful relationships, personalismo bolsters community and belonging. One generation ago, people were not as mobile, lived in intact communities, and knew each other's familias. Many had the type of relationships personalismo espouses.

In our fragmented world, building a sense of community is a key function of leadership. In fact, Robert Greenleaf in his profound book *Servant as Leader* lamented that "building community was the lost knowledge of our times."[5] Personalismo can lay the groundwork for more meaningful and authentic relationships as well as a renewed sense of community.

Because Latino leadership is community based, where leaders motivate and encourage people to work together, personalismo and confianza are indispensable. The seven practices outlined here gain trust and establish the leader as someone who is genuine, and caring, and connects personally. This lays the stepping-stones to a community leadership process based on mutual respect and equality.

Perhaps these basic courtesies should be extended to all people, but when these hallmarks of personalismo are skipped with non-Latinos, it may not make a big difference in the outcome of the relationship or of future encounters. Failure to connect personally with a Latino, however, can mean a loss of trust and credibility. They may seek a different person (or leader) to work with or go somewhere that is more culturally friendly to obtain services or make purchases.

¡Ahora! Reflection and Application

Seven Personalismo Practices

Here are seven practices that help leaders cultivate relationships and gain confianza, all of which enhances personalismo.

1. *Bienvenido!* Be welcoming! Give a natural, friendly smile and make brief eye contact when meeting someone. Stand up and shake hands, both when greeting and when saying good-bye. This indicates respect.

2. Remember the Hispanic hospitality golden rule: "*Mi casa es su casa.*" My house is your house. Invite people to sit down and make themselves at home. If possible, serve them something to eat or drink.

3. Spend time building rapport before discussing the issue at hand, dealing with problems, or making requests.

   - Meet with people individually or in small groups.[6]

   - Establish a person connection. Find out about family history, where they are from, their values and traditions. Remember: building confianza takes time!

   - Cultivate relationships by knowing people's interests, goals, good qualities, and challenges.

   - Emphasize personal dignity, honor, and one's "good name"; be sensitive to a person's pride.

4. Be open! Share your own background, family history, and experiences as a way of making a personal and mutual connection. Include your cultural background.

5. Learn and practice cultural values and behaviors that foster Latino relationships, such as *respeto* (respect), being *honesto* (honest), and *simpático* (congeniality).

6. Listen carefully when a person is speaking and take care not to appear distracted or uninterested. Do not do other things like checking your email or text messages.

7. Use a few words in *español*, especially if you are non-Latino. This conveys the willingness to reach out to people in a way that respects their culture, language, and preferred form of communication.

Learning Personalismo

Ask yourself, Who do I know in my sphere of relationships that practices personalismo? Or have I observed this in others? If possible, ask these people questions about how to do this well.

Showing respeto for people is integral to personalismo. List three ways leaders show respect for people.

1.

2.

3.

Leadership is a "people business"! How do these seven practices further enhance a leader's relationship with people?

Know Your People

A good leadership practice is to know at least three personal things about people, such as family history; hobbies; favorite sports, food, or podcasts; movies and music they like; and so on. Take time today to practice personalismo with coworkers, friends, and neighbors by asking about these special interests and sharing yours. How did they respond?

CHAPTER 4

Conciencia: Knowing Oneself and Cultivating Personal Awareness

THE BRILLIANT MEXICAN ARTIST Diego Rivera created a powerful black-and-white etching entitled *Conciencia*. In it, he rendered a young teacher holding beautiful apples in her mantle, surrounded by eager children. Rivera, a symbolic artist, included an open book, suggesting the quest for knowledge. The title *Conciencia* implies that we must look for deeper meanings. *Conciencia* can be translated as "consciousness," "awareness," or "self-knowledge." Rivera's portrayal suggests the teacher as our inner guide. The children symbolize our pure and receptive self, poised to learn and grow. The apples are pearls of knowledge.

The concepts of *confianza* and *personalismo* point to two critical questions for Latino leaders: Who are you, and what kind of person are you? Answering these questions requires the practice of conciencia, or in-depth reflection, self-examination, and integration. Conciencia is the connection the leader has with their inner core—the reliable, consistent self that provides direction and guidance. Conciencia is the mechanism for the leader's character formation and personal development.

Conciencia entails knowing oneself. This requires tapping into the intuition that allows one to be aware of one's motivation, values, intention, and inner dynamics. Robert Greenleaf calls attention to this when he writes, "The intuition is the most reliable part of the servant leader."[1] A National Community for Latino Leadership survey indicated that the number one trait people wanted in their leaders (chosen by 58.9 percent of respondents) was character, depicted as being honest, demonstrating integrity, and having strong moral values.[2] The word *integrity* comes from the Latin root *integer* and refers to wholeness or being complete. Such wholeness (integration) is possible only by cultivating the practice of conciencia—paying close attention to one's intuition, impulses, and inner voice. To cultivate conciencia, leaders must also uncover any personality flaws or desires that might get in the way.

Conciencia reflects a leader's personal clarity and fosters congruence. My mentor Bernie Valdez oozed conciencia. He asked questions that helped me define why I wanted to be a leader and what I wanted to accomplish. Because he was my first Latino mentor and teacher, Bernie also helped me incorporate my culture into leadership. This was essential to my personal integration and indispensable for becoming a Latina leader. Bernie believed leadership was helping our people find pride in their cultural roots and tapping into their inner power.

Conciencia is the connection the leader has with their inner core—the reliable, consistent self that provides direction and guidance. Conciencia is the mechanism for the leader's character formation and personal development.

Conciencia Rests on Cultural Identity

WHILE SELF-AWARENESS IS AN essential part of leadership preparation for all people, for Latinos it includes integrating one's cultural identity and knowing one's roots and family heritage. Moreover, since US Latinos have grown up as minorities and have experienced exclusion, leadership requires healing any scars or insecurities that have resulted.

In 1967, Rodolfo "Corky" Gonzales, a civil rights leader, poet, and boxer, wrote the epic poem "I Am Joaquin," which powerfully depicts the struggles of sorting through negative societal messages, grappling with the pull of assimilation, and seeking a positive Latino identity. The poem laments that Latinos are "lost in a world of confusion" and "caught up in the whirl" of a strange society.[3] Gonzales's remedy was to embrace Hispanic history and tap into the greatness of the culture.

Much has changed since the 1960s, when Gonzales penned his call for cultural preservation and pride—a time when Latinos did not even have a collective identity. Ensuring that the culture is preserved for future generations, however, is still an essential function of leadership. Through national and community-based organizations, leaders support cultural integration, pride, and a collective identity.

A crucial aspect of conciencia, then, is being secure in one's cultural identity. By integrating positive cultural aspects, leaders can function effectively in mainstream society without losing their heritage, sense of self, or commitment to their people. They can then teach others how to do likewise.

For many Latinos, becoming culturally secure requires resolving the internalized effects of discrimination and exclusion that result from growing up Brown. Latinos have been termed "minorities," a euphemism for people who historically have been in subservient or in oppressed positions. Minorities are on the outskirts of the dominant culture, always seen in reference to and measured by dominant norms and values.

In the United States, White culture is presented as the standard, even the ideal, and innately superior. Anglos are the top dogs. The media, school system, and society reinforce this message. White people reap disproportionate economic benefits, have a higher standard of living, and enjoy greater opportunity and certain privileges. In addition, in a materialistic culture, the high significance placed on wealth and status is connected to individual value and worth. People who have higher economic status are simply treated as if they are more important, special, smarter, or more talented. White privilege has structured society to favor some groups and to make access more difficult for others.[4] Moreover, there is a general ignorance about the culture and contributions of Latinos, as they along with other minorities were never integrated into US education or history. (I hope part I of this book has contributed to a greater understanding of these antecedents.)

 While self-awareness is an essential part of leadership preparation for all people, for Latinos it includes integrating one's cultural identity and knowing one's roots and family heritage.

Resolving the Barriers of Exclusion

Because of cultural domination, success for Latinos meant cloning the behavior and thinking patterns that White society taught in schools and other institutions. This social conditioning can result in Latinos rejecting their culture, becoming "whitewashed," and distancing themselves from their own group. One way that Latinos and other people of color have tried to escape negative cultural images is to assimilate into the dominant society. Assimilation erases one's cultural identity and can create feelings of inferiority that function at an unconscious level. The fact is, however, that no matter how hard Latinos and other people of color tried, they could never totally fit in.

When I was seven years old, my family bought a small house in a newly developed section of town. I was uprooted from West Tampa, where the

"Spanish" people lived, and walked into second grade to see a whole sea of White faces. Like other children, I wanted to be accepted and to succeed in school. So, little by little, I stopped speaking Spanish, learned to act like the other kids, and even became embarrassed by my immigrant family. Likewise, many Mexican Americans in the Southwest forgot Spanish and even changed the pronunciation of their names.

The psychological pain of rejecting one's own group, together with the confused or splintered identity that can result, was termed the "pedagogy of the oppressed" by the perceptive Brazilian thinker and educator Paulo Freire. His concept built on the "psychology of oppression," a process by which Latinos and other "minorities" internalize the society's negative messages and beliefs about their people and come to believe that these messages and beliefs are true. This operates at an unconscious level, so that many are unaware of how these function in their personal lives or affect their self-esteem. Once this occurs, they are held hostage by their own thinking and begin to collude with the society that keeps them "in their place." They may believe their culture is inferior and thus readily accept the social, mental, and behavioral consequences of oppression.[5]

For an individual, the feeling that one may not measure up can be confused with a lack of initiative or abilities. However, when an entire culture cannot compete equitably and must battle the obstacles of discrimination, this becomes a systemic or social mechanism.[6] Conciencia requires a clear awareness of how exclusion affects Latinos both individually and collectively.

Conciencia entails addressing the subliminal messages about White privilege, resolving the internal barriers of exclusion, and integrating one's cultural identity. As a young girl, I struggled with this. As an immigrant growing up in a lower-income family, I did not know the social manners associated with White people or the middle class. Children like me who didn't have the "right" clothes, know the "right" people, or live in the "right" neighborhood often felt inadequate. The language my family used, their table manners, and their jobs put me at a disadvantage. I remember as a young girl feeling inferior. One occasion was especially difficult.

The Red-Striped Dress

Even as a child, I could total up my "social disabilities." I was poor, Brown, small boned, short, and a girl. My mother spoke broken English. I didn't think I was very smart. All in all, this added up to what I later termed a cultural inferiority complex.

As budding teenager, a very sensitive time in my life, I was invited to a special party by a well-to-do Anglo cheerleader. My mother took me to Lerner Shops to buy a dress for the event. Going to Lerner was like a Saks Fifth Avenue expedition! I still can't imagine how my mother got the money to do this. There on the rack was a beautiful red cotton dress with black and brown stripes and a little bow tie at the collar. My mother and I were so happy that I tap-danced around the store. Such a treasured moment.

What a trauma to my young soul when I walked into the party and saw the rich girls dressed in fancy taffeta and silk! I was mortified and hid in a bathroom all night, refusing to come out. Years later, I saw a TV special on how poverty affects self-image. It told the story of a little girl who hid in the bathroom during lunch because she didn't have money to eat. When the teacher asked why she did this, she said, "I felt ashamed." This was the same embarrassment I felt that night. Experiences are internalized by minority children, and they think, "I am not good enough," "Something is wrong with me," "They are better than me," or "I won't amount to much."

By the time I entered high school, I had decided "I must succeed. My parents and *familia* are counting on me and have sacrificed so much." While I was thinking about this, I saw a cartoon that had a wise old owl singing "It is not what you got. It's what you do with what you got." This became my mantra. *Wow!* I thought. *I may have been born with limitations, but I am going to make it!* I became involved in school activities and sports, wrote for the school paper, and was even elected an officer in several clubs. (Actually, if the truth be told, I assimilated, but more about that in part IV.)

I ended up going to college and then, through the transformative experience of the Peace Corps, learned about my great culture. Today, I know that as an immigrant growing up in a low-income family, I was resourceful, scrappy, talented, and street smart. In fact, check it out: I learned to speak English when I was six years old. I now draw energy, pride, and strength from the obstacles my parents and familia overcame. My mother came here with no money and no education, and yet those obstacles couldn't stop her. If she could do that, think of what I can do!

Latino contributions were never taught in school, portrayed in the media, or acknowledged by people in authority. I had to search for them, talk with others who had similar experiences, and then find these within myself. The decision to be proud of my heritage is one of the integrating factors of my life and work. Conciencia entailed redefining myself by acknowledging my cultural strengths and embracing my Latino identity.

Latinos today must consider their values and upbringing through a new lens—one that portrays the positive attributes of the culture. They need to know their history and unearth the real story of Latino people in the United States. By definition, becoming a Latino leader involves the integration of one's culture, history, and personal background.

Leadership preparation in the dominant culture typically does not entail learning about and tapping into one's cultural identity or resolving issues of discrimination or exclusion. Although doing this would certainly expand a person's ability to understand the deep imprint of culture and race, Anglo leaders today are challenged instead to increase their understanding of other cultures and to expand their ability to relate to and appreciate diverse people.

Today, I know that as an immigrant growing up in a low-income family, I was resourceful, scrappy, talented, and street smart. In fact, check it out: I learned to speak English when I was six years old.

From Conciencia to Action

MANY TIMES, OPPRESSED PEOPLE that believe they can't change their situation and that circumstances are too great to overcome. To be a leader, a person must heal their own wounds—find out how past circumstances have made them stronger and more capable. Then they can use this awareness to help other people believe that they too can change their lives for the better. This was a hallmark of Raul Yzaguirre's leadership: "The leader has to build his self-confidence. You have to believe in yourself first. You have to convince yourself you can do it before you can convince others."

Personal integration, a secure identity, and self-confidence are not possible if one's reference group and ancestry are rejected. Many younger Latinos might not have experienced discrimination personally and can relate to this only by talking to their parents or grandparents. But they can ponder the fact that Hispanics still lag educationally and economically and are scarce at the higher levels of leadership. These are flashing indicators that discrimination and White privilege persist.

Conciencia must be a collective process, because otherwise a person keeps internalizing, believing that they are the only one with the problem or even that these limitations are inherent in Latinos as a whole. As people talk about and release the effects of internalized oppression, cultural pride and a stronger identity emerge. Leaders remind people that historically their salvation came from their culture and community, which sustained and nourished them. Latino leaders are alchemists, transforming oppression into energy for positive change and harnessing frustrations to create passion. They understand that hardships bring vitality, resilience, and spiritual strength.

Conciencia must be a collective process, because otherwise a person keeps internalizing, believing that he is the only one with the problem or even that these limitations are inherent in Latinos as a whole.

Latino leadership programs must also teach the skills that make people successful in the dominant culture. Latinos value modesty, humility, and staying part of the group. However, if a person does not know how to distinguish oneself or toot one's own horn, they may not be promoted or seen as a leader. For this reason, when I was the director of Mi Casa Women's Center, every participant took an assertiveness training course. The Young Hispanic Corporate Achievers program has a special "branding and marketing yourself" segment—an essential skill to move up the corporate ladder. Ruben Gallego, the young congressman, emphasizes, "Latinos need to learn to promote themselves. One thing I've learned, whether its business or politics, people who know how to sell themselves are the ones who end up getting the jobs and political positions."

When Latinos master dominant-culture skills and integrate their cultural identity and assets, they have a competitive advantage. As more Latinos become educated, they have these skills. (Anna Escobedo Cabral, Ruben Gallego, and Lisa Quiroz all graduated from Harvard.)

Conciencia Is Other Centered

Conciencia implies that a leader has contemplated questions such as Why do I do what I do? Many cultures believe that a person's intention—the *why* or the desired end result—is the nucleus from which integrity and power flow. In a collective, people-centered culture, leaders have a natural propensity to serve their communities. Furthermore, since most traditional leaders have sprung from the public and nonprofit arena, their leadership is other centered rather than about money, personal gain, or advancement. Cabral notes this tendency: "There is this basic value that whatever you do, you do for the community and the family. Yes, it is important to do well, but because it will enable others to do well."

Bernie Valdez encouraged me to tap into my conciencia when he said, "First, a leader has to be really secure. You have to know who you are and have respect for yourself." Knowing oneself engenders consistency and predictability. Then actions can align with words.

César Chávez grew up in the migrant camps of California and continued to live humbly throughout his life, never making more than the farm workers he led.[7] Latinos saw him living a simple life, taking personal risks by leading demonstrations, and many days fasting. A spiritual man, he manifested his inner work in his speeches, behavior, and action. These demonstrations of his personal values led people to believe in him as a person, and so they followed and tried to emulate him.

"There is this basic value that whatever you do, you do for the community and the family. Yes, it is important to do well, but because it will enable others to do well."

—Anna Escobedo Cabral

¡Ahora! Reflection and Application

Personal integration, a secure identity, and self-confidence are difficult when your reference group and ancestry are marginalized or rejected. Programs and organizations that aspire to create environments that support Latino inclusion can take the following steps:

1. Study US Latino history and learn how Latinos overcame discrimination and progress.

2. Explore cultural concepts, strengths, and assets. (See chapter 6, "*De Colores*.")

3. Learn about current issues that affect Latinos as well as political and social-change strategies to address these. (Chapter 10 covers this in more depth.)

4. Deal with the aftermath of discrimination and exclusion and learn about White privilege and the psychology of oppression.

5. Build a support network that understands and can explore and address collective oppression.

6. Connect with and hear the stories of leaders who have overcome discrimination and demonstrate personalismo and conciencia. (Some of these are included in this book.)

Practicing Conciencia

Conciencia requires in-depth reflection, self-examination, and integration—a leader's connection to his or her inner core. Reflect on these questions:

What values are core to how you lead your daily life?

Where did these come from in your family or community? How might they be helpful in your leadership today and tomorrow?

When thinking about yourself as a leader, what strengths can you identify?

Where do you need to grow or what do you need to learn to bring conciencia into your leadership?

Who could help you do that?

Understanding the Psychology of Oppression

The psychology of oppression is the pain of rejecting one's own group, internalizing the society's negative messages and beliefs about your identity group, and believing they are true.

What are some of the negative messages Latinos might have because of marginalization, being classified as "minorities" and not part of the dominant culture? I have included examples from my life.

List some negative messages you have observed or experienced. For example, I did not think I was smart, especially in my early years.

What is the effect on individuals and/or Latinos as a whole? For instance, I worked harder. I did not have high educational goals—no one in my family had gone to college—and began to think my *padres* were "uneducated."

What steps might transform and resolve these issues? For example, I learned to speak *inglés* correctly; I got a scholarship; I came to see my parents' determination, hard work, and sacrifice as being smart and resourceful.

CHAPTER 5

Destino: Personal and Collective Purpose

A S A CHILD I didn't believe in *destino* at all. In fact, I thought God had gotten it all wrong. If I had designed my life, it would have been a different movie. Take the first act, for instance.

I was born on a hot, humid, clothes-sticking August night in the middle of the Nicaraguan jungle. Most people in those days didn't even know where Nicaragua was—and if they did, they didn't much care. The mining town of Bonanza spurred the emergence of a small community living in little wooden houses that leaned into the rocky hills. Across from the company's commissary, overlooking a lush green ravine, my mother lay down on that hot summer night to birth her seventh child.

Whose plan was this? What happened to divine providence? Why was I born to a Spanish Indian woman with a fifth-grade education who was as thin as a rail and at forty didn't need another child? My mother was one of those tall coastal women whose strength often allowed them to laugh in the face of the strenuous life they were dealt. But she was buckling under the stress of this untimely pregnancy and the uncertain future that wobbled before her.

My father had brought the *familia* to Bonanza a few years earlier, after yet another dervish hurricane and tsunami had whipped the coast, ripping out trees and homes, turning lush tropical jungle into slithering mud. Cabo Gracias a Dios, which had been our home for generations, was wiped as clean as a chicken bone after our dog Chocho was done. Exasperated, my father came to the Bonanza mine to run the commissary, save money, and take his familia to America—the promised land!

Concerned for my mother's health, the *partera* (midwife) prepared the herbs that would induce contractions. I guess I must have sensed my number was up. The herbs would make me nauseated and drowsy, and then I might never know how to get out of here. A small voice must have whispered, "It will be better if you go of your own volition." Holding my breath, I descended like a locomotive in a tunnel. Bonanza, here I come! Being born in the Nicaraguan jungle as a Hispanic girl, the seventh child of a struggling family who had lost their home, was not exactly my idea of "the right stuff" or the ticket to a fulfilling life. Whose idea was this, anyway? How would I get from the middle of nowhere to a place where I could get an education, live a halfway comfortable existence, or make a contribution to the world? There was not even a library or a high school. *No way, José*, this was not happening.

Today I know that every particle of my life was precisely what was needed for me to become who I am today and to be a leader in my community . . . this was my destino. I would only understand this through *conciencia*—doing a great deal of soul searching, reflecting on my life, and humbly understanding that I know very little about how a life unfolds (or even what is good for me).

¿Qué Es Destino Anyway?

Leadership guru Stephen Covey recognized the connection between conciencia and destino when he stated, "You can't become principle-centered without a vision of and a focus on the unique contribution that is yours to make."[1] Consciousness, he said, is the ability to detect our own uniqueness. The essence of conciencia is to know oneself well enough that one's life and actions are in alignment with one's purpose and destino.

Because every person is unique, one's destino is as distinct as their fingerprints or DNA. As a person embraces their life's journey, destino grows, becomes clearer and more encompassing. Like an acorn that becomes a great oak, the seeds of our destino must be nourished, and they flourish only with patience and persistence.

The search for destino brings a deeper understanding of one's special calling and a clearer sense of direction. When Covey urges leaders to examine their values and principles and to develop a personal mission statement for their lives, he is asking them to explore their destino. This type of reflection provides firm footing when waters are turbulent or life throws a curveball. Appreciating what makes you unique—your history, life path, and destino—is the true way to know yourself and to understand the special leadership contribution you are called to make.

Because every person is unique, one's destino is as distinct as their fingerprints or DNA. As a person embraces their life's journey, destino grows, becomes clearer and more encompassing.

Why Destino Is Not Fatalism

ANTHROPOLOGISTS WHO STUDY AND categorize cultures deem the tendency to believe that outside circumstances or outside forces control one's life to be fatalism.[2] Could it be that most anthropologists come from an individualistic perspective and do not understand that destino does not mean that a person cannot mold or change their future? Fatalism implies being stuck, unable to choose. Destino is not fatalism, because it does not prescribe or determine. People can still choose how to respond to and utilize life's experiences. Latinos dance with their destino. Like the right, left, right of salsa dancing, it is a back-and-forth interchange.

Destino differs from the Anglo-American belief in individual effort and self-determination. In fact, one of the distinctions between *We*-oriented cultures and those that are more *I* or individualistic, revolves around the question "How much control do I have or assume in my life?" The independent focus says, "To a very great extent, I control my life, choose my experiences, and shape my destiny. I am the captain of my ship." Self-identity, self-determination, and self-interest are keystones in *I* cultures. Freedom and personal choice forge one's destiny or future. Rugged individualism dictates that people can become whatever they set their mind to and work hard for.[3]

The basis of White privilege is that Anglos have an advantaged position in society just by the nature of their color and race. Ironically, however, these social assets remain largely invisible and unconscious partially because Anglos have traditionally *not identified* as a culture or race. In reality, then, even in the strongly *I*-oriented Anglo society, people's destiny is shaped by outside forces such as social privilege, which gives a head start.

On the other hand, people from collectivist *We* cultures believe that some things just happen to them, and external influences affect their lives. Latinos know it is impossible to control chance, fate, natural disasters, or unplanned events (like the hurricane that was responsible for my family leaving Nicaragua). Serendipity—good fortune, luck, or coincidences, such as meeting a person "by accident"—happens to all of us. Latinos see life as an interchange between individual effort and the experiences, gifts, surprises, and lessons it brings. I may be the captain of my own ship, but the sea of life determines much of my course.

It is important to remember that US Latinos often got the short end of the social opportunity stick and had to make compromises simply because of their heritage, social class, or lack of English fluency (over which they had limited control). Acceptance was a survival mechanism. When people are enslaved, colonized, or marginalized, they can't always change their status. Patience and learning to make the best of your lot might be the best plan.

But doesn't that imply passivity? Isn't this exactly the feared fatalism, the dreaded anthropologists' diagnosis, which sideswipes Latinos like the wet handkerchief crossing my father's brow in the tropical heat? No! When the hurricane and tidal wave wiped out Cabo Gracias a Dios, a natural disaster that no amount of individual determination could have prevented, my father moved his familia to Bonanza to earn money to bring us to a new land. He defiantly looked destino in the face and followed a new path. There is always a choice about how to respond to situations. Latino optimism and the ability to celebrate life under duress are surefire testimonials to steering around life's circumstances and overcoming barriers.

In reality, destino is another reflection of the paradoxical nature of the Latino worldview. Try as you might, it is impossible to control your life, because you were born under certain circumstances, with unique gifts and temperament, into a certain family and at a specific time in history. On the other hand, you can still forge your destiny and chart your life. The great numbers of immigrants who leave their homeland searching for a better life, and the scores of leaders who have rallied against social inequities, are testimony to this. People must wrestle as well as dance with their destino.

Destino is not fatalism, because it does not prescribe or determine. People can still choose how to respond to and utilize life's experiences. Latinos dance with their destino.

Leaders Seek and Embrace Their Destino

ESTINO IS THE REASON a person was born, the central core or nucleus, the unique pattern and life path. It is always greater than the individual. Like an unseen current, destino ties the past, present, and future together. While it remains constant, it is not static. As a leader matures, her destino unfolds, becoming richer and more encompassing. Destino is an integrating force, fostering congruence and clarifying choices.

Destino is more than personal vision. *Vision* speaks of imagining and anticipating what will be, while the seed of your destino is already inside you, waiting to reveal itself, and awaits acceptance. Many people can work to fulfill a great vision. However, a person can never adopt another's destino—each is personal and unique.[4] For instance, César Chávez's dream of fairness and equality was shared by multitudes. His destino, however, was to be the prophetic voice and inspiration for the farm laborers' movement and civil rights for Latinos.

In the American Indian vision quest a person goes alone into the wilderness to seek their life's purpose. Searching for one's destino is not so direct. Latinos are kinesthetic learners who prefer a practical, hands-on approach, learning from experience, and from others through the oral tradition.[5] Likewise, seeking one's destino is an activity entailing retrospection, learning, and fortuitous situations.

There are certain markers indicating a leader is on the right path to unfolding her destino. When a leader's talents and skills are uniquely suited for the work she is doing, that means she is on target with her destino. When a leader is passionate about something—well, that's the powerful engine of destino providing energy to do the work. Here are five indicators that help leaders understand and get in tune with their destino:

- Begin with your family history and traditions (the roots of your destino).

- Tap into your heart's desire or passion (the fire and energy to follow your destino).

- Identify your special skills and talents (your destino knapsack).

- Open the door when opportunity knocks (it's your destino calling you).

- Honor your legacy and personal vision (the destino magnet that pulls you forward).

Begin with Your Family History and Traditions

OUR EARLY LIFE IS the rich soil from which our destino grows. Our ancestors' lives point us in a certain direction and beckon us to follow. My parents' lives were dedicated to giving their eight children a better future. No sacrifice was too great. This same passion fuels my life today. I aspire to contribute to young people and to ensure they will have more opportunities—just as my parents did for me.

Examining your ancestry, family history, circumstances of birth, early experiences, significant events, talents, and inherent gifts or attributes can steer the way to a deeper understanding of your destino. Because I am the youngest daughter, I had more opportunities than my older brothers and sisters. Growing up in Florida, I met Hispanics from many countries. That would not have happened if my family had settled in the Southwest, which is predominantly Mexican American. These circumstances etched my destino and the work I do.

The backgrounds of the national leaders I describe here show that their destino was being shaped even before they were born. Likewise, your own history and traditions point the way to your destino. Aligning with your destino assists you in determining the special attributes you bring to leadership and how to best serve your community.

A Tradition of Community Leadership

San Antonio's Julián Castro was the youngest mayor of a top 50 American city. He is the son of Rosie Castro, a 1970s firebrand who was among the leaders of La Raza Unida, the political party started by Texas Chicanos in the 1960s. A single mother, Rosie raised Julián and his identical twin, Joaquín, who was elected to the US Congress in 2012, to be leaders with a community spirit.

Julián often accompanied his mother to political and community events, where he met key figures in the Latino political world, learned community organizing, and worked on political campaigns.[6] While he follows the leadership example set by his mother, the times in which he lives are shaping a different type of destino.

Today, Latinos make up 39 percent of Texas and 64 percent of San Antonio; Latinos are on the inside of power.[7] Born in 1974, Castro is part of a new breed of Latino politicians—intellectual, self-contained, serious, and even-tempered. Much like Barack Obama, he comes out of a broader American experience and was educated at Stanford and Harvard Law School. Yet his destino is grounded in a tradition of community leadership. "I believe in destino," he says. "I am where I belong. I am in my place. I was born in San Antonio. I grew up here and want to bring opportunity to the people here." As his destino unfolds and political future grows, he will always be rooted in the Westside barrio of San Antonio. Castro was tapped as US secretary of Housing and urban Development in 2014 and was a 2020 presidential candidate.

"I believe in destino. I am where I belong. I am in my place. I was born in San Antonio. I grew up here and want to bring opportunity to the people here."

—Julián Castro

The Footprints of Our Ancestors

Federico Peña's family settled in Texas over 250 years ago. His great-great-great-grandfather was a founder of Laredo. His grandfather had a seat on the city council. One ancestor served in the first Texas legislature, another was elected mayor of Laredo, and yet another was president of the school board. Peña has built on this legacy by choosing the path of public service: "I saw my life as one of helping people who were being discriminated against and had no voice."

In 1983, he was elected Denver's first Hispanic mayor and the first mayor of a city in which Hispanics were only 6 percent of the population. Peña said of his broad appeal, "The way I saw it, I was a servant. I didn't become mayor because I was great but because people voted for me. So, I was there to serve them and the Denver community."

After serving as mayor he was appointed US Secretary of Transportation in the Clinton administration. Peña now directs a private equity fund, investing in companies that provide clean energy and alternative fuels. Public service is central to his life. He served as the vice chair of the 2008 and 2012 Obama for President campaign and has led efforts to reform the Denver schools. Peña has spoken out for immigration reform, urging compassion and decency for undocumented workers.

Family Roots Become Great Vision

Raul Solis was a union steward in México. After immigrating to California, he met Juana Sequeira from Nicaragua in a citizenship class. They married in 1953 and raised seven children in the barrio of East Los Angeles, a community that was 97 percent Hispanic. Raul worked at the Quemetco battery recycling plant and organized workers to seek health benefits. Due to the hazards of the work, he contracted lead poisoning. Meanwhile, Juana was an assembly line worker at Mattel and outspoken about labor issues.

These working-class champions rocked the cradle in which Hilda Solis's destino was born. The first in her family to finish college, she ran a state-wide program for disadvantaged youth. People urged her to run for office. In 1992, she was elected to the California assembly and later became the first Latina in the state senate. In 2000, she was elected a US congressional representative and served four terms. President Obama appointed her the twenty-fifth US Ssecretary of Labor in 2009, where she was staunch advocate for workers and fair labor laws.[8]

True to her working-class roots, Solis lives in a modest home not far from where she grew up. A young woman encouraged by her high school counselor to work as a secretary ended up as a secretary, all right—the US Secretary of Labor. How is this possible? Many Latinos would answer, "She is following her destino." In 2014 and 2018, Solis was elected to the Los Angeles Board of Supervisors and continues to serve people in this powerful position.

Tap into Your Heart's Desire

IN THE PAST FEW years, numerous young Latinos have left lucrative corporate jobs to head up nonprofit organizations. Their common themes are finding a greater purpose, wanting to give back, and believing that this is a strategic time for Latinos to make their mark.

A native of Cuba, Carlos Orta was an executive at Anheuser-Busch and Ford Motor Company before taking the helm of the Hispanic Association on Corporate Responsibility (HACR) in 2006. While in corporate America, he saw too few Latinos in high-level positions and wanted to open corporate avenues for Latinos. A true believer in leadership development, Orta served on the board of Leadership Florida, as chair of the Greater Miami Chamber of Commerce.

In 2007, combining his passion for integrating business savvy and nonprofit service to enhance both sectors, he launched the Young Hispanic Corporate Achievers program. To date, more than six hundred of the brightest Latinos in corporate America have completed this program and now have a powerful network, are culturally connected, and are committed to work for community advancement. After serving as president of HACR, Orta returned to the corporate arena and continues to promote corporate responsibility and nonprofit business acumen.

One thing is certain, following one's destino will ignite the fire that inspires and motivates. Tapping into one's passion requires mulling over questions such as What do I value? What do I love to do? What inspires me? Answering these questions will assist you in identifying your passion and motivation.

Sometimes it takes courage to follow one's passion. Lisa Quiroz was working at Time Warner when she had a brilliant idea. She talked to the CEO and persuaded him to launch a news magazine, *Time for Kids*. The magazine, now widely used in schools, motivates kids to read, learn about real-world topics, and build writing skills. Quiroz, who graduated from Harvard with an MBA, had qualms about working in corporate America because she was passionate about education and thought nonprofit work was a better venue. Today, the award-winning *Time for Kids* has gone digital and spawned a generation of "kid reporters" and a host of educational aids. By being true to her passion, Quiroz found a powerful way to influence education and support reading and literacy for millions of children.[9]

Lisa went on to become the founder and publisher of *People en Español* magazine, in 1996, the largest Spanish-language magazine in the United States, reaching 7.1 million readers with each issue by 2009. She passed away at only fifty-eight years old, but by staying true to her passion, she found a powerful way to influence education and support reading and literacy for millions of children. Lisa left such a lasting legacy, something that very few Latinas have been able to do.

Identify Your Special Skills and Talents

THE FASCINATING REALIZATION THAT there will never be another person just like you can be a source of power and determination. Each of us truly is one of a kind. But tapping into our uniqueness requires an honest and thoughtful examination of our talents, gifts, and abilities. I like to call this our "destino knapsack," because if destino is the job you were sent here to do, you will have certain innate skills and talents to help you accomplish this. Yes, you must develop your talents, but first you must know what they are. Then, interestingly, life circumstances will provide the training ground to grow these.

Uprooted by the Cuban revolution, Carlos Orta lived in Cuba and Spain by the time he was five, and then the familia settled in Miami. His father held down three jobs even though he had been a professional in Cuba. His mother worked in a factory and went to school at night. Carlos was raised by his grandmother, who taught him traditional manners. "I was raised to be courteous—a *modelo*—a model child." As an only child, he was used to being with adults. He became self-contained and observant. Orta emerged as a poised adult, with a broad perspective, and able to talk to anyone. Today he converses with a corporate CEO or congressperson as easily as a community volunteer or a young professional. His early childhood was the perfect training ground for the work he does.

Leadership has been described as the ability to stay cool under fire—to perform under pressure and in the face of adversity. In the corporate realm, "executive temperament" signifies a similar trait. Orta's natural composure was further developed through experiences in politics and corporate America. As a child, he recalls, "I would see things as they could or should be and had a fascination with building things. Although I am not an architect, I am builder of sorts. I like growing organizations, developing structure, and creating a comfortable space for people."

Orta combined his natural abilities, education, and experiences to embrace a very strategic destino when he was president of HACR: lead a coalition of the sixteen largest Latino national organizations that aim to change the way corporate America includes and supports Latinos.

"I would see things as they could or should be and had a fascination with building things.... I like growing organizations, developing structure, and creating a comfortable space for people."

—Carlos Orta

Communicating with people and being able to get ideas across is a cherished leadership trait. As members of a relationship-oriented culture that values the oral tradition, Latinos value the charisma that allows leaders to connect with and motivate people on an emotional level. Janet Murguía has a fiery charismatic style, which was evident at a very young age. She grew up in a family of nine, where her ability to talk to others was honed at home. Murguía improved her speaking skills when she ran for student body president in high school, became a leader in college, and then went to law school. These experiences sharpened her natural ability to speak in a powerful, passionate, and convincing manner.

A roadblock for Latinos in embracing their special gifts and talents is that they value modesty. Bragging is not a positive trait. However, acknowledging your gifts can be a practice in humility. You were born with these. They were given to you, so there is no need to boast. And people must know their gifts for collective and shared leadership to work.

In fact, part of a leader's job is to identify and utilize each person's special skills and talents, including their own.

Open the Door When Opportunity Knocks

ONE SURE WAY TO clarify your destino is to look at opportunities that come out of the blue or seem like a lucky break. We all have had times in our lives when opportunity knocked—a favorable prospect appeared, an offer you could not refuse. Perhaps it was a new job or promotion, a special assignment, the chance to learn a special skill, or "accidentally" meeting a mentor. This is your purpose calling you and opening doors.

Then there are special or unique circumstances, like living in another country or growing up in the barrio. Many Latinos of my generation, for instance, grew up in neighborhoods where they were minorities, causing them to adapt at a very early age. This allowed us to be front-runners in functioning successfully in the dominant culture and to change Anglo perceptions of Latinos as being unable to speak English well or being poorly educated.

Then there are also those special moments when things just seem to come together—or what might be called coincidences converge in a meaningful way. Joe Jaworski, founder of the American Leadership Forum, called this "synchronicity" and urged us to pay close attention—this was life guiding us on our path. When we respond to these situations, things begin falling in place almost effortlessly, because we are allowing our life to unfold.[10]

After returning from the Peace Corps in Chile, I moved to Madison, Wisconsin, with my new husband, who was going to law school. With my papers and commendations in hand, I went to the Department of Social Services to apply for a job as a social worker. In Chile I had organized production cooperatives in low-income barrios. (Today these are called microenterprises.) I was fired up! If I could do this kind of work with almost no resources, I could tackle any barrier. The interviewer seemed overwhelmed by my enthusiasm. He stopped me and said, "Look, I can see you are motivated and talented, but we only hire people with a master's in social work."

I was stunned. I was the first educated person in my family. I had a college degree, and in my world that was *el ultimo!* I gathered my courage, picked up my papers, and emphatically put them on his desk. "You don't understand," I said. "I was born to be a social worker."

He looked astonished. "Well, if you can go down to the University of Wisconsin and get into the social work master's program, we will provide an educational stipend if you come back and work for us." That was my destino opening the door and preparing me for my life's work. And it wasn't even my idea!

Murguía sees opportunities like these as "angels in my path along the way." One was Jerry Rogers, the financial director at the University of Kansas.

> This angel of a man would sit down with us and make sure our financial aid package worked. He really saw our potential. Maybe he was fascinated because we were the "Mexican twins" going to school and had the same majors. There wasn't any form of student aid he didn't help with. We did work-study, got scholarships and student loans, and kept our grades up. Getting into law school was the same thing. We couldn't afford it. At one point my parents had five children in college. But here was the law school admissions officer who believed in me and helped me. He fought to keep me in that school.

 One sure way to clarify your destino is to look at opportunities that come out of the blue or seem like a lucky break.... This is your purpose calling you and opening doors.

Honor Your Legacy and Personal Vision

IN HIS BRILLIANT EXPLORATION of personal transformation, the renowned scholar Joseph Campbell identified the "hero's journey" as the search for true identity—"to become what we were meant to become—to achieve our 'vital design.'"[11] While the seeds of your destino were present at your birth, understanding your "vital design" requires reflection and integrating your life so congruence becomes apparent. Just as utilizing a muscle will make it stronger, embracing your destino will make your life plan clearer and more encompassing.

For your destino to expand, continue asking, Where is my life leading me? Or as Greenleaf counseled, "How can I best serve?"[12] Then again, particularly for Latinos and leaders who are committed to future generations, consider what you want your legacy to be. This will begin shaping your choices and life's journey. Covey encouraged people to cultivate the habit of beginning with the end in mind. What are your hopes and dreams for the future? What contributions do you want to make? How will you make this a reality? Covey urged, "Honor the vision of what you will become."[13] In the Latino worldview, this is your destino and becoming who you were born to be!

Murguía believes that she has been guided by the values instilled in her as a child: family, faith, community, hard work, love of country, and sacrifice. These values converge in her desire "to help open the doors of the American dream like they were for my family and for me." Therefore, she took the helm of the largest Latino advocacy organization in the United States, UnidosUS. "I think with my own career and life it has been very mission oriented. I am responding to a calling, and you know, for us, we're always trying to make sure we're fulfilling that destiny which lies ahead."

Tapping into one's destino requires soul searching and trusting that the inspiration you need will be forthcoming. Just as nature is the great conserver and recycles every leaf, so too will every aspect of your life be incorporated into your unique life's purpose day by day.

The first time Arturo Vargas appeared in the *Los Angeles Times*, he was ten years old and holding a picket sign. His elementary school had minimal resources and no playground, and because of overcrowding had gone to double sessions, during which children attended school only half a day. His immigrant parents, who had come to the United States so their children could get an education, joined a group called Padres Unidos. They began picketing the elementary school with the baby in a stroller and Arturo at their side. Padres Unidos changed these conditions, and Arturo learned at a young age the power of activism. Today he continues fighting for the full participation of Latinos in the political process, including elective office, active citizenship, and public service. His destino surfaced at a very young age and was even documented in the *LA Times!*

"I think with my own career and life it has been very mission oriented. I am responding to a calling, and you know, for us, we're always trying to make sure we're fulfilling that destiny which lies ahead."

—Janet Murguía

¡Ahora! Reflection and Application

Five steps to tap into your destino:

1. Begin with your family history and traditions.

  - What is the "story" of your familia? Where is their ancestral land? (You might need to talk to the oldest member of your familia.)

  - How does your familia identify? How has this influenced your life?

  - What is the name of an ancestor you want to remember, and what life lessons did you learn from him or her? How do you utilize these today?

2. Tap into your heart's desire or passion.

- What did you want to be when you were growing up? What inspired you about this?

- If you could wave a magic wand and do what you really wanted to do with your life, what would that be?

- Make a list of things you like to do—these give you energy and revitalize you. How might these be connected to or give you the energy to follow your destino?

3. Identify your special skills and talents.

- Natural abilities: list three gifts you were born with.

- What skills have you learned through education and training? (Example: technological savvy.)

- How does this support and help you in your life today?

- Complete this sentence: "I am really good at . . ."

4. Open the door when opportunity knocks!

- Think about a time in your life when you were offered an opportunity, were in the right place at the right time, experienced something fortuitous, or thought, *What a lucky break!*

- Describe what happened. How was this a surprise or unexpected?

- How did this opportunity enhance what you want to accomplish in life?

- As you look back, why was this your destino calling you?

5. Honor your legacy and personal vision.

- Reflect on and answer the following questions (these will change and expand as you follow your destino):

  - Where has my life been leading me?

  - How can I best serve?

  - Imagine you are at the end of your life . . . what do you want your epitaph to say?

PART III

The Cultural Foundations of Leadership

ULTURE DEFINES REALITY. Even as a baby, you were swaddled in your cultural loincloth—a tight serape close to your mother's chest, a papoose carrier that kept you strong and upright, a cradle rocking by your parents' bedside, a bold, colorful kanga hanging from your mother's back, or a buggy strolling through an urban neighborhood. Sounds, language tones, music, family size, food, home—all were determined by your cultural patterns. Most likely, everything you were taught and believed in was framed by a cultural lens.

Culture provides the focus through which groups of individuals define their world. It is described as collective programming.[1] Culture is tradition, customs, ethos, philosophy, and a way of life, the cloth that dresses our human experience. Culture is the norms—the dos and don'ts. One of its most significant functions is teaching values—the cultural ideal of how one should live.

Values are enduring beliefs describing ways of acting or being that are preferred by a given group. Cultures organize value systems and reinforce them through symbols, myths, education, role modeling, and oral communication. As noted, *dichos* (adages) are a shorthand way to infuse norms and values.

Two strong cultural streams that integrate Latino values are a humanist (people) orientation and a love of diversity. These dynamics fashion an accessible, inclusive culture that celebrates people's uniqueness. Most Latinos value people and community before material wealth or individual achievement. Relationships are the heart of the culture! Many values, therefore, emphasize the way in which people should relate to and treat one another. We will explore the role that values play in framing Latino leadership. Leaders must model these values to be seen as part of the community and as someone people would want to follow.

Chapter 6 begins with the intriguing story of how a conglomerate of races, cultures, and nationalities became identified as Hispanics. Before the 1980 census, the 14.8 million people who identified as Hispanics were in a cultural no-man's-land. In the next four decades, because of their inherent diversity, Latinos would restructure the US census and the way culture, race, and ethnicity are defined across the United States.

CHAPTER 6

De Colores: Culturally Centered Leadership

LATINOS ARE A RICH culture of synthesis and fusion. With such a colorful array of fiesta-loving, family-centered, hardworking, tamale- and salsa-eating Latinos, one might wonder what could possibly keep this sundry group together. What are the connecting points that give a shared identity to this cohort of thirty distinct subgroups in the US census?

Much like the Jewish community, Latinos are an ethnic and cultural group. Latinos are bound together by the Spanish language, a shared history, a spiritual tradition, and common values that stem from both their Spanish and their Indigenous roots. Cultural values are fastening points—the nucleus—shaping a collective identity from the many ingredients of the delectable Latina *familia*. As Arturo Vargas, president of the National Association of Latino Elected and Appointed Officials, observes, "I've met Latinos all over the country, and diverse as Latinos are, there's a set of core values we hold. It's about family, and the face of their children, and the face of the future. There's a level of optimism and a sense of community."

This chapter highlights seven key values: familia, *simpático* (being easy to get along with), generosity, respect, honesty, hard work, and service to others. The central value of faith is explored in chapter 7. These deeply intertwined values form the substance of Latino leadership. Hilda Solis notes, "My leadership is based on my upbringing and cultural values— what I was taught as a young child."

Before delving into cultural values, let us explore the multifaceted Hispanic identity. Since our vast diversity includes many nations of origin and mixed-race ancestry, there remains the puzzling question about exactly what it means to be Latino. The story of how Latinos came to be recognized as a cultural and ethnic group offers historical insights into the racial underpinnings of the US census.

"I've met Latinos all over the country, and diverse as Latinos are, there's a set of core values we hold. It's about family, and the face of their children, and the face of the future. There's a level of optimism and a sense of community."

—Arturo Vargas

Latino, Hispanic, Mexicano, Cubano, Latinx—Who Are You?

FILLING OUT MY FIRST US census form in 1970, I searched for a category that would acknowledge my culture and ancestry. I felt a loud thud in my heart as I finally checked the "Caucasian" box. As I filled out the forms, I heard my *abuela*'s sweet voice, "Ay, mi hijita, nunca olvides quien eres y de donde venistes" (Oh, my dearest little daughter, never forget who you are and where you came from). But remembering your history and embracing your identity is a difficult feat when there is no acknowledgment that your people even exist.

We all have a deep need to know who we are. This is particularly true for Latinos and other people of color, who have been relegated to a minority status and measured by a White ideal. As we have noted, Latinos are *de colores* (of many colors) and have a *bienvenido* spirit—they are inherently inclusive and diverse. The mainstream culture, on the other hand, values homogeneity, uniformity, and categorization.

The story of how the "Browns" (Hispanics) became a category in the US census illustrates the unique history of this cultural medley. (Of course, members of other ethnic groups, such as South Asians, Pacific Islanders, Middle Easterners, and Native Americans, may also consider themselves Brown, but we are using *Brown* to refer to Hispanics and Latinos.)

Adding "Hispanic" restructured the census categories to offer many more choices for racial and ethnic identities and tilled the soil for our emerging multicultural identity. In fact, according to the 2020 census, the "Two or More Races" population (also referred to as the multiracial population) is now almost 34 million people—a 276 percent increase since 2010.[1]

The Evolving US Census

FROM THE EARLIEST DAYS of the Constitution, one of the ways the US government categorized people was by race and color. This was enumerated and sanctified by the US census, in which every ten years census counters scoured the countryside, tallying the people that made up this great land. After the national count in 1970, the census counters, pulling their hair in frustration, asked, "What do we do with this disparate group, the Browns, who are reporting all kinds of concoctions? They were supposed to check one of the existing four categories: Caucasian, Black, Asian, or Native American!"

The Browns were identifying themselves as Mexican, Cuban, and Spanish (in the Southwest, many trace their heritage to the Spanish land grants). Others identified themselves by the place they, or even their grandparents, were born, such as Brazil, Chile, Colombia, El Salvador, or Puerto Rico. The list was *ve-e-ery* complicated, because the Browns had kinship with twenty-six countries, and indeed they liked to mix it up!

The census takers were quickly finding out that the Browns valued something called *personalismo*, which meant everyone was *único*—an individual with a story to tell. Diversity and differentiation were core to their identity.

Then the census bureaucrats had a bright idea: let's ask *them* what they want to be called. A big council was organized in the nation's capital, and leaders from the Browns were flown in. One was Leo Estrada of UCLA, a leading demographer.[2] The census counters thought he would know what to call these people, since he was one of them. The leaders deliberated for a very long time. Finally, in the wee hours, a compromise was reached. The government could use the term *Hispanic*, referring to Hispania, the old Roman name for Spain. *Hispanic* was English, not a Spanish word, so the census counters were *muy contentos* (content or happy)!

So it came to pass that President Richard Nixon's OMB Statistical Directive 15 ordered the addition of a Spanish-origin self-identifier to the 1980 census.[3] From then on, there would be five colors in the American palette. The conglomerate of people spanning five hundred years of the *mestizaje* was baptized Hispanic.

Just Check the Box

THE DEBATE AMONG HISPANICS, however, continued, reflecting their diversity and the difficulty of finding one Communion wafer everyone could swallow. Many prefer the term *Latino*, even though it can be traced to the Roman occupation of Spain centuries ago. *Latino* is politically and culturally a more useful term because it connects people to Central and Latin America and unites them through culture, kinship, and the Romance languages. And it is a Spanish word. *Latino* was added as a designation in the 2010 census.[4]

For the census takers, the saga of the naming of Hispanics continued like a roller coaster on Coney Island. Since Hispanics are an ethnic group and not a race, they can be Black, White, Yellow, or Red. The census takers took out their racial microscope and surmised that all the categories needed to change to really capture the essence of America's genetics. People now had to indicate their race based on their non-Hispanic iden-tity—White non-Hispanic, Black non-Hispanic, American Indian, Eskimo and Aleut non-Hispanic, Asian and Pacific Islander non-Hispanic.

Hispanic, which was once a strange mutt that needed a name and had been excluded from the census from 1790 to 1980, now became the standard-bearer for all other racial delineations, giving new meaning to the biblical phrase "The last shall be first."

Unlike African Americans, Native Americans, or Asian Americans, whose blood content defines them, Latinos are the only group that *self-identifies*. According to F. James Davis in his book *Who Is Black?*, anyone with any known Black African ancestry is considered Black.[5] In the racist South, this was the basis for the "one-drop rule," which came to mean that anyone with *any* Black blood was considered Negro. Native Americans have blood quantum, imposed by the treaties, which means a person must have legal proof of their bloodline to be enrolled in a tribe. *Asian* refers to a person with origins from any of the original peoples of the Far East, Southeast Asia, or the Indian subcontinent.[6]

On the other hand, according to the US census, "An individual's responses to the race question and to the Hispanic origin question were based on self-identification."[7] This was reinforced by the Pew Research Center in a 2021 article entitled "Who Is Hispanic?" According to the article, the answer to the titular question is "Anyone who says they are. And nobody who says they aren't."[8]

It could be said, then, that to identify as a Latino you simply check the box on the census. Raul Yzaguirre surmises, "America needs a different paradigm of what it means to be Latino. The prototype of the Native or African Americans, where your blood content defines who you are, doesn't work. Latinos are a culture, not a race. Culture, it must be remembered, is learned and not inherited. My definition of *Latino* is anybody who wants to be a Latino. Bienvenido—welcome to the family." (The invitation to become a Latino by affinity, or *corazón*, will be considered in chapter 13.)

While many non-Latinos might be confused by this definition, more than 62 million Americans, or 19 percent of the population, identified as Hispanic in the 2020 census. This validates Latino heterogeneity and the ability to incorporate differences into a common cultural core.

To gain a better understanding, let's explore the dynamic values that unite Latinos and frame this diverse culture. These values are also the driving force for the people-centered leadership of the Latino community.

"America needs a different paradigm of what it means to be Latino.... Latinos are a culture, not a race. Culture, it must be remembered, is learned and not inherited. My definition of Latino is anybody who wants to be a Latino. Bienvenido—welcome to the family."

—Raul Yzaguirre

La Familia—A *We* Orientation

TRADITIONALLY IN SPAIN, LARGE extended familias lived in the same community for generations and relied on each other for daily essentials and special needs. Likewise, in American Indian cultures today, as with previous generations, the tribe takes care of its members, land is held in common, and everyone is seen as a relative. The Aztec civilization was made up of multiple ethnicities and organized into small family groups who governed themselves and worked together as a unit. Thus, the many roots that nourished the Latino tradition had strong family ties and community bonds.

These ancestral connections anchor a *We*, or collective, orientation. *We* cultures have been on the earth for a very long time. Tightly woven, stable, and integrated, *We* cultures center on group welfare, interdependence, and cooperation. The family, community, or tribe takes precedence; individual identity flows from the collective. People work for group success before personal gain or credit. It is no wonder that Latinos cherish belonging, mutual benefit, and reciprocity.

We cultures revolve around people-centered values. For Latinos, these values include generosity, being of service, and respecting others. To keep relationships strong (the fabric of We cultures), Latinos strive for unity, harmony, and pleasant social interactions. They like politeness and good manners.

The *We* orientation is evident in the familia, which is not exclusively bonded by blood or legal relationships but broadly refers to a group with a special affinity for one another. The familia is e-l-a-s-t-i-c and expands to include *padrinos* or *madrinas* (godparents) at baptisms, weddings, confirmations, and other special events. *Tíos* and *tías* are honorary aunts and uncles and close family friends. *Primos*, or cousins, include anyone who is even vaguely (and sometimes mysteriously) connected to your family. Ask who someone is that you don't know at a family reunion and a common response is "Es tu primo." And this is accepted.

Then again, while you're simply walking down the street with a close friend, another person might suddenly be introduced as a *compadre* or *comadre*, indicating that he or she is now part of the familia. This goes unquestioned, as family connections are elaborate and expansive where close friends are considered relatives. I just became a *tía abuela* (grandmother aunt) to my goddaughter's baby. I always like to add that these relationships imply responsibility, meaning you are expected to assist when a need arises, which can range from contributing to weddings and special occasions to providing emotional support.

This tradition of open and inclusive family relations reflects the bienvenido spirit, which means to receive or accept with pleasure, approve or appreciate, even embrace. The bienvenido spirit is the source of Latino hospitality, generosity, and receptivity to differences. Bienvenido welcomes immigrants into the Latino community and is the wellspring for an intergenerational approach to leadership. (More on this in chapter 9.) Bienvenido invites non-Latinos to partake in the culture and become part of the familia as Latinos by corazón. Latino leadership centers on this We, inclusive, or other-centered orientation encapsulated in the bienvenido spirit.

Hispanic Value: Simpático—Being Congenial

*¡Q*UE SIMPÁTICO! IS A prized Latino compliment. It means people think you are likable, easy to get along with, and charming. Having smooth social relationships is of biblical importance to Latinos, who tend to acquiesce to the wishes of others in order to be seen as congenial. Being respectful and courteous, making small talk, and

taking a personal interest in people are ways to be simpático—coveted traits in a people-come-first culture.

When Latinos enter a room, for instance, the polite thing for them to do is to say hello to each person, inquire how that person is doing, and ask about his or her familia. When leaving, Latinos make the rounds again, this time expressing how good it was to see everyone. ("Con permiso"— with your permission—requests approval to make an exit.)

"Relationships take time" could be a Latino mantra. At some events, everyone in the room has to be recognized and thanked, which means things can go on and on and on. This is when the observance of LST, or Latino Standard Time—time that revolves around connecting with people and not just getting things done—tests your good manners.

In surveys, Latinos respond that they tend to carry out socially desirable actions and attitudes.[9] A person who is *bien educado*, for instance, is polite and gracious and takes people's feelings into consideration. The literal translation of *bien educado* would be "well educated." However, for Latinos it means a person was raised right! How a person treats others (personalismo) is more important in garnering respect than university degrees, wealth, achievements, or the status symbols a person has attained.

People who are simpático are usually good at recognizing and complimenting people's special traits and contributions.[10] Latinos call this *echando flores*—literally, "giving people flowers." Verbal flores express gratitude and celebrate a person's achievements. The genuine affection Latinos show toward one another helped sustained them through centuries of living in a society that undervalued their contributions or misunderstood their cultural effusiveness. Acknowledging people's good qualities and accomplishments is an essential ability for Latino leaders.

¡Que simpático! is a prized Latino compliment....Being respectful and courteous, making small talk, and taking a personal interest in people are ways to be simpático— coveted traits in a people-come-first culture.

Hispanic Value: Generosity and Sharing

My sister Margarita was raised in Nicaragua and was culturally more traditional (or less assimilated) than I am. When I was in my thirties, she was visiting when my next-door neighbor dropped by. He casually admired a poncho hanging on the wall. "Gracias," I said, and I smiled as I remembered its origins. "It's handwoven, and I got it in Chile." When he left, my sister scolded me. "Have you forgotten everything you were taught? You were supposed to give him that poncho!"

This jostled my memory, and I flashed back to a fiesta a few years earlier, when Margarita lived in Guatemala. The hostess flung open the door and gave me a big *abrazo* (embrace), even though I had never met her and hadn't really been invited. "What beautiful gold earrings," I gasped, somewhat stunned at her generous welcoming.

"Here," she said. "You must have them—they're yours." Then she smiled, took them off, and handed me the treasured gift without a moment's hesitation.

The Latino saying "Mi casa es su casa" is the first commandment of generosity. It encapsulates the joy in sharing and implies "What I have is also yours." In collectivist cultures, possessions are more fluid and communal. People take pleasure in giving things away. Generosity, however, is not just a two-way street; it is a busy intersection where everybody meets. A good illustration is the way strangers are always made to feel welcome. One can rest assured that this kindness will come back to you. Even if a particular individual never reciprocates, someone else will surely return the kindness one day.

Latino fiestas are a testament to collective hospitality. All who attend bring gifts, flowers, food, wine, and special treats to share. Many times, when I have a social gathering, it is something akin to the parable of the loaves and fishes in the New Testament. Everyone contributes and the food keeps coming—there is more to eat and drink at the end of the fiesta than at the beginning. For weddings, graduations, and special celebrations, there is the tradition of being a *madrino* or *madrina* (sponsor) and paying for the photographer, banda (band), cake, or bar. At Mexican weddings, people pin money on the bride's dress or pay to dance with the bride or groom.

In traditional families, it can be embarrassing to "have more" or to advance ahead of the group. Having more means a greater responsibility to share more (which is not a burden, but a task undertaken with grace and kindness). When my brother John became a successful music executive, he was the go-to person when a family member had a special need, such as money for school or for travel expenses to attend a family reunion. Cooperation, sharing resources, and helping others keep ties solid.

Generosity is the glue that holds *We* cultures together. Mutuality ensures that people give to each other, and everyone is taken care of. Almost unanimously across collective cultures, it is understood that the accumulation of vast wealth and power by a few hinders the well-being of the community as a whole. People taking more than their share, and the sharp accumulation of money by some at the expense of others, rips apart the community fiber. For this reason, true wealth is defined as being able to give to others.

Unless one has experienced contagious Latino generosity, people from individualistic cultures may find it difficult to understand or to aspire to this level of sharing. From a *We* perspective, since the self emerges from the collective, generosity toward others is actually giving to oneself.

The Latino saying "Mi casa es su casa" is the first commandment of generosity. It encapsulates the joy in sharing and implies "What I have is also yours."

Latino Value: Respeto—Showing Respect

Latinos believe everyone should be treated with dignity and courtesy, regardless of wealth or status. The belief that every person has inherent worth resonates with their people-come-first values, which was highlighted in the section on personalismo. And as we will see, this is the foundation for the leader as equal.

Prolific movie producer Moctesuma Esparza, whose credits include *The Milagro Beanfield War* and *Selena*—a tribute to "the queen of Tex-Mex music"—emphasizes, "Along with respecting elders, a quality my father passed on to me was to treat everyone the same, that is, with respect, no matter what their station in life was, no matter whether they were a president, a rich person, a farm worker, a dishwasher, or anyone else."[11]

While everyone is treated with respect, being looked up to depends on how a person lives, acts, and treats others. Latinos show respect through their body language, tone of voice, deference, apologies, and explanations (even when not really warranted). Of course, all this is interwoven with behaving courteously, offering profuse thanks, and giving compliments. Mutual respect fosters harmonious relationships, cooperation, and reciprocal support.

Respect is even more important with elders and people in positions of authority, such as doctors, priests, teachers, and leaders. They respect a person's title, contributions, education, or authority.[12] Paradoxically, people in positions of power must not assume airs or act as though they are better than others, or they will lose this respect. Plumbers, electricians, bricklayers, gardeners, and people in many trades are respected as well. Someone who is good at a craft or profession is called *maestro*, or master, indicating they are eminently skilled at their craft. The beautiful work many Latino laborers and tradespeople do is indicative of the pride they take in being maestros.

Latinos may communicate indirectly and circuitously if it will spare a person's feelings. Again, this is somewhat paradoxical, since honesty has such a high value, but in this case, courtesy has a higher one. Ask a Latino for directions, and of course they will try to help. You are probably going to get into a conversation even if they don't have a clue where you are going. Taking time to be friendly and maintaining congenial relationships is the best way to ensure that Latinos will participate, be committed, and give well-thought-out, honest responses. These are building blocks for people-oriented leadership.

Hispanic Value: Ser Honesto—Being Honest

Latinos honor the oral tradition. Agreements made verbally were considered just as binding as legal documents. Traditionally, Latinos did not rely on lawyers or contracts to make agreements or do business—a word and a handshake were sufficient. This worked because people usually knew each other or had mutual acquaintances. As Carlos Orta has observed, even today, "Latinos have to get to know a person and trust them before they can do business with them. Latinos don't do business from a transactional perspective but from a relational one."

When buying a service or making an agreement to purchase something, Latinos will routinely not ask for the money or talk up front about costs. This reflects trust in the person's fairness and in the unspoken but binding agreement that they will keep their word. It is also a cultural test—to determine whether this person is honest and someone to befriend. (Of course, in the end, setting a fair price becomes part of the conversation. The essence of bartering is conversing, exchanging, and ensuring everyone feels good about the exchange.)

The phrase "hombre de palabra"—a man of his word—is like the Latino *Good Housekeeping* seal of approval. Keeping one's word is a value upheld in many cultures and certainly is an indispensable leadership trait. But in *We*-centered cultures, the threads holding relationships together would unravel if people did not keep their word. People depend on one another for survival, and honoring commitments is essential.

Honesty or being truthful has been identified as the single most important ingredient determining a leader's credibility because it engenders trust.[13] The bankers letting their greed precipitate the housing and banking crises, politicians breaking their promises, corporate executives not accurately disclosing a company's finances—all indicate that many leaders today simply do not tell the truth. Raul Yzaguirre characterizes honesty as aligning words with action: "There are a lot of inconsistencies with leaders today who articulate American values but don't live them. Latinos are living their values every day. As a culture, we believe that you do what you say you are going to do."

"There are a lot of inconsistencies with leaders today who articulate American values but don't live them. Latinos are living their values every day. As a culture, we believe that you do what you say you are going to do."

—Raul Yzaguirre

Hispanic Value: Trabajar—Contributing Through Work

Even though a growing number of Latinos are now middle class, historically most families, like mine, were working class. In fact, today Hispanics account for 17 percent of total employment but are substantially overrepresented as painters and construction and maintenance workers (36 percent); as miscellaneous agricultural workers (43 percent); and in food preparation and serving (27 percent).[14] This is in part because immigrants often start at the bottom of the economic ladder.

Yes! Latinos continue doing all kinds of tedious jobs—putting on roofs in the searing summer sun, cutting lawns, digging ditches, cleaning hotel rooms, and cooking food. Many times, they might be listening to a radio blasting salsa or Mexican *ranchera* music, having noisy conversations, ribbing each other, or even singing a Spanish tune. What is it about Latinos that enables them to take jobs that people in other cultures might find "beneath" them and to be happy and singing while doing these menial and sometimes physically difficult tasks?

In a collective culture, where *We* is more important than *I*, work is not just a person's livelihood; it is a way to take care of the familia. Since familia is the highest value and concern, work has meaning and dignity. A person will do what they have to do: "As long as I can feed my familia, I feel good about myself. I am honorable." Perhaps for this reason, Latinos have an impeccable work ethic, which translates into the highest participation of any group in the labor market.[15] Work is not just a job; it is a way to contribute to others. Latinos believe in the rewards of hard work. More than 8 in 10—including 80 percent of Latino youths and 86 percent of

Latinos twenty-six and older—say that most people can get ahead in life if they work hard.[16]

 Eighty percent of Latino youths and 86 percent of Latinos twenty-six and older say that most people can get ahead in life if they work hard.

The *dicho* "Los que no trabajan no comen" (Those who don't work, don't eat) underscores that everyone has the responsibility to work and to give of one's efforts. Taking advantage of others by freeloading or not doing one's share runs contrary to helping others. Doing a good job is also the main way to contribute to one's employer. This connects to Latino generosity—what better way to share than to do one's work with gusto—to give it your best shot!

An interesting dimension is that Latinos have traditionally not been part of the elite class; they have not attained benefits, reaped rewards, or assumed privileges they did not earn. They have gotten ahead through their own efforts, especially by working hard and proving themselves. Equality asserts that every person should contribute and earn privileges or rights. Chapter 8, "*Juntos*: Leadership by the Many," builds on this by describing how to ensure that everyone has a place at the table and is invited to contribute.

Hispanic Value: Serving and Helping Others

The values described above converge into cultural directives that spell out how people should relate to and treat one another. *We* cultures emphasize taking care of and contributing to others.

When you first meet a Mexican American, she might greet you by saying, "A sus ordenes" (at your service). When a request is made, she might reply, "Para servirle" (I am here to serve, and how may I help you?). When someone asks for something, the response might be "Mande." *Mande* literally means "Tell me what you want me to do." The cultural translation is "I will do it if I can."

These traditional responses are deeply rooted in the Latino Indigenous background and create a collective spirit where people "serve" one another. Consider that the Nahuatl language of the Aztecs had no word for the concept of *I*. Their sense of relatedness and helping others was the basis of their worldview. So, too, the golden rule of the Maya, "In Lak'ech," signifies "You are in me, and I am in you." This saying reflected their belief that human beings are one people and that what one does to another affects oneself.[17]

Serving is intricately linked to generosity, group benefit, and reciprocity. People understand that what they give to others will certainly come back to them. While it is not tit for tat and people do not *expect* anything in return, they know that the cultural covenant is to help one another. Cyclical reciprocity means that what you give will eventually circle back to you and that, by sharing, everyone will have enough.

In *We* cultures, relationships always imply responsibility toward others. This engenders a sense of duty and is evident in the work ethic I have described. Service is the nucleus around which Latino leadership revolves. Anna Escobedo Cabral has seen this tendency in her extensive work with Latino leaders: "Our ultimate motivation is a concern for the people we serve."

"Our ultimate motivation is a concern for the people we serve."

—Anna Escobedo Cabral

De Colores—of Many Colors

IN THE 1960S, WHEN the humble farm workers marched with César Chávez, they sang "De Colores," a traditional and beloved song that is thought to have been brought over from Spain in the sixteenth century. *De colores* literally means "of many colors." The song celebrates the incredible beauty of diversity—the multicolored birds, the radiant garden flowers, the luminescent rainbow. The chorus of "De Colores" says that because life by its nature appears in so many colors, *so too great love also comes in a multitude of colors.*

The love of diversity in this song is deep within the Latino soul because Latinos are *de colores*. The many colors of humanity are part of our *familia*. While the US census took more than two hundred years to recognize the multifaceted Latino identity, the song "De Colores" clearly defined it centuries ago. We are a diverse and inclusive people that represent the beautiful colors of humanity.

As we noted, Hispanic identity also diversified the US census. Consider that the 2000 census was the first time people had the option to identify as more than one race. By the 2020 census, the "Two or More Races" (multi-racial) population was almost 34 million people—a 276 percent increase since 2010. This is now the fastest-growing racial and ethnic category, and Latinos are leading this change.[18]

We have surmised that Latino *destino* is shaping the diverse and inclusive society. De colores offers a pathway to accomplish this—to integrate our kaleidoscope society and to embrace the gifts of all people, including every generation. Latinos offer an antidote to the exclusion, inequity, and homogeneity of the past. For this reason, I believe "De Colores" is the Hispanic national anthem.

¡Ahora! Reflection and Application

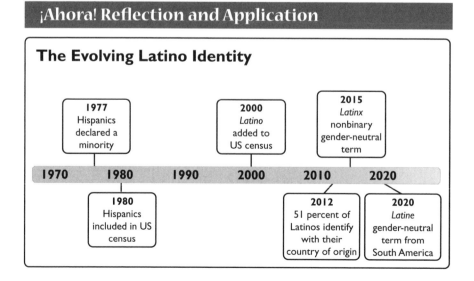

The Evolving Latino Identity

1977 Hispanics declared a minority

1980 Hispanics included in US census

2000 *Latino* added to US census

2012 51 percent of Latinos identify with their country of origin

2015 *Latinx* nonbinary gender-neutral term

2020 *Latine* gender-neutral term from South America

1970   1980   1990   2000   2010   2020

How do you identify? (As we will see in chapter 11, young Latinos use an intersectional approach.)

Three steps I will take to explore, strengthen, and share my Latino identity . . . *or* three steps I will take to learn about and better understand the multiple identities Latinos have in the United States.

1.

2.

3.

From I to We—Building a Collective History and Sharing Our Narratives

- What did you perceive to be the distinction between *I* and *We* cultures?

- How do We cultures strengthen community, collaboration, and inclusion?

- As we begin to explore Latino leadership, what distinctions might you surmise between leaders who come from a We orientation one as compared to those who come from an individualistic one?

Cultivating a We Identity—Sharing our Stories Group Activity

Participants bring the oldest picture of their grandparents or *antepasados*. Each person shares the story reflected in the picture. (In the Latino oral tradition, people embellish lavishly.) They share gifts they inherited from their family. Pictures and gifts can be placed on a table, creating a collective history.

- People comment on what they learned about each other's unique family backgrounds.

- What were the commonalities and differences?

- What are the benefits of creating a collective history with people?

Learning and Incorporating Latino Values

If you worked for a marketing or branding company promoting the Latino culture, what positive values and attributes would you emphasize?

The Latino culture is rich in proverbs, or *dichos*. The following five dichos frame the values overviewed in this chapter. What can you learn from these and how can these dichos enhance your life and work?

Value/dicho	What this teaches	How can I apply this?
Generosity	*"Mi casa es su casa"* My house is your house	
Respect	*"Cada cabeza es un mundo"* Every mind (person) is unique	
Honesty	*"Un hombre de palabra"* A man of his word	
Work	*"Los que no trabajan no comen"* Those who don't work, don't eat	
Service	*"Para servirle?"* I am here to serve, and how may I serve you?	

CHAPTER 7

Fe y Esperanza: Sustained by Faith and Hope

IN MY *FAMILIA*, THE phrase "Está en las manos de Dios" (It's in God's hands) was never far from my mother's lips. My brother Chris needed a baseball outfit; a stray dog wandered in, and David couldn't bear to part with him; my class needed costumes for the school play. And where were the cookies for the church social? "What are kookees?" my mother would ask. No matter what the challenge, somehow she always managed to get what was needed for her eight children and to help others in the community as well.

God looked after her. How else could Celia María Bordas have ended up in the three-bedroom house at 3713 West Platt Street in Tampa, Florida—not far from the same ocean waters that lapped up onto the Caribbean shores where she was born—if God hadn't put her there?

Generations of Latinos simply believed in God's providence and guidance. In fact, my Tía Anita summed up her *fe* (faith) in six words. When asked about what was going to happen or something that was planned, she always prefaced it with "Sí Dios quiere" (If God wants this to happen). After the event happened, her response was "Gracias a Dios" (Thanks be to God). So, coming or going, she had it covered.

The waters of Hispanic spirituality run deep. Fe is a deep-seated thread that permeates everyday life and prescribes how people should treat one another. Building on the generosity, mutuality, and service orientation of their *We* cultural roots, Latino spirituality is a mandate for social responsibility—to do good for others and to help others in need. Arturo Vargas recounts, "Even to this day, my mother is packing up a bag of nonperishables to take the church because it's the first Sunday of the month. We're supposed to take food for the hungry, and I'm thinking, 'Mama, you don't have that much yourself.'"

Esperanza—Hope, Gratitude, and Celebration

WHEN I WAS A child, *mis padres* sang a favorite lullaby, "Ay, ay, ay, ay, canta y no llores" (sing, don't cry). They taught me that when you're facing hard times, singing will change your attitude and get you through them. How amazing that despite their hard work and meager resources my parents were telling me to sing and be happy. *Canta y no llores* also nurtures a can-do attitude, fosters perseverance, and encourages people to stick together—all valuable leadership traits.

In his book *Emotional Intelligence*, Daniel Goleman defines optimism as the greatest motivator, because it expresses a strong expectation that things will turn out all right despite setbacks and frustrations. He cites research that optimistic people tend to be more successful.[1]

Optimism is *esperanza* (hope), an essential Latino quality. This was validated by a *New York Times*/CBS News poll noting that 75 percent of Latinos believed their opportunity to succeed was better than that of their parents. Only 56 percent of non-Hispanics thought this was true. Additionally, 64 percent of Latinos thought life would be better for their children. This jumped to 83 percent for Hispanic immigrants but was only 39 percent for non-Latinos.[2] Optimism is Hispanic immigrants coming to a strange land, struggling to learn English, and working difficult jobs while never faltering in their belief that things will get better. Hispanic optimism is being sustained by younger generations: 75 percent of Latinos ages eighteen to thirty-five believe the standard of living for their children will be much better or somewhat better than their own.[3]

One of our young leaders, Congressman Ritchie Torres, speaks on how hope sustains him, "How I grew up I call Mission Impossible. A single mother raising three children on a minimal income remained hopeful in the face of real deprivation. In some sense it was a miracle. It's the triumph of hope that inspires and sustains me every day."

Latinos are optimistic because of our upward mobility. Compared to the low-income situation many Latinos grew up in, our future is bright. My house is the nicest I have ever lived in. I have more disposable income and nicer things than my parents. Optimism is kept alive by our sense of gratitude and celebratory nature, which we will consider as we continue.

Way back in the early eighties, as a young leader, I designed Mi Carrera (My Career), a nontraditional jobs program for high-risk teenage Latinas, funded through the US Department of Labor. The program was chosen to be replicated across the country. That year, however, President Ronald Reagan was elected. Federal funds were frozen. Mi Carrera was kaput. But we had to do something to save this valuable program! We gathered supporters, threw a big community fiesta to celebrate our accomplishments, and announced Mi Carrera's continuation. Like a magnet, this optimism drew supporters and funders. (We operated on 36 percent of the previous year's budget—a testimony to Hispanic do-more-with-less and resourcefulness.)

And *milagros* (miracles) happened! I was sitting in my office, pondering how to pay a counselor to monitor summer jobs. In walked Lisa Quiroz, a student at Harvard University, who wanted to work for the program that summer. "¡*Dios mío!* You would be perfect, but we don't have money to pay you," I exclaimed. Her mind started clicking, "If you can pay me a stipend, I can get another job and make it work." Lisa was the perfect role model. And as we noted in our section on *destino*, she graduated, worked for Time Warner, and established *Time for Kids* magazine, which melded her concern for youth and education. Latinos believe that doing good comes back to you.

Canta y no llores reminds Latinos that by staying positive, by singing and dancing together, we can overcome difficult situations. Leaders tap into this optimism to inspire and motivate people to work together even when the odds are stacked against them.

Gracias—Gratitude and Thanksgiving

Gratitude was deeply ingrained in early Mestizo-Hispanic culture, in which just surviving was a blessing indeed. Even before the European conquest of this hemisphere, the seeds of gratitude were nourished by Indigenous people. The two meanings of *gracias* ("grace" as well as "thank you") imply that to be happy and to live in what Christians refer to as "a state of grace," one must be grateful. *Gracias a Dios*, a cherished philosophy of life (and my Tía Anita's mantra), was always a common refrain in conversation. Gratitude encompasses an appreciation for parents, familia, the community, the *antepasados*, and the blessing of children.

"Gracias a la Vida" (Thanks to Life), a treasured song by Chilean artist Violeta Parra, is steeped in this spirit of thankfulness. The song thanks life for our ability to see and hear and to have feet to walk with; for cities, puddles, beaches, deserts, mountains, plains, the stars in the heavens; for the alphabet and words so we can communicate; and for our mothers, friends, brothers, and sisters. We are grateful for both smiles and weeping because they allow us to distinguish happiness from sorrow. The ending affirms, "Thanks to life that has given me so much."[4]

Expressing gracias is a great gift that Latinos bring to America—an antidote to the raging materialism that is dividing our nation into a land of haves and have-nots. It is the opposite of taking more than one's share. Gratitude allows people to be generous and give back. Like a spiritual salve, gracias can soothe the cultural angst that comes from always wanting more "stuff" than one has. By focusing on thankfulness, Latinos have been able to maintain a deep-seated optimism among people who sometimes had little economic means or resources. Gracias anchors the Latino Sí se puede (Yes we can!) spirit.

Expressing gracias is a great gift that Latinos bring to America—an antidote to the raging materialism that is dividing our nation into a land of haves and have-nots.... Gratitude allows people to be generous and give back.

Spirituality as Celebration

Gozar la vida (Enjoy life), a principle we will explore, encompasses leadership as celebration, and this tendency springs from Latino spirituality, which has many community celebrations, ceremonies, and rituals that stem from their Indigenous tradition and the Catholic Church.

In the Catholic tradition, Latinos are named for saints, and each saint has a special day on the calendar. Your saint's day is akin to your birthday—and another reason to celebrate! Every Latin American country also has a patron saint, and people get a day off to commemorate their *santo*. (Note: my feast day is June 24, the feast of St. John.)

The small island of Puerto Rico has only 311 miles of coastline, but it may have more patron saints per capita than any other place on earth. Each town has a *festival patronal* (patron saint festival). Add up the number of towns on the island and you're talking about a festival every week. Throw in the fact that the party tends to go on for days, and you will understand the lively tropical spirituality of Puerto Rico.

Rituals such as El Día de los Muertos (Day of the Dead) glow with elaborate altars, special foods, marigold flowers, multitudes of candles, music, and remembrances of people's ancestors. On the night of November 1, people pray, eat, and ask for guidance from their ancestors. The next day, there is a community celebration during which people dress up in costumes and dance all night, traveling from house to house with a *banda* in tow. These festivals weave history, culture, and community into a spiritual celebration that strengthens people's ability to collaborate and do the hard work of community organizing.

When I was a budding teenager, my *abuela* came to visit from Nicaragua. Every night, she would gather us together and my hands would go up like a church steeple as we repeated the mantra "Holy Mary, mother of God," praying the rosary. The holy mother was our protector and nurturer and ensured that our life would be good.

Celebration was evident in the farm workers' strikes of the 1960s. Their long marches and demonstrations were spiritual processions, with a statue of Our Lady of Guadalupe leading them as they sang "De Colores." César Chávez encouraged them: "Let us bring forth song and celebration so the spirit will be alive among us!"[5] Hope, gratitude, and celebration transformed oppression and need into an enduring faith in life's goodness.

Spirituality as Responsibility Toward Others

THE HUMANISTIC, PEOPLE ORIENTATION of Latinos, their values of service, compassion, and responsibility toward others, and their profuse generosity are all grounded in their spiritual beliefs. Janet Murguía reflects, "Early on, my parents helped me develop a sense of responsibility in caring for others. They really instilled in me and my brothers and sisters a sense of caring not only for the family but also for our neighborhood and community." Chávez made the connection between individual contributions and community service: "Being of service is not enough. You must become a servant of the people."[6] This was part of my upbringing as well. If I was unhappy, my mother, in her simple but wise way, would say, "Get busy and do something for somebody else."

"Early on my parents helped me develop a sense of responsibility in caring for others. They really instilled in me and my brothers and sisters a sense of caring not only for the family but also for our neighborhood and community."
—Janet Murguía

Latino spirituality centers on relationships and responsibility for others. In fact, the truest sentiments of the Christian faith follow in this vein. People are described as brothers and sisters and are urged to feed the hungry, give shelter to those in need, and take care of the sick. Spirituality is a moral obligation to ensure others' well-being and the collective good. For Latinos and other communities who have dealt with inequities, spiritual responsibility implies removing the obstacles that limit opportunity. Social and political action is intertwined with spiritual responsibility.

Archbishop Óscar Romero of El Salvador was part of the liberation theology movement that interlaced social justice and responsibility, particularly for the poor in Latin American countries.

Federico Peña adhered to this commitment: "I saw my life as one of helping people who were being discriminated against and had no voice." Speaking out on immigration, he connects religious faith with how we treat others: "For those of us who attended religious worship this past weekend, we should conduct a full moral gut check as we watch immigrant workers wither in our deserts, drown in our rivers, and die on our highways. . . . I believe that great people live by their moral and ethical principles every day. I believe that a nation earns respect when it shows compassion and decency."[7]

"I believe that great people live by their moral and ethical principles every day. I believe that a nation earns respect when it shows compassion and decency."

—Mayor Federico Peña

César Chávez elevated the farm workers' strikes with such traditional religious practices as pilgrimages, fasting, retreats, public prayers, and worship services. Perhaps Chávez explained the integration of faith and social action most succinctly. During the *huelga* (farm workers' strike), when asked how they would achieve their goals, he said, "We're going to pray a lot and picket a lot."[8] The leader as community steward and social activist is rooted in spiritual responsibility.

Three Spiritual Virtues: Courage, Humility, and Forgiveness

THE INTEGRATION OF FAITH, social responsibility, activism, and celebration is the spirit of Latino leadership. Now let's consider three virtues that flow from this orientation: courage, humility, and forgiveness.

Faith Inspires Courage

Latino advancement has required hard work, determination, and the courage to do what is right. Vargas reflects on this: "We must be bold—make unpopular decisions and battle infrastructures that keep our community from progressing." Social activism requires courage, which gives people the strength to face dangers and difficulties. Courage is required every time we try something new, battle the odds, or stand up for injustice. Immigrants, for instance, show tremendous courage by coming to a foreign land.

Courage also comes from having strong convictions: right makes might. Moral courage is developed through right action and by making choices and decisions that align with our values and beliefs.[9] This underscores the significance of leadership preparation and *conciencia*. Like the roots of the great ponderosa, your core values, your history, and the trials and tribulations of those who came before can ground you and give you courage when you have difficult decisions to make or must go against the tide.

Murguía finds courage in her faith: "Con Dios por adelante, todo es posible [With God's help, forward, all things are possible]. And so, for me it was a sense that we shouldn't believe people anytime they say 'You can't do that' or 'No,' but to know all things are possible with God's help." Murguía went from a humble barrio in Kansas City to working in the White House—all the while keeping faith and service central in her life.

Hilda Solis concurs, "We are a very spiritual people. I look to my faith to guide me in many decisions. I'm able to rely on that when I am in difficult conversations, when I'm being challenged, or when I may have to set myself apart from other people because I'm going to say something or do something that may not sit well with a lot of people. My faith gives me courage." (Solis was the first woman to receive the Profile in Courage Award from the John F. Kennedy Foundation.)

"I look to my faith to guide me in many decisions. I'm able to rely on that when I am in difficult conversations, when I'm being challenged, or … I'm going to say something or do something that may not sit well with a lot of people. My faith gives me courage."

—Hilda Solis

Without the gift of hope, Latinos would not have had the courage to stand up against the inequalities of the past. Leaders must dispense hope, because if people are not hopeful, they won't act to change things. Hope and courage are the keystones for the social activist nature of leadership.

Humility

I asked Raul Yzaguirre what he would say if he were speaking to a group of Latinos about our special contribution and what we should hold on to. His answer surprised me: "A sense of humility, modesty, and courtesy." And then he went on to say, "A truly complete human being is one who treats the maintenance worker with the same kind of respect and dignity that he affords the president or CEO." Yzaguirre was defining the leader as equal, which we will detail as we continue. To embody this perspective, leaders must be humble, accept their own shortcomings, and appreciate the inherent worth of others.

Arturo Vargas also recognizes humility as essential. "Leadership—for me it's about clarity of purpose, courage, and being humble. Without humility there is the risk of leadership becoming a cult of personality." US Representative Lucille Roybal-Allard certainly could have taken that path— many people in power do. Instead, she was groomed by her father, Edward Roybal, the first Hispanic elected to Congress in California. He served thirty years and was a staunch advocate for civil rights and people's issues. Her father would remind her, "Never forget where you came from." Today, Roybal-Allard remains true to her father's advice. "I can see where it would be very easy to get caught up in the glory of Washington. It's really important to remember who you are, who you represent, and why you are there."

Leaders who are clear on their purpose, who put an issue or a cause first, and who serve something greater, lessen their self-importance. Anna Cabral observes, "Latino leaders think about the broader good and are not so focused on individual success but rather, How do we achieve success for the larger community?" This shifts the focus from the individual leader to the people he or she serves. Humility is the essence of servant leadership, where the people's needs come first.[10]

Many Latino leaders come from or have family members from a lower economic status and humble background. Their *padres* or *abuelos* overcame Herculean obstacles to provide the opportunities they have today. Latinos, therefore, value humility and look for that quality in their leaders. In collective cultures, humility allows the leader to connect with people and to be seen as one of them. If a leader focuses on *I* rather than *We*, this damages the collective identity and group empowerment. Carlos Orta says, "Good leaders have empathy. They've put themselves in other people's shoes. It goes beyond caring. You have to understand where people are coming from and how your decisions are going to impact them."

Humility does not imply that a leader does not know her worth. It is an understanding that the gifts one was given should be placed at the service of others and that in the last analysis everything a person accomplishes is because of the support and help she has received. Murguía clearly understands this: "In the Latino community, we have this sense that we never do this alone. We rely on family, we rely on community, but in the end we rely on that higher being to help get us through the darkest times and to illuminate our path, and for me that's always been true."

"Good leaders have empathy. They've put themselves in other people's shoes. It goes beyond caring. You have to understand where people are coming from and how your decisions are going to impact them."

—Carlos Orta

Forgiveness and Healing

In part I, we explored the history of the conquest and the colonization of Hispanic ancestors. These antecedents provided the backdrop for leadership aimed at changing oppression. This chapter surmises that it was the spiritual roots of Latino people that gave them the hope and strength to overcome adversity. Now we will consider forgiveness, which entails the healing of historical traumas. Forgiveness has strengthened and nourished the spiritual roots of Latino people.

The story of Our Lady of Guadalupe brought together Catholic and Indigenous beliefs and laid the foundation for the unique brand of Latino spirituality that emerged in this hemisphere. Guadalupe's message was one of perseverance, hope, compassion, and racial and cultural integration. These qualities are intrinsic to Latinos' faith today and are reflected in their leadership practices.

Guadalupe's lowered eyes and supplicating hands invoke humility. She speaks to a peasant and not a Spanish high official, thus negating the church hierarchy in which access to God was through the priests and sanctified officials.

As a Mestiza, Guadalupe represented the vision and promise of the future—a healing force that planted seeds of forgiveness and compassion. Today, Latinos recognize that the blood of the Spanish conquistadores runs through our veins—they are our ancestors. Their influence is present in the language we speak and in many positive aspects of our culture. Rejecting this heritage would be to deny an integral part of ourselves. Bringing the Spanish into our cultural familia, however, requires the reconciliation of historical transgressions (including the trauma of my grandmother and so many other Indian women).

Our Lady of Guadalupe is the face and image of the *mestizaje*, of the forced cultural integration and fusion that took place. Yet her message is of compassion, hope, and inclusion. She is perhaps the reason that Latinos are the only people of color in the Americas who have made peace with their oppressors, embraced their multiple racial backgrounds, and courageously look their history straight in the eye.

Forgiveness allows people to begin anew, to birth new understandings and new pathways. Forgiveness releases and heals the past. The vibrancy, resilience, productivity, and energy of the Latino culture is the result of the complex, historically painful, and yet genetically powerful mestizaje. Forgiveness has allowed Latinos to reconcile the past, have gratitude for what we have today, and be optimistic for the future. Forgiveness is also a wise and magnanimous leadership trait.

Latinos are the only people of color in the Americas who have made peace with their oppressors, embraced their multiple racial backgrounds, and courageously look their history straight in the eye.

Part IV offers five principles that structure leadership with a higher sense of community, deep social responsibility, and a strong sense of service. Leadership is a collective process that builds internal and external coalitions. This is the foundation for *juntos*, leadership by the many, which garners the critical mass needed for social change. It is a blueprint for the civic engagement and citizen participation urgently needed today.

The hard work of leadership is renewed through gozar la vida, which brings people together in celebration and replenishes their resolve to work for long-term change. Chapter 11, "*El Cìrculo*: Inclusiveness Across Generations," accentuates the new dimensions young Latinos bring to leadership. They are following centuries of Latino activism and are dedicated to dismantling social structures that hinder equity, inclusion, and the common good.

¡Ahora! Reflection and Application

Gozar la vida renews people's dedication and long-term commitment to tackling difficult things together.

What are ways in which you have seen the Latino celebratory spirit?

Why has this been particularly useful for Latinos as they have struggled with discrimination and a history of oppression?

Gratitude and Thanksgiving

Gratitude allows people to focus on what they have rather than what they lack or need. This week, take time each day and list five things you are grateful for.

Can you identify a challenge or life situation that may have been difficult but that taught you a lot and made you a stronger and better person? Why is this an important leadership trait?

Have you been a recipient of Hispanic hospitality? How does gratitude allow Latinos to be generous and give back, regardless of their financial means or status?

Can being grateful be an antidote to the raging materialism in our country today? And how does gratitude promote a sense of well-being?

Spiritual Responsibility

For many Latinos, spiritual responsibility implies addressing the obstacles that limit opportunity for people. Social and political action is intertwined with spiritual responsibility.

> During the *huelga* (farm workers strike), César Chávez was asked how the strikers would achieve their goals. He said, "We're going to pray a lot and picket a lot." How does this simple quote capture the deep faith and relentless activism Chávez brought to his work?
>
> Have you observed this tendency in other leaders? What would be different if political and corporate leaders were truly concerned with the welfare of others and saw this as their responsibility?

Courage, Humility, and Forgiveness

Reflect on a leader who you believe is humble and does not aggrandize his or her importance. Now consider one that toots their horn loudly and has a big ego. What is the difference in how you feel about these leaders? Who would you follow? How does lessening self-importance indicate to people that they too could lead?

Group Activity

> Discuss forgiveness and reconciliation. What does it take? Where have Latinos demonstrated that it is a process and that it can be done?

> How does Guadalupe foster this process? Are there other similar stories of "a healing force" that influenced your familia or community or our nation?

> Where else can forgiveness be applied in society and in other ethnic and racial clashes?

PART IV

Putting Leadership into Action

WE ARE NOW READY TO learn about the leadership principles that have propelled Latinos forward. Looking at mainstream leadership is a good starting point, because we will find connecting points between this and how Latinos have traditionally led.

For generations, the centerpiece of mainstream US leadership was the individual leader. This fashioned a hierarchical form, which was very effective in an assembly line economy where people followed orders and looked to a boss for direction. Today, our economy centers on service, technology, communications, and industries such as health care and education, where people skills, joint problem solving, and on-the-spot decision making are required. To address this, leadership has become collaborative and team oriented.

Leadership is also changing due to the external environment. Civil rights, changing demographics, higher educational levels, and political awareness have transformed leadership into a more inclusive and participatory form. Additionally, the diverse, better educated, tech-savvy, and increasingly young workforce expects to participate and function more autonomously. This resonates with Latino inclusiveness—diversity is simply a Latino leader's competitive edge.

We should also consider that in our rapidly changing, super complex world, even the smartest, most experienced leader will simply not have all the answers. Leaders must craft environments in which people work together to generate viable solutions and achieve results. They must hand over the reins and shift the locus of control from *I* as the leader to *We*—the people served by the leader.

Latino leadership aligns with today's collaborative orientation. Latinos are natural collaborators, having learned to work and cooperate with others at an early age. Values such as reciprocity and generosity encourage collaboration. Leaders serve people and share responsibility—a rich foundation for creating inclusive and empowering environments. Perhaps, then, we can say that leadership by a few is being replaced with leadership by the many—a revered Latino leadership principle that we will learn about.

Latinos know that the journey to social justice and economic equality requires ardent community organizing. Advancement has only come because of the struggles and dedication of our leaders. Latinos find examples of this right in their *familias*. Just as I honor the sacrifices of my mother and father, so too can Latinos look back and learn from the leadership of their *antepasados*.

Janet Murguía follows such *consejo* (counsel). "I think my parents, in their own humble ways, taught me a lot of the great skills of leadership. They were honest and hardworking, sacrificed for their children, helped their community, and taught me responsibility for others. These are valuable cultural assets. If we embrace these, they will serve us well."

The leadership principles that follow describe proven ways to engage, inspire, and mobilize people who desire to create a more just and inclusive world. Latino leadership has passed the test of time and has a centuries-old track record of collaborative, collective, and activist leadership. *The Power of Latino Leadership* honors this tradition and lays the foundation for the evolution and expansion of this dynamic form of leadership.

CHAPTER 8

Juntos: Leadership by the Many

T HE ANCESTRAL GROUPS THAT melded into the Latino culture had strong family ties and community bonds and were centered on *We*, the collective. Leadership flows from this orientation and is based on a communal process by which people work together to uplift their communities. This spirit is captured in the word *juntos*, which means "union, being close, joining, being together" and is expressed in the principle of leadership by the many.

Whether *I* or *We* is central to a society contours the shape of its leadership. In an *I,* or individualistic, culture, I become a leader because of my initiative and competence as well as my winning personality. I am a can-do, take-action person. Because I call attention to myself—my accomplishments and skills—people believe I am competent and follow me. Unanimity or group consensus follows the leader's decisions. The leader strives for self-mastery—as I become empowered, I can empower others. Leaders maintain status by remaining youthful, vigorous, attractive, and able. Seniority is secondary to performance.

In contrast, a *We* identity prompts a collective view of leadership in which people acknowledge that the community has nurtured them.

In individualistic cultures, there is a belief that I made it on my own. Collective cultures understand that success is due to the *familia*, the community, and opportunities they have been given. Antonia Pantoja understood this: "I am interdependent. I was nurtured to be who I am and am responsible and accountable to a community of others." Pantoja urged an aspiring leader to answer this question: "Am I a leader that is going to be accountable to my people, to the community from whence I came? If you decide to be that kind of leader, then your skills, energy, and endurance are for the well-being of your community."

The heart of leadership, therefore, is sustaining, educating, and advancing the community. Anna Cabral describes this commitment: "What motivates people in our community who are doing great work and leading efforts is that they are looking out for the collective. The collective good drives them."

"What motivates people in our community who are doing great work and leading efforts is that they are looking out for the collective. The collective good drives them."

—Anna Escobedo Cabral

From Servant Leadership to Community Stewardship

BECAUSE LATINO LEADERSHIP IS rooted in serving the community, it resonates with the prophetic work of Robert Greenleaf, who wrote *The Servant as Leader* in 1970. Greenleaf set the stage for a collaborative process in which the leader serves people. A philosophical and reflective man, he surmised that the hierarchical approach he had witnessed in his career at AT&T did not nurture people's leadership skills, and in fact did not develop the leader's higher capacities, either.

Greenleaf began reflecting on why a person aspired to lead. Thus, he tapped into the practice of *conciencia*, in which a person's intention—the *why*—is the central core from which other actions flow. In an individualistically oriented society, people are taught that personal motivation, the *why*, is generated by self-interest. Leadership brings privilege, status, position, and financial rewards. Greenleaf concluded that these types of leaders did not have a lasting influence on society or the people they led. In fact, leaders who have made the greatest contributions to humankind sought to serve first and then became leaders in order to expand their capacity to serve.

In looking at the leaders profiled in this book, and the thousands of community collaborators who are working to advance Latinos, we can agree with Greenleaf. Having a lasting impact means serving people, communities, and the ideals a leader seeks to further. Greenleaf called people with these intentions "servant leaders." Carlos Orta describes this commitment: "My drive and motivation come from a place of service and righting wrongs. I truly believe that I have been given many opportunities and have the responsibility to give back."

Greenleaf also believed that the litmus test of whether someone was a servant leader was his or her effect on people: Do people become freer, more autonomous, and more capable of serving others? In other words, were people empowered? Greenleaf added another caveat, which was a revolutionary departure from the hierarchical leadership of previous times: What was the leader's effect on the less fortunate members of society?[1]

This connection to the social good and to people's needs repositioned leadership, bringing it back to the beliefs of Indigenous people and to a model closely aligned with the Latino community. In *We* cultures, leaders function as stewards of their communities. Federico Peña echoes this sentiment. "I saw my life as one of helping people who were being discriminated against and had no voice."

Latinos are therefore expanding the focus and scope of servant leadership to community stewardship. Community stewardship develops the capacities of many people to work for the public good.

"My drive and motivation come from a place of service and righting wrongs. I truly believe that I have been given many opportunities and have the responsibility to give back."

—Carlos Orta

The Leader as Equal

Creating a community of leaders is essential when a group's advancement depends on people power and collective resources. Social action requires a critical mass of skilled and motivated people. Ironically, one way leaders develop people is by staying a part of the group and never thinking they are above or better than others. Being humble, not taking oneself so seriously, and not getting snarled in the web of power or money ensure that leaders remain part of the community. This facilitates people's identification with the leader as "being one of us" and reflects the Latino value of *igualdad* (equality, fairness, and justice). The leader is one among equals.

Such leaders must roll up their sleeves, stuff envelopes, clean up, serve food, and attend community functions. Any type of elitism or projection that one is above a certain task lessens credibility and reestablishes hierarchy. For Latinos who struggle with exclusion and discrimination, this would reinforce the psychology of oppression and their "minority" status. Standing out too far from others or calling too much attention to oneself can damage the group cohesion so central to collectivist cultures. Leaders are expected to accomplish extraordinary things but remain ordinary and humble.

In the hierarchical system, a leader might take big bonuses, fancy perks, or fat salaries. The leader as equal, however, cannot take more than their share. When leaders become too wealthy, an economic and social chasm can open that disconnects them from people. Many leaders and politicians today are disengaged from real people because of this.

There also seems to be an unwritten agreement that leaders can make their own rules or even break the law. (Politicians who continue to get wealthy at the public trough are an example.) If people can become rich through legal measures or by nature of their position, then this is an entitlement. A leader as equal, on the other hand, adheres to the same rules as everyone else. Raul Yzaguirre reflects, "You've got to be fair. You've got to say, 'These are the rules. I will abide by them.' You need to be willing to sacrifice if you want others to sacrifice."

Personalismo, the quality of leaders who are respected because of their character and the way they live, prescribes treating everyone equally, fairly, and with respect. Mayor Julián Castro lives by this code: "My values include family, service to others, and a deep respect for other individuals. I need to be respectful and even deferential to others."

When the leader assumes no special status and works side by side with people, this levels the playing field. Others believe they too can become leaders. The result is authentic collaboration where people work as equals to attain mutual goals. Since everyone can contribute, leadership is rotated depending on the task or function, and is much more distributed. Thus, leadership by the many and the critical mass to pursue social change emerges. In a truly equitable environment, the *We* identity is strengthened and the spirit of mutuality flourishes. People reinforce each other's motivation and commitment.

"My values include family, service to others, and a deep respect for other individuals. I need to be respectful and even deferential to others."

—Julián Castro

Leadership Is Conferred

The leader as equal turns the hierarchical pyramid of traditional leadership upside down. A Latino leader's authority and designation come from the people they serve and to whom they are accountable. While there is no formal ceremony or ritual, there are standards for conferring leadership. As noted, personalismo implies that leaders are chosen because of their character—they must be the type of person people want to emulate and follow. And because Latino leaders serve as spokespeople for their communities, they are held to a higher standard. When Peña was mayor of Denver he noted, "I knew I had to conduct myself above reproach, always keep my composure, and work harder because I was the first mayor of color."[2]

Second, the leader must demonstrate results. Leadership does not refer to a position; instead, it is a lifelong commitment to advancing the community, as validated by the leaders in this book. This means that a Latino can be a leader in a group or organization, but not necessarily a Latino leader. It is only when people see this dedication and sanction a person as a trusted role model that they are acknowledged as a leader.

Third, people must believe that the leader is serving something greater—a cause, an issue, a higher calling—and is addressing people's needs. In other words, they are not seeking power for their own aggrandizement. Congressman Torres clearly states this commitment: "Activism is not a hobby. It is my vocation. It's my mission. My source of meaning in life. I have no interest in the title or trappings of public office. I have an interest in public office as a vehicle for effecting the change that I want to see."

Anna Cabral speaks to this focal point: "César Chávez was working in the fields and saw people who were being badly mistreated and needed someone to advocate for them. He rose to the occasion, and it was very difficult. He wasn't educated in leadership techniques; he learned these afterward. But that wasn't his goal—to name himself as leader of the farm workers and assume a position of power. He was really addressing a tremendous unmet need in a specific population."

Sometimes leaders are even enlisted through the pleas of their followers or drawn to leadership to address the injustices of their times. Consider Mayor Castro: "I did not want to run for office," he recalls, "but then saw the potential to make a real difference in people's lives. Now I see politics as a way to construct and create a better community. For instance, I believe we need to preserve the Latino culture. As a policy maker I can work to create mixed-income neighborhoods—make it attractive so Latinos move back to the neighborhoods they grew up in."

When people see a leader rising to the occasion and answering the call to serve, then that person is designated a leader. An overwhelming majority of the Latino leaders with whom I have worked during the past five decades have kept their promise to serve. Evidence of their labor is the vast number of community leaders they have nourished, and the incredible progress Latinos have made.

Leadership by the Many

J AMES MACGREGOR BURNS, IN his Pulitzer Prize–winning book *Leadership*, argues that we are living in a time of "post-heroic leadership."[3] The "great man" theory of leadership is finally over! This resonates with Latinos who are striving to generate a critical mass of engaged people—leadership by the many.

While some people might lament that there is not one leader—a Martin Luther King Jr. or a César Chávez—others believe that an individual, one-person leadership model is not effective for such a diverse and growing community. Activist leadership requires the *fuerza*, or strength, of many hands and many voices. As Arturo Vargas observes, "We're not going to have this one charismatic leader who's going to bring everybody together. It's thousands of leaders. It's thousands of movements in thousands of communities across the country, whether it's the immigrants who are organizing at a local level or the head of a nonprofit organization that is mobilizing his community or the young politician that gets elected to office. It's a different kind of leadership."

Vargas continues, "The challenge for Latinos is not to find a single spokesperson to unite the many disparate communities and causes found among a people sixty-two million strong. The challenge is to coordinate these efforts, to build on successes, and to support communities that are most in need—and it can be done!" This was evident in the passing of DACA, which brought millions of people together and spurred a new generation of activist leaders. There are myriad examples of collective action, which we will explore more in-depth in chapter 10, which focuses on coalition building.

Sylvia Puente, who heads up Chicago's Latino Policy Forum, understands the power of leadership by the many, declaring, "Our strength lies in our numbers, in our collaborative work with hundreds and hundreds of community members. Every day we're working to train hundreds of community members in parent education, fair housing, and to understand the complexities of immigration reform. Then they become community leaders in these areas."

Murguía predicts, "I think that we are going to see a rising tide of Latino leaders in the next generation that is not only going to serve our community but serve our country as well." Vargas concurs: "If people are waiting for the great Brown hope, give it up. It ain't gonna happen! Instead, we have thousands and thousands of leaders working collectively every day throughout our communities. That's the new model of Latino leadership." Latino leadership is of, by, and for the many.

"We're not going to have this one charismatic leader who's going to bring everybody together. It's thousands of leaders. It's thousands of movements in thousands of communities across the country."

—Arturo Vargas

Let us remember that, historically, Latino leaders had to bring large numbers of people together and motivate them to work on issues of discrimination and social marginalization even though they were not getting paid, knew these changes would not happen in their lifetimes, might be penalized for their activism, and were struggling with low-paying jobs.

Such was the case with the League of United Latin American Citizens (LULAC), the oldest Hispanic organization in the United States, founded in the 1920s because Mexican Americans were not allowed to learn English, were paid less for their work, and were being lynched by the Texas Rangers. Many Mexican American families worked in fields, on farms, and on ranches, and their children never went to school. Yet despite these dire circumstances, LULAC was able to organize and fight for equal rights.

This type of action depends on promoting leadership by the many—a community-organizing approach that relies on mass involvement, long-term action, and passing leadership from one generation to another. LULAC today is the largest Latino civil rights organization, with one thousand councils (chapters) across the United States and Puerto Rico—a testament to the resolve of early Latino leaders.[4]

Leadership by the many evokes widespread inclusion, cooperation, and motivating of people. Since leaders identify with, arise from, and depend on people for their authority, leadership is group driven. Yzaguirre notes, "A Latino leader's effectiveness depends almost entirely on their ability to work with people and engage them in community issues." People power and combined resources are how Latinos get things done, whether it's planning a family reunion or a community event, building an organization, or electing more Latinos to office. Latino unity and empowerment today are not dependent on a single leader or a small cadre of influencers but on creating leadership by the many.

And how do these diverse leaders bring people together and get things done? Latinos utilize a collaborative community process. As Hilda Solis describes, "Leaders have to educate our community about issues and do this in a way that is not top down but connects people and brings them together." Then the work is distributed based on skills and abilities, interests, and resources. Collaboration promotes ownership, shared responsibility, and accountability and builds a critical mass of leaders.

Four practices anchor the collaborative community-building process: the power of shared vision; the power of history and cultural traditions; *compartir*, or the power of participation and shared responsibility; and *paso a paso*, or the power of a step-by-step approach.

Leadership by the many is a community-organizing approach that relies on mass involvement, long-term action, and passing leadership from one generation to another.

The Power of Shared Vision

To inspire many people to lead requires a collective process that speaks to a broader vision that springs from the community, fosters involvement, and aims to improve people's lives. Values such as inclusiveness, cooperation, and mutuality facilitate the shared-vision process.

When the Latino Policy Forum in Chicago strove to develop "an American agenda from a Latino perspective," they brought together eleven organizations and six hundred civic leaders, including religious organizations, businesses, elected officials, and community activists, for a series of meetings. By listening to different points of view, communicating in an open, give-and-take fashion, and welcoming new ideas, the forum was able to weave common threads and integrate people's contributions into a collective vision and a comprehensive agenda.[5]

In San Antonio, Mayor Castro invited citizen participation. "You have to ask people what they want to accomplish. That's what gives the vision life. People also define the terms and mechanics of how things get done. And then leadership entails motivating people and supporting collaboration toward realizing that common vision."

A shared vision also links the past, present, and future—it integrates history, addresses today's challenges, and points to future advancement. Anna Cabral observes, "Leaders in our community have a really good sense of the past and how it relates to the present. However, they know that in the end they have to address the challenges the community is facing today and be concerned with the future. Our past guides us. It is important to know the struggles our community faced, but we cannot live in the past. The challenge is to make sure our community is evolving and creating a better future."

Grounded in people's collective experience, a shared vision articulates possibilities and opportunities and spurs people into action. The Latino Policy Forum's vision, for instance, casts a wide net: "Advancing Latinos advances a shared future." It envisions "societal prosperity, unity, and equity in our nation and in the global community." And how will it accomplish this? By building "the power, influence, and leadership of the Latino community through collective action to transform public policies that ensure the well-being of our community and society as a whole."[6] The power of this inclusive vision galvanized busloads of people to travel to the Illinois state capitol in Springfield to successfully advocate for funding early education—a critical issue, given the large, youthful Latino population.

A shared vision is the substance of leadership by the many, a magnet fostering unity and consensus. With a compelling vision, people are willing to assume higher risk, work harder, make sacrifices, and believe they will succeed! Leaders are then spokespeople communicating the vision with passion and conviction and inspiring people to get on board. They are trustees of their community's future and guardians of tomorrow's children.

The Power of History and Cultural Traditions

To bring their cultural assets into the mainstream, Latinos must have a strong identity, be proud of their heritage, and be rooted in their history. This nurtures a feeling of family and unity, so that a sense of continuity and wholeness emerges. Knowing the struggles of the past provides an understanding of what needs to be done to keep advancing. Julián Castro emphasizes this: "Many young Latinos don't know who César Chávez is. I feel blessed that I grew up with a mother who was an activist, who understood what it took to get to where we are. I attended Chicano rallies as a child, and I learned about the sacrifices made by previous generations."

Hispanic history is very complex. Since it is not taught in schools or integrated into American history, Latinos are at a disadvantage. Often, they do not know the leaders who advanced their people or the seminal events that shaped the Latino experience. Unlike dominant-culture leadership, which emphasizes acting in the present, understanding one's past is key to Latino leadership. The expansive diversity makes this historical connection a necessary prelude to united action.

I begin all Latino leadership programs with a history of Latinos in the United States. While it would be impossible to describe this lengthy process, the following summaries offer a snapshot of the historical footprints of US Latinos:

- The first Latino organization was the League of United Latin American Citizens. The second was the American GI Forum, founded in 1948 because of discrimination against Hispanic veterans who fought and died in World War II but were denied burial in White cemeteries.[7]

- At this time, Mexican American children could not attend school with Anglos, and the Texas landscape was peppered with signs saying "No Mexicans, No Dogs."

- In 1954, *Hernandez v. Texas* challenged the belief that Hispanics were not being discriminated against because they were considered White. The US Supreme Court ruled that Hispanics are "a class apart" that could indeed suffer discrimination.[8]

- Puerto Rico became a commonwealth in 1952, after years of war, colonization, and uprisings. This status means that Puerto Ricans are US citizens. They frequently return to their beloved island, reinforcing a strong cultural identity and Spanish fluency.[9]

- The influx of Cubans seeking political asylum in the 1960s shaped Miami into a bilingual international city and the heartbeat of a vibrant Cuban community. Cubans have the highest Latino educational and economic level and tend to vote more conservatively.[10]

- The 2020 census validated Latino diversity, which includes Puerto Ricans (10 percent), Cubans (4 percent), Salvadorans (4 percent), and Dominicans (3.8 percent). Mexican Americans represent 60 percent of the Latino population, due to the proximity of México to the United States and the fact that more than one-third of the continental United States was historically México.[11]

Promoting an understanding of Latino history is the first step in recognizing commonalities and honoring differences. Leaders assist people
in identifying points of cohesion, such as shared values, traditions, and
language. Unlike Black Americans and American Indians, whose identity is
defined by blood and biological heritage, Latinos as a conglomerate culture
must choose to embrace a common identity. (They check the box!) Leaders
bring people together to share common experiences as minorities, as immigrants, and as a mixed people from many races, faces, and places. Forging
Latino identity is a critical function of leadership today, and this begins with
tapping into the power of history and cultural traditions.

Compartir—The Power of Shared Responsibility and Participation

COMPARTIR MEANS "TO SHARE," and it reflects a collaborative
approach in which people are encouraged to take responsibility.
Arturo Vargas notes, "When I am asked to make a decision, I've
got to check with the people who are going to do the work. For people to
follow your leadership, they also need to be an integral part so that they're
leading as well." Compartir encompasses Latino values such as cooperation, generosity, and service. As Julián Castro observes, "Latinos are
simply more communal and more inclusive. If everyone chips in and does
his or her part, things get done quicker, relationships become stronger,
and we can have a good time."

Compartir also extends to sharing and distributing rewards. While
many espouse collaborative leadership today, there is still great income
disparity and privilege. When one succeeds in a collectivist culture, however, the good fortune is shared. Since the purpose of leadership is to benefit the community, the rewards must benefit everyone as well. This was
affirmed by a Nationwide Mutual Insurance Company employee benefits
survey, which found that Hispanic businesses are 23 percent more likely
to offer benefits to their employees, including medical and retirement
benefits, than non-Latino companies.[12]

Latinos love to work, and they especially relish working with others. There also is the desire to *hágalo con orgullo* (do it with pride), to add a little passion and energy, to give it your best shot. This not only drives excellence but also urges people to enjoy what they are doing! For Latinos, compartir—sharing responsibility—strengthens relationships, allowing everyone to contribute and to enjoy the process. Latinos add the spice and salsa to collaborative and collective leadership. (More about this in chapter 11.)

Ruben Gallego credits his successful run for the US Congress to his ability to work hand in hand with people. "We would do it together, and that was the biggest equalizer. As a leader, you can't stand back and let people do that hard work. You should be able to show 'I'm willing to do it, and therefore I hope you'll do it too!' I was the person that would hit the doors campaigning in the 110-degree summer's heat."

Mayor Federico Peña's campaign slogan, way back in the 1980s, was "Imagine a Great City!" What a pipe dream! Denver was then a cow town with a faltering economy. But Peña got people involved. "When I was mayor, I always invited people to participate and to be part of the solution. There was a great deal of community involvement. People would say, 'Why is the mayor putting together another task force?' Well, I understood that you get things done by involving people and working as a community. Now people reflect back and say, 'By having that task force, you saved fifteen years.' When people become part of the effort, they want to support the effort, and then they are helping to shape their destiny."

During his tenure, Denver passed more bond issues than any city in the United States had previously, and it achieved great feats: a new airport, a convention center, a performing arts center, a Major League Baseball team, an expanded library, and a revitalized downtown.[13]

"Latinos are simply more communal and more inclusive. If everyone chips in and does his or her part, things get done quicker, relationships become stronger, and we can have a good time."

—Julián Castro

Paso a Paso—The Power of a Step-by-Step Approach

LIKE SLOWLY SIMMERING A pot of green chili so the spicy ingredients meld into a delicious dish, keeping people involved and motivated takes a great deal of patience and perseverance. In a community that grapples with historical disparities, countless needs, many interests, great diversity, and bourgeoning growth, cultivating a sustained commitment is an ongoing process. Raul Yzaguirre, who basically wrote the handbook for Latino advancement, advises, "We have to have a strategy of little victories. We can change things, but in bite-size pieces. Leaders need to think big, but it is the little success that builds people's self-confidence. Having both a long-term vision and building sequential steps, paso a paso, keeps people moving and motivated. As people succeed, their vision of what is possible to accomplish becomes wider and more expansive."

Paso a paso—taking it step by step—recognizes that it took generations for Latinos to be where we are today. By remembering the struggles of their parents and grandparents, people find the resilience and courage to continue working for Hispanic progress. The past has made Latinos stronger, wiser, more resourceful, and determined. Hilda Solis captures this spirit: "We are persistent and continue to move along even in the hardest and worst times," she says. "We move forward and we're relentless. We don't give up."

"We have to have a strategy of little victories.... It is the little success that builds people's self-confidence.... Sequential steps, paso a paso, keeps people moving and motivated. As people succeed, their vision of what is possible to accomplish becomes wider and more expansive."

—Raul Yzaguirre

As an intact community, Latinos have a sense of *destino*, of being part of a greater force. In the late nineties, María Antonietta Berriozábal served on San Antonio's city council, and she would use a dynamic metaphor: she saw herself in the middle of a stream of change. It began with her ancestors, flowed through the many leaders who had gone before her, and continued through the community leaders she currently worked with. As the stream continued to flow into the future, it would gather strength and momentum and would be there when she was gone. "I do my part, and others do theirs. Eventually we will make the current so strong that it will sweep away the old and make things ready for a new world." The belief that they are part of a historical movement is the power of Latino leaders. It keeps leaders moving paso a paso and sustains their lifelong commitment.

Paso a paso is a strategic leadership tool that requires planning, analytical thought, careful execution, and incremental building on progress. It reminds people that by staying on track and remaining focused, small contributions add up and collective efforts pay off. Leadership by the many is only sustained when people persevere step by step and day after day. Janet Murguía reflects on how this prepares people to be advocates for change: "Leadership is having a sense of responsibility but also having a shared vision for the change that you want to see in society, then creating that change and executing ideas into action by building a sense of unity with people." (Chapter 10 discusses this aspect of Latino leadership.)

"Leadership is having a sense of responsibility but also having a shared vision for the change that you want to see in society, then creating that change and executing ideas into action by building a sense of unity with people."

—Janet Murguía

Latino inclusiveness and a penchant for diversity are evident in our next principle: *¡Adelante!*—immigrant spirit, global vision, and multicultural identity. Historical connections across the world give the Latino culture an international flair that is being revitalized by immigration, technology, travel, communication, and globalization.

In addition, Latino growth has been fueled by immigration. America is a nation of immigrants whose ancestors came seeking freedom and prosperity. This same desire exists in Latino immigrants, who come seeking a better life and bring optimism, hard work, and enduring contributions to our nation. Latino immigrants are revitalizing the cultural core.

Finally, Latinos today are embracing their multiracial and multicultural identities. This is in sync with young people, whose fastest-growing identity is mixed race.[14] This positions Latinos to lead our transformation to a multicultural nation.

¡Ahora! Reflection and Application

Servant Leaders and Community Steward

Reflect on two leaders. The first is a servant leader who benefited people. The second attained position, power, and maybe wealth but did not put people first.

How did these leaders differ?

What was the impact on the people they led?

Note ways in which servant leaders empower as they serve . . .

The Leader as Equal/Leadership by the Many

The leader as equal works side by side with people. How does this concept uproot hierarchical leadership and dismantle dominance? List three ways a leader could demonstrate being "one among equals." (Example: the leader follows the rules.)

1.

2.

3.

~~~~

Group Activity

Review the four practices that anchor the community-building process and grow a critical mass of leaders (leadership by the many). Now complete this exercise.

You are leaders of a community group and want to inspire participation and commitment. Brainstorm two steps under each practice that would motivate people to work together to grow their leadership ability.

Shared vision

- Step 1:

- Step 2:

Honoring history and cultural traditions

- Step 1:

- Step 2:

Compartir, participation and shared responsibility

- Step 1:

- Step 2:

Paso a paso, a step-by-step approach

- Step 1:

- Step 2:

CHAPTER 9

¡Adelante! Immigrant Spirit, Global Vision, Multiracial Identity

MY FIRST MEMORY IS of being in the hull of a banana boat as we rocked and swayed across the Gulf of México. My mother, four brothers, my sister, and I hunkered down in bunk beds as we left our beloved Nicaragua. Scared, excited, and hopeful, we were on the way to the land of opportunity! This immigrant dream has been the promise of America and the wellspring of its greatness. No one knows this better today than the millions of Central and South Americans who have made the long trek across deserts, oceans, rivers, and mountains to share in the bounty of this great country.

Anna Cabral remembers her grandparents' stories about their perilous crossing of the Rio Grande and then walking all the way from Texas to California with no money. They took jobs in the fields to care for the family. Julián Castro's grandmother was five when she came from México. She worked as a maid, cook, and babysitter so his mother could go to Catholic school and eventually complete college. Hilda Solis's mother fled the turmoil of the wars in Nicaragua to work in factories in East LA.

After leaving their possessions behind to escape Fidel Castro's regime, Carlos Orta's father worked three jobs to support his family. Arturo Vargas's parents met on a bus in Chihuahua, México. They moved to El Paso seeking a better *vida* (life) for their children. Decades later, Cristina Jimenez's family left Ecuador because of a lack of food and jobs, high inflation, and political turmoil. Her mother cleaned houses and her father worked in construction and factory jobs.

For Latino leaders such as these, immigration is a recent experience, molding their worldview and influencing how they approach leadership. Immigration roots run deep and strong—they shape the Hispanic psyche. Consider that in the past century more than 40 percent of all Hispanics were foreign born.[1] According to the 2020 census, this remains at 33 percent, or 1 out of 3 people.[2]

Unlike US Latinos, who have been minorities and only recently emerged as a recognized group, immigrants were raised in countries where identity, language, and culture are central. Because of this, immigrants keep the Latino cultural memory alive, reinforce core values, and foster an indomitable can-do spirit. This is one of the main reasons Latinos today are not assimilating as other groups have done. (More on this as we continue.) At the same time, immigration presents daunting leadership challenges.

This chapter reviews three core dynamics that shape the US Latino experience today and strongly influence leadership: immigration, global connections, and a growing multicultural identity. We begin by considering the status of past immigration and how that has changed for those from Central and South America who aspire to achieve the American dream today. (Multiracial is being composed of, or having a mixture of, multiple races. Multicultural is a conscious choice to relate to or adapt to several different cultures.)

Immigrants keep the Latino cultural memory alive, reinforce core values, and foster an indomitable can-do spirit.... At the same time, immigration presents daunting leadership challenges.

The Immigrant Spirit

I MMIGRANTS THROUGHOUT HISTORY HAVE been willing to pay extraordinary costs and take enormous risks. Just over a century ago, most immigrants arrived via a hazardous sea journey. Today's immigrants often cross the desert, not the ocean, but the risks are the same and the costs just as high. And why do they take these risks? Immigrants seek economic security, education, opportunity, and freedom. Many are fleeing oppressive regimes, natural disasters, and poverty. Yet they persist. They are pioneers, front-runners, dreamers, and achievers. Most of all, they have courage and a vision for a better future.

The United States is a nation of immigrants. No other country has ever absorbed so many people from so many different places. "E pluribus unum"—to make one out of many—is the heart of the American experiment. Immigrants gave us the values we hold most dear: initiative, hard work, tolerance, freedom, optimism, and faith. The immigrant spirit endowed us with the belief in endless possibilities and people's ingenuity.

The early waves of immigrants in colonial times came mainly from northwestern Europe—England, Ireland, Scotland, Germany, France, the Netherlands, and Scandinavia—and were welcomed with open arms. They had a common heritage of being White, Anglo-Saxon Protestants. Immigrants today look more like my family, and yet they make the same sacrifices and pursue the same dreams that brought the early pioneers and colonists.

But the doors of opportunity have slammed shut. The last immigrant reform law was passed under President Ronald Reagan, in 1986, and provided amnesty for immigrants who arrived prior to 1982. This was the last law passed by the US Congress to ameliorate the immigrant crisis. For forty years, undocumented immigrants have languished in the shadows.

Jimenez, whose family was undocumented, recalls, "As a high school student I lived with fear every day that I would come home and my parents would be gone. After 9/11, people were detained, deported, and disappeared." It is estimated that about 4 million Latino children in the United States—25 percent to 28 percent of all Latino children in the country—have an undocumented immigrant parent.[3] These children are experiencing the fear and anguish associated with having a parent who could be deported *at any moment.*

In the past ten years, a wall of exclusion has jutted up across the Mexican border and in the hearts and minds of some. People cannot migrate legally and so they make the perilous trek and risk their lives, sometimes ending up in detention centers. Their children are taken from them, lost in an inhumane system or even put in cages, as was the case during the Donald Trump administration. Today, it is estimated, there are 10 million to 12 million undocumented immigrants living in the United States with no pathway to legalization.[4]

Immigration is central to the heart of Latino leaders. We know that people like my *familia* are part of a Latino diaspora who came hoping for a better and safe life for their children. Immigrants give up their extended families, homeland, culture, language, and the respect they had in their communities.

The United States is a nation of immigrants.... Immigrants gave us the values we hold most dear: initiative, hard work, tolerance, freedom, optimism, and faith.

The "New" Hispanic Immigrant

THE YOUNG HISPANIC CORPORATE achievers is a dynamic, well-educated, community-minded group that is bringing Latino assets to corporate America. I have worked with the group since its inception fifteen years ago, and I see an interesting shift occurring. Although 63 percent of the US Hispanic population is of Mexican descent,[5] many participants in recent classes were born in Central and South America. They come from Bolivia, Chile, Colombia, Cuba, Ecuador, Honduras, México, Puerto Rico, and Venezuela. About 70 percent of South American Hispanics in the United States are foreign born.[6]

A steady stream of educated young Latinos are leaving their countries seeking opportunity in the United States. This is an unforeseen legacy that started in the 1960s, when John F. Kennedy launched the Alliance for Progress to create a strong, highly educated, technically skilled middle-class sector to modernize oligarchic societies, stabilize economies, and spur democracy.[7]

Unfortunately, there were limited professional opportunities for the growing educated class in South and Central America. A brain drain started in the 1970s and continues today.[8] These immigrants are known as the "new economic exiles" and are arriving at a time when organizations and businesses are eager to tap the assets of educated, bilingual, and globally oriented Latinos. This wave of educated South and Central American immigrants is enhancing the global identity of US Latinos and engendering a stronger, more diverse leadership cadre.

Approximately 36 percent of adult South American immigrants have a bachelor's degree or higher; this is slightly greater than the number among the native-born adult populations in the United States, which is 33 percent. Fifty-six percent of immigrants from Venezuela, 44 percent from Brazil, and 41 percent from Argentina and Chile each are college graduates. And, likely owing to their college education and better English, a significant share of these immigrants works in management, business, science, and arts occupations.[9]

At the same time, working-class and rural immigrants from Latin America continue to make up the majority of the newly arrived. Measured in raw numbers, the modern Latin American immigration wave is the largest in US history. Nearly 59 million immigrants have come to the United States since 1965, when the Immigration and Nationality Act was passed. About half are from Central and South America.[10] When asked why they came to this country, 55 percent say for economic reasons, while 24 percent cite family reasons.[11]

The Latino community continues to benefit from the optimistic and enduring immigrant spirit. Latino immigrants are adding a new cultural zest and vitality and reconnecting us with our ancestral countries and traditions. Latino immigrants are breathing new life into our economy, culture, and democracy.

Why Don't Latinos Assimilate Like Other Groups?

WHEN WHITE IMMIGRANTS LANDED on Ellis Island, they were urged to shed their cultural skin, change their names, lose their language, and merge into the melting pot. The message was "Assimilate—don't look back!" Because they had common racial, cultural, and religious roots, they were able to do this. Most disconnected from their countries of origin, forgot their language, and lost their culture. Perhaps this was a small price to pay to partake in the American dream, and it may have been necessary when our young country was forging its identity.

As noted previously, because of exclusion, discrimination, and racism, Latinos were marginalized and historically did not assimilate. They acculturated. Latinos kept their communities, culture, and language and remained connected to their countries of origin. When Latin American immigrants arrive, therefore, they have a cultural oasis waiting and can partake in the US Latino culture whose inclusive values say *bienvenido*. Furthermore, the newly immigrated are a critical mass, numbering around 20 million.[12] Thus, because of their sheer numbers, Hispanic immigrants today can keep their identity and acculturate.

Since the Spanish conquistadores imprinted themselves not only on the United States but also on much of the entire Western Hemisphere, Latinos have strong cultural and historical affinities that other US immigrants do not have. The proximity of Hispanic homelands and the relative ease of modern communication and travel also have reduced the need to assimilate. Our growing realization of the benefits of cultural diversity may encourage modern immigrants to keep their ethnic identity, whereas this previously was seen as a handicap. Finally, the Latinos' demographic growth and rising influence offer many advantages to immigrants who wish to become bicultural rather than assimilate.

The Latino community continues to benefit from the optimistic and enduring immigrant spirit. Immigrants are adding a new cultural zest and vitality and reconnecting us with our ancestral countries and traditions.

Immigrants Are Building Our Future

BEFORE EXPLORING HOW LATINO leaders are fighting for immigration reform, let's look at how immigrants contribute to the vitality and viability of the United States.

According to the research organization New American Economy, immigrant entrepreneurs made up 21.7 percent of all business owners in the United States. Moving to another country is inherently courageous and risky, requiring stamina and determination. So it comes as no surprise that immigrants are more entrepreneurial. Immigrant businesses create jobs and boost our economy, employing 8.1 million people and generating $1.1 trillion in spending power in 2019.

And they pay taxes even when undocumented! Collectively, undocumented immigrants pay an estimated $11.64 billion in state and local taxes yearly. Because they are starting over, immigrants buy household goods, furniture, cars, and clothing, so they pay $6.9 billion in sales tax each year. And check it out: they pay personal income tax of $1.1 billion. Immigrants are stoking up our economy![13]

Most critical is that new immigrants and their children are projected to account for 82 percent of population growth in the coming half century.[14] But is this cause for alarm? Will this dilute the United States' distinctive characteristics? Will we lose our economic prominence?

Quite the contrary. Demographers are predicting that without immigration, the declining US birthrate and the graying of the White population would result in a dearth of workers and drain the economy.

The dependency ratio—the number of elderly people and children relative to the number of people of working age—is set to rise sharply, mainly because of the increase in the elderly population. By 2050, assuming trends continue, the ratio will rise to 72 dependents for every 100 Americans of working age. The current ratio is 49 percent.[15] If the United States' working-age-to-senior ratio is not maintained, more resources will be needed for the aging population, decreasing economic growth.

A study by George Mason University proposes that US gross domestic product could double by 2050 if today's immigration levels were doubled to more than 2 million new permanent and temporary immigrants each year. *And listen up:* this would lead to a 3 percent increase in average income by 2050 for all Americans.[16]

Even at current immigration levels, by 2050, new immigrants and their children will account for 83 percent of the growth in the working-age population. Since México is the top country for US immigration, and other Latin American countries make up an additional 25 percent, this will augment the Latino population in coming decades.[17] Add this to current predictions that the US Latino population will more than double by 2060 and we can understand the critical role Latino growth will play in sustaining the US economy.[18] Janet Murguía notes this importance: "The growing Latino population ensures the steady supply of future workers and taxpayers needed to maintain the social contract between generations."

As far as preserving distinctly US national characteristics, we have already seen that in our global and diverse world the old patterns of ethnocentricity and cultural conformity are antiquated responses. Instead, leaders need to know how to effectively deal with and adapt to people from many cultures and many parts of the world. Immigrants can be prototypes for cultural adaptation, because to succeed they must become bicultural, learn the "American way of life," and fit into mainstream society. Immigrants bring new perspectives, a global mind-set, and cultural gifts that enrich our society and prepare us to navigate successfully in our world village.

"The growing Latino population ensures the steady supply of future workers and taxpayers needed to maintain the social contract between generations."

—Janet Murguía

Advocating for Immigration Reform

ACCORDING TO A REPORT from the Pew Research Center, most immigrants (77 percent) are in the country legally, while almost a quarter are unauthorized.[19] During the Trump administration, US Immigration and Customs Enforcement (ICE) policy was that all undocumented immigrants had committed a crime, either by entering the United States illegally or by staying after their visa expired. The result was a 150 percent spike in arrests of undocumented immigrants without a criminal record.[20]

This policy made the 10 million to 12 million hardworking undocumented immigrants de facto criminals and goes against the grain of our founding values as the country where the world's "huddled masses" were welcomed. It is also not in sync with the majority of Americans (76 percent) who believe immigrants strengthen the country "because of their hard work and talents."[21]

US Latinos could have turned a blind eye to the current immigration crisis, lamenting the profound fear and misery it brings to millions but doing *nada*. This, however, would be contrary to our values, unravel connection with our relatives and *amigos* in other countries, and diminish our political and economic potential. Instead, immigration is front and center in the Latino activist agenda.

The League of United Latin American Citizens, the oldest Latino advocacy organization in the United States, has a strong immigration initiative that mobilizes its one thousand chapters to pressure the US Congress to create a path to citizenship for undocumented workers. LULAC also provides legal assistance and needed resources, such as the Hispanic Immigrant Integration Project, to help low-income, Spanish-dominant, and underserved immigrants relocate to the United States.[22]

The platform for UnidosUS, the Latino civil rights organization, states, "We fight for an immigration system that values every person's dignity and human rights. We support policies that broaden ways for people to enter the country legally." This advocacy is needed today more than ever. The immigration court system has a 1.7 million–case backlog, the largest in history, making citizenship an elusive and painful process.[23]

Recognizing the paralysis of the federal government on immigration reform, Latinos are taking action at the state level. Illinois has the sixth-largest immigrant population in the country. The Latino Policy Forum recognizes the power of partnership and has brought together an alliance of twenty organizations to work on immigrant issues and public policies that address these. Cochaired by former congressman Luis Gutierrez, the son of immigrants, the alliance lobbied for the passage of the Illinois Trust Act, which closed immigrant detention centers, increased protection for immigrants, and ended local partnerships with federal immigration enforcement authorities. California and Washington State have passed similar laws.[24]

Chapter 11, on intergenerational leadership, tells the story of young undocumented Latino immigrants who are on the front lines fighting for immigration reform. Likewise, we will learn about Voto Latino, which lobbies public officials to fix the broken immigration system and to treat immigrants with respect and dignity.[25]

Immigrants not only are reinforcing the cultural core but also are strengthening the international Latino identity. This next section looks at the skills required for global leadership, and the unique contributions and assets Latinos have because of their historical, cultural, and linguistic connections across the world.

Global Leadership—A Latino Advantage!

WE LIVE IN AN interconnected world where globalization requires leaders to have the knowledge, attitudes, and skills to deal with diverse people from many nationalities and cultures. While many mainstream leaders are learning these capacities, people from communities of color, and particularly Latinos, because of our mixed background and international antecedents, already know how to connect with a multitude of nationalities, races, and cultures.

This section reviews five behaviors/skills gleaned from books and articles, including *What Is Global Leadership?* and *Leadership Is Global*, that define the intercultural capacities leaders need in our world community.[26] These five behaviors/skills are developing cultural awareness, discerning cultures within cultures, putting relationships first, the ability to frame shift, and setting a personal example.

I want to emphasize that none of the sources reviewed included or even referred to leaders from communities of color or to Latinos as having international capabilities. This is a glaring gap that disregards the enormous contributions these communities can make in advancing global leadership. Latinos can serve as ambassadors, mentors, resources, and valuable connectors to our world community.

Developing cultural awareness, the first behavior, is the ability to discern differences among people. Cultural awareness flows from the realization that our leadership practices are formed by the environment around us—our background, upbringing, and cultural orientation. A culturally self-aware person realizes how these differences impact leadership and the way things get done. While a person's leadership orientation is a product of a particular cultural context, self-aware leaders know that they must adapt to and operate in new environments.[27]

For Latinos, cultural awareness is a survival tactic—to succeed, they have had to adjust to and function in mainstream society. Latinos develop cultural awareness, as I did, when they walk into their elementary school and the teacher, the other children, the language, and the learning methodology are as foreign as white bread. And if they or their parents immigrated to the United States, as in the case of Jimenez, Murguía, Orta, Pantoja, Solis, Vargas, and my own family, cultural awareness and adaptation were an integral part of our lives.

In the Latino community, cultural self-awareness and adaptation are referred to as "crossing over," implying that a person can traverse between the Latino culture and the mainstream one. They straddle two worlds. Moreover, as discussed, Latino have ancestry from twenty-six countries, and the US census identifies thirty Latino subgroups. This impels Latino leaders to develop a deep cultural awareness and adaptability to relate to this immense diversity.

The second trait global leaders need is the ability to *discern cultures within cultures*, to take a flexible approach to leadership that accommodates the behaviors of people who identify with different cultural spectrums. "Cultures within cultures" is described as internal diversity.[28]

Vargas, whose parents were from Chihuahua, México, recalls growing up in south Los Angeles in a mixed White and Black neighborhood that was becoming more Mexican by the day. Later it became a migration point for Salvadoran war refugees. By the time he was eighteen, Vargas attended Stanford University and was adept at maneuvering within cultures—internally in the diverse Latino community and externally in the dominant culture. Today, as president of the NALEO Education Fund, he uses these skills to bring Latino subgroups together and to build coalitions with other groups to work on political empowerment and citizen participation. (The next chapter describes coalition building, which necessitates being able to discern differences, build on commonalities, and focus people on mutual action.)

Promoting internal diversity is not integral to the mainstream White culture. Instead, homogeneity, cultural dominance, and ethnocentricity have been the norm. In this restricted cultural environment, the knowledge and contributions of Latinos and other communities are not validated or utilized. Latinos and other communities of color, on the other hand, had to incorporate internal diversity to survive and succeed in the dominant culture. Now they can serve as valuable resources in showing mainstream leaders how to adapt to cultures across the globe.

The third intercultural capacity is a Latino cultural and leadership strength: *putting relationships first*. In foreign environments, leaders must rely more on strong, trusting relationships than they would have to in more familiar territory. Putting relationships before tasks is a "practice that is considered common sense in many parts of the world." Leaders must be willing to join in and become part of the group.[29] To be authentic, this needs to happen at a personal level and not just at work.

Excuse me, but putting relationships first is the heartbeat of *We* cultures! For Latinos, practices such as *personalismo*, developing *confianza*, being *simpático*, and remaining a leader among equals are mainstays of leadership and underscore that relationships come first.

Moreover, these practices are also key to our fourth ability, *the ability to frame shift*, to modify perspectives and leadership methods to fit different circumstances and people. Frame shifting for traditional Anglo leaders is learning to interpret indirect communication, to be comfortable with emotionally expressive styles, to demonstrate personal loyalty and interdependence, to change the pace of work or slow down, and to deal with cultural complexity.[30] This list is a recipe for White leaders to learn how to adapt to traditional *We* cultures and the Latino experience. It is an invitation to cross over, to experience cultural fluidity and flexibility!

The fifth competency, *setting a personal example* (or, for Latinos, personalismo), enables leaders to inspire people from different countries. The many challenges of global leadership require leaders to rely on others to assist them, especially as cultural guides. Perhaps we should do a little frame shifting here; we do not need to cross national boundaries to find cultural guides or to learn global leadership skills. Latino leaders can serve as prototypes. They are already utilizing the five intercultural capacities described. In fact, we might say that Latinos have a global advantage.

Our five competencies enable global leaders to bridge cultures, disciplines, and sectors and to foster an external frame of reference (that of other countries). The many immigrants, nationalities, and countries of origin that compose the multidimensional Latino community in the United States demonstrate these competencies. Including the practical experiences and global perspectives that exist within the culture of Latinos and other communities of color would expand the United States' ability to effectively partake in our world community. As Julián Castro surmises, "My vision is that Latinos can be America's greatest asset to compete in a global context."

"My vision is that Latinos can be America's greatest asset to compete in a global context."

—Julián Castro

Embracing a Multicultural Identity

IMMIGRATION IS FUELING A multicultural, multinational, and multiracial Latino identity that is reinforcing the Latino propensity to keep connected with their countries of origin. Even though my family emigrated when I was a child, I still see myself as Nicaraguan with Mexican roots (as well as a Latina and a proud American). A study by the Pew Research Center found that 51 percent of US Latinos identify with their family's country of origin, using such terms as *Mexican*, *Cuban*, or *Dominican*.[31]

This trend is continuing among Latinos ages sixteen to twenty-five. When asked about the first term they use to describe themselves, 52 percent say their family's country of origin. Acculturation allows Latinos to have multiple identities and to value every single one! These identities function as bridges or crossroads allowing a person to bring forth the best from each culture. What an asset in our global village! (Intersectionality, which recognizes the interconnected nature of social identity such as race, class, ethnicity, and gender as they apply to a given individual or group, is looked at in chapter 11.)

The Pew Research Center *Between Two Worlds* report also documents that even second-generation Latinos (41 percent) identify first by the country where their parents were born. Young Latinos are more likely than older Latinos to say their parents raised them with a more Hispanic focus than an American one. More say their parents have often spoken of their pride in their family's country of origin. Sixty percent note that their parents encouraged them to speak Spanish as well as English. This makes sense, considering that Latinos were only acknowledged in the 1980 census and that Latino pride and identity have kept increasing since that time. Young Hispanics are growing up in family settings that place a strong emphasis on their cultural roots. In chapter 11 on intergenerational leadership, we will note how Latino millennials and Generation Z have already crossed over and now identify as multicultural, which in no way denies their *Latinidad!*

Latinos—The Mixed-Race People

PRESENT-DAY LATINOS STAND AS living proof of the genetic vibrancy and resilience of cultural fusion. Latinos integrate Black, Indigenous, Asian, and European ancestry. The mixing of African slaves in such countries as Puerto Rico, the Dominican Republic, Cuba, Colombia, and the Caribbean coast, and the subsequent migration of these populations, have resulted in 24 percent of US Latinos reporting African descent.[32]

As the progeny of the original inhabitants of this hemisphere, 24 percent claim Indigenous or American Indian ancestry. And catch this! Forty-two percent say their racial background includes White due to their European lineage, the majority being Spanish. But the grand slam is that 34 percent identify as mixed race.[33] Since a tipping point or critical mass can happen at 25 percent, this indicates that Latinos are already driving our identity as multicultural people.[34]

There also is the fact that US Latino experience is distinct from that south of the Mexican border. I like to say that my Central and South American amigos should pity their Latino relatives in the United States. *We were colonized twice:* once by the conquistadores and then by the Anglo-Saxons, who annexed one-third of the United States from México, the beautiful state of Florida, and way up the Northwest to the San Juan

Islands and Valdez, Alaska. My South American amigos usually respond with "*Pobrecitos,*" which literally means "You poor things" but is meant to connote sympathy and support!

US Latinos, therefore, have a cutting edge. We were educated in dominant-culture schools, have worked in organizations constructed from an Anglo perspective, and live in a society crafted by White norms. To be successful means integrating the Anglo worldview, as I did as a child. This adds another dimension to our multicultural cachet.

The Future Is Mixed

WE ARE LIVING IN a fluid time in history. By the middle of this century there will no longer be a dominant race or culture in the United States. The emergence of our multicultural nation is a profound transformation that will transmute every aspect of our society.

This transformation, like any birth, is not without pain and resistance. The roots of racism go deep into the bowels of our country and into every aspect of our society, our institutions, and our whitewashed mentality. There is a racial reckoning happening today, however, calling us to reconcile this past—to end the inequities, discrimination, and White dominance that has ruled for the past five centuries.

We are aware that Latinos were born of cultural fusion and are composed of many races, cultures, and nations. While the United States struggles with racism and White privilege, many Latinos have transcended racial exclusion and revel in multiple identities, including being multicultural or mixed. Latinos, then, can be the nucleus for our nation to come together, forge a multicultural identity, and birth a mosaic nation. Furthermore, Latinos will be 1 out of 4 US people in the next twenty years, providing the people power to actualize our multicultural transformation.[35]

Like small streams forming a powerful river, the forces driving our multicultural transformation are converging into a new social reality. Evidence of this is a phenomenal change in White identity. Between 2010 and 2020, according to the US census, the "White and Some Other Race" population added 17.6 million people to the multiracial count, a change of more than 1,000 percent.[36] This indicates that people, and in particular Whites, are digging into their identities, unearthing diverse heritages, and are ready to be part of our multicultural future. A new world in which all cultures, races, and ethnic groups are respected as equal—and with special contributions to make—is being born.

It is a core concept of this book that Latinos, due to our inherent diversity, our inclusive, people-centered values, and our bienvenido spirit, are the prototype for our transformation to a multicultural nation. Latinos survived the conquest, overcame the obstacles of being minorities and immigrants, mastered *inglés*, maneuvered through the Anglo school system, and learned to survive in the dominant culture. *And yet we thrive!* If any group is a living example of the benefits of racial and cultural integration it is Latinos! Our ancestry, our history, the mixed blood in our veins has prepared us to launch a new beginning that heals racial divisions and brings greater unity and understanding to humankind.

Leading from a Social Change Orientation

THE NEXT PRINCIPLE, *Sí se puede*, describes a social activism and coalition-building approach to leadership. According to Solis, the first Latina California senator, Latinos are adept at working with different groups and networks around a shared goal. "I learned early on that bringing people together meant more strength. When I wanted to pass the first environmental legislation in California, I had to involve Blacks, Latinos, labor, women's organizations, and environmental groups and help them understand why this was beneficial to them. I learned from my father that a good organizer reaches out, persists, and serves people's needs."

In the first edition of this book, we highlighted organizations that shepherded Latino advancement in the last century. In the next chapter, we welcome organizations such as Voto Latino and Mijente, launched after 2000, and the National Latina Institute for Reproductive Justice, founded in 1994. These organizations express the formidable ways in which young Latinos lead, which we will review in depth in chapter 11 on intergenerational leadership.

¡Ahora! Reflection and Application

The Immigrant Experience

What are your ancestral roots? Can you identify the country of origin and/or the cultural background your family comes from?

Did your ancestors immigrate to America? What attitudes were shared with you about their homeland or their immigration process?

What are the contributions immigrants have made to the United States and how has this benefited our nation?

Our Multicultural Identity

The data from the 2022 census indicates that US identity is becoming more multicultural and mixed.

Have you noticed changes in how people are identifying themselves as compared to the past, and if yes, how would you describe these changes?

What three steps would you recommend to someone who wants to become more multicultural and inclusive? (Example: participate in Hispanic heritage activities in your community.)

1.

2.

3.

The Future Is Mixed

> Do you believe the future is mixed? And if yes, what does this mean, and what exciting benefits does this bring? (I call it the Marvelous Multicultural Mambo!)

> Why are Latinos described as a multicultural, mixed-race people? And what is the Latino Global Advantage?

Inclusion Means Inclusion

We noted that global leadership (and mainstream leadership books, as well) overlook the experience and abilities of Latinos who have advanced for centuries under dire circumstances and remain connected to countries across the world. You have been selected to make a presentation to a group of White leaders on why including Latino leadership and the principles in this book would enhance and expand US leadership. What are the five points you would make?

An Inclusion Conversation

In dyads, complete the following exercise.

One person believes "looming demographics" means White people will be replaced. We will lose our national character. And as Manifest Destiny indicated, non-Whites do not know how to govern themselves. The other person believes that becoming a multicultural country is an "add-on" experience—everyone will have a seat at the table. Diversity brings expansion, growth, and learning. Many of our children already relish being multicultural.

> What are the three major points each person will make?

> Can you find connecting points?

> How does this exercise indicate the widening gap in our ability to dialogue, learn from one another, and build a diverse future together?

CHAPTER 10

Sí Se Puede: Social Activism and Coalition Leadership

L EADERSHIP BY THE MANY brings people together, reinforces a strong sense of culture and community, and articulates a shared vision that inspires people. This is the prelude to the real work of Latino leaders: concerted and collective social action. As "minorities," Latinos have experienced discrimination and exclusion. This drives an activist leadership form, which builds coalitions and cultivates a critical mass of people with the purpose of changing the social and economic conditions that perpetuate inequality.

Latinos become activists because of the inequities they saw in their own families and communities. When Arturo Vargas joined his parents in picketing his overcrowded barrio school, which had only half-day classes, this was preparing him for his life's work. "Leadership, for me, is about clarity of purpose and courage. I think we need to be very clear that the purpose of leadership is for the progress and improvement of the collective and the community. Courage, because true leadership needs to be bold, to sometimes make unpopular decisions, and to battle infrastructure and institutions that keep our communities from progressing."

Hilda Solis learned advocacy from her father, a union steward. "My father took a leadership role—he was a fighter. There were three hundred workers, most of whom were Mexican immigrants who couldn't speak a word of English. He helped to organize and mobilize them and won some great concessions. He did not get there by sitting in the back of the room quietly. He was outspoken. He knew he could make a change and a difference, and he did it."

Raul Yzaguirre became determined to organize Latinos because he grew up in the poor areas of the Rio Grande Valley in south Texas. He remembers those signs in restaurant windows that said, "No Mexicans, No Dogs." His grandmother talked about the "race wars" in which the Texas Rangers systemically beat up and killed Mexican Americans. His grandfather was almost lynched for being on the streets after the curfew they had imposed on "Mexicans."

Janet Murguía remembers her father showing his children how to stand up for themselves. "My dad wouldn't let people push him around. He worked very hard at a steel plant for thirty-seven years. In those days he was denied access to the bathroom because he was Mexican. I remember when my dad faced down some of those guys. They never stopped him from going to the bathroom again."

"Leadership, for me, is about clarity of purpose and courage. I think we need to be very clear that the purpose of leadership is for the progress and improvement of the collective and the community."

—Arturo Vargas

Advocating for *We*

T HE SHAPING OF LEADERSHIP as social activism was a natural evolution for collective cultures, in which protecting and sustaining the
We is the crux of a leader's responsibility. This emphasis is one of the
sharp distinctions from mainstream American leadership, where there is
a strong focus on developing the individual, managing organizations, and
running businesses. Addressing the public welfare, social institutions, or
community change is not integral to this approach. In fact, public service
usually pertains only to government, public office, or the nonprofit sector.

In contrast, *Sí se puede* is a roll-up-your-sleeves kind of leadership—
good old-fashioned community organizing, coalition building, and
advocacy. Yzaguirre reflects on this challenge: "Oppressed people have
been taught they can't get things done. 'It's impossible and going to end
in failure.' They must be convinced they will succeed and can do it! So
the first step—the ultimate, all-important step—is to build their faith in
themselves."

Murguía, who was groomed by Yzaguirre to take the helm of the
National Council of La Raza (now UnidosUS), is a master at motivating
people and reinforcing the *We* identity. "For too long we have counted on
others to be our champions. We need to be our own champions. We need
to empower ourselves. We are a community of 62 million people. . . . We
need to start acting like it. If we organize, if we engage, if we mobilize, if we
vote, we won't need to hope our issues get addressed. We will guarantee it."

*"Oppressed people have been taught they can't get things
done.'It's impossible and going to end in failure.'They must
be convinced they will succeed and can do it! So the first
step—the ultimate, all-important step—is to build their
faith in themselves."*

—Raul Yzaguirre

Antonia Pantoja, an early pioneer working with Puerto Rican immigrants in New York City, reflected on this form of leadership in her autobiography, *Memoir of a Visionary*. "I had to find a way to become an agent of change working in partnership with the community," she wrote. "I learned that we could work collectively to find solutions to our own problems."[1]

Leaders as advocates and change agents require determination, commitment, and utter reliability. This is reflects consistencia—fierce determination and consistency—the promise that leaders will never give up or abandon the community or people.

"I had to find a way to become an agent of change working in partnership with the community. I learned that we could work collectively to find solutions to our own problems."

—Antonia Pantoja

Consistencia

WHILE *PERSONALISMO* AND *CONCIENCIA* are the inner preparation for leadership, the long-term goal is external action. Leaders must demonstrate essential traits such as consistency, follow-through, and honesty. Consistencia is the public dimension of the leader's character. It is perseverance and commitment. Regardless of obstacles or personal sacrifices, the leader will do whatever it takes for as long as it takes to deliver. A leader's reputation as being reliable, dependable, and accountable is anchored in consistencia.

In their groundbreaking book *The Leadership Challenge*, James M. Kouzes and Barry Z. Posner surveyed thousands of business and government executives to determine the characteristics people look for in a leader. The survey, which has been conducted since 1987, remains constant over time. It is not surprising that the most valued trait, chosen by 89 percent of respondents, is honesty—being truthful and reliable and aligning words with action. According to the survey, honesty engenders trust so that people believe in and, therefore, follow a leader.[2] Honesty and keeping one's word foster the coveted trait of credibility, establishes a track record, and reflects the leader's consistencia.

Since leadership is not a position or a passing stage, consistencia reflects lifelong relationships. Trusted Latino leaders are regarded as part of the *familia*. And like familia, these relationships are enduring. This bond assures people that they can count on their leaders and it is validated by the many elders who continue playing a prominent role. Bernie Valdez kept fighting for Hispanic progress until he passed on at eighty-five. His consistencia was reflected in more than sixty years of activism. The absolute assurance that he would be there for the long haul encouraged people to follow him—from street demonstrations to the boardrooms of high-level organizations. Likewise, Pantoja continued leading into her eighties. And I am honored to still be serving people even though I, too, am in my eighties!

At its heart, consistencia is a commitment to keep the values you were raised with and to always remember where you came from. For leaders who work to keep the culture alive, consistencia means nourishing people's identity, pride, and connections to the past. They weave an intergenerational force through which leadership lessons are passed from one generation to another.

Consistencia is the public dimension of the leader's character. It is perseverance and commitment. Regardless of obstacles or personal sacrifices, the leader will do whatever it takes for as long as it takes to deliver.

Consistencia Is Collective Action

TENACITY USUALLY CONNOTES THE resolve of an individual leader. For Latinos who lead from a collective perspective, tenacity is instilling consistencia into the community and into organizations. Long-term commitment is sustained by having a strategy for sequential success and by building a community of leaders, as discussed in chapter 8, "Juntos: Leadership by the Many." By practicing *paso a paso*, leaders divide the work into small pieces, strategically choosing issues where success is probable. Then people will say, "Well, if I can do this, I can do twice as much, and then I can be four times as good."

Consistencia engenders loyalty to the leader. Working side by side and experiencing success also develops people's confidence in each other. Consistencia fosters long-term incremental progress, continuity, and stability.

Luz Sarmina is barely five feet tall, but don't let her size fool you. She is small but mighty. As president and CEO of the community health center Valle del Sol for over sixteen years, she grew the organization into one of the largest nonprofits in Arizona. Her ability to build partnerships across communities and sectors was essential, as was transforming the agency's vision to serve individuals from diverse backgrounds.

Today, Valle del Sol's mission is helping people achieve a better life while emphasizing culturally sensitive services. As a strategic leader, Luz understood that long-term security for the organization meant acquiring a large facility. But how would she secure those kinds of funds in an economically tight era? Working with community partners, she positioned the organization as a much-needed resource and built political alliances. Then, when Phoenix passed its 2006 citizen bond to invest in the community, she was at the forefront, and $4 million was allocated to help Valle del Sol acquire a three-story service center. Now almost twenty years later, Valle offers it services in seven locations. Relentless consistencia, cultivating a community of supporters, and building political clout through sixteen years of hard work had paid off.

Consistencia follows the *dicho* "Con gotas se llena el valde" (The barrel fills up drop by drop). Every small contribution, every little victory, every success adds up. Then one day the barrel will be full. *Con gotas* refers to a collective process by which people patiently work one day at a time. If they try to do too much or get spread too thin, they might fail. The barrel represents the container, the community reserve, where everyone's contributions and collective endeavors build the momentum for change. Through consistencia and a collaborative community process, Latinos continue to advance.

An Inclusive Latino Agenda

EVEN THE DOCUMENT'S TITLE, *An American Agenda from a Latino Perspective*, speaks to the inclusive vision of Illinois's Latino Policy Forum: "Parallel to a political agenda, our society must articulate a moral agenda to fulfill its obligations to the public good and to transcend the racial and ethnic tensions that prevent us from taking responsibility for one another and our collective future."[3]

Likewise, Julián Castro connects Latino progress with American progress. "I believe if we recommit ourselves to doing the hard work that it takes to mobilize our communities, if we work at that harder than ever, then we can ensure that this twenty-first century is a time of prominence, global superiority, excellence, and economic prosperity for our entire nation."

I use the phrase "leading with a *bienvenido* spirit" to capture Latino inclusiveness. Vargas is adamant that this is the correct course: "I have heard people talk about how we are now the largest minority group so let's start pushing our weight around. I'm like, 'No, no, no!' We need to express and develop a new style of leadership that is much more inclusive. We need to be prepared to provide leadership not just for Latinos but for everybody—that is the new frontier."

By crafting an inclusive agenda that speaks to the welfare of all Americans, leaders ensure that people from other groups understand how their interests and those of Latinos intersect. Vargas speaks to this: "We are the future workers of America, and we are not going to succeed if we're not educating our children today. We need to convince people to begin investing in younger generations, to understand that the Hispanic dropout rate is not a Hispanic problem; it's an American crisis."

Leadership with a bienvenido spirit is evident in the way Latinos reach out to other groups and build coalitions. This was a trademark of Solis's terms as a congresswoman: "I learned to engage with people in other communities and include them in helping me address issues and develop policies. Leaders have to build networks, to always be inclusive, to show people that good things can come out of working together, that there is more strength in numbers."

Solis is masterful at launching coalitions: "I was able to get legislation passed because I had previous experience working with many different people on issues. They knew me and trusted me. I brought people together that had never really talked to each other before—Latinos, women, African Americans, labor unions, environmentalists. As a leader, I knew we had to break down barriers and find the common ground."

'Leaders have to build networks, to always be inclusive, to show people that good things can come out of working together, that there is more strength in numbers.'

—Hilda Solis

Building Partnerships and Coalitions

Latino leaders reach out and cultivate the critical mass to propel social change by building coalitions *internally* with Latino sub-groups and *externally* with other groups. Coalitions increase the power of collective action by bringing people and organizations together to impact specific issues or causes. Let's look at how developing internal and external coalitions fosters social change and grows community capacity.

UnidosUS is the largest civil rights and advocacy organization in the country, representing a coalition of over three hundred community-based nonprofit organizations from every Latino subgroup. These organizations joined forces to have a national influence on issues such as education, jobs, employment, immigration, health, and homeownership. UnidosUS is a political watchdog and strong advocacy arm that speaks for Latinos on Capitol Hill and in the mainstream media. Murguía, who has led UnidosUS since 2005 (demonstrating *consistencia*), aims to expand Latino political strength through action alerts to mobilize people, political advocacy, voter mobilization, and affecting national public policy.

While UnidosUS mobilizes people at the grassroots level, working with community-based organizations, the Hispanic Association on Corporate Responsibility brings national organizations together with a very specific purpose. Realizing that one organization trying to influence corporate America would be a voice crying in the wilderness, a group of leaders, including Yzaguirre and former New Mexico governor Jerry Apodaca, started HACR in 1986. HACR builds internal coalitions within the Hispanic community and external partnerships with corporate America. As a coalition of the fourteen largest and most influential national Latino organizations, HACR represents such diverse constituencies as Hispanic businesses, youth-serving organizations, veterans, publishers, women's leadership, and Hispanic-serving colleges and universities.

HACR's mission is to advance Hispanics' inclusion in corporate America at a level commensurate with our economic contributions in four areas: at the board level, in employment, in philanthropy, and in procurement. More than thirty-five years later, HACR has made a strong business case for Hispanic inclusion and has established partnerships with many of the largest corporations.

Building external coalitions requires leaders to assume the role of cultural brokers who can identify resources and organizational supporters. Brokers maneuver multiple cultures and articulate the mutual benefits of partnerships and coalitions. Carlos Orta, who served as HACR'S president, previously worked for three Fortune 500 companies and is an adept cultural broker, helping businesses to understand the need to tap into the growing Latino workforce, lucrative market, and talents. At the same time, he encourages corporations to augment their social responsibility efforts and diversity and inclusion efforts.

Coalition building is a tactic that is being continued by young Latinos. For instance, Latino congressman Ritchie Torres, who is in his early thirties, is forging coalitions in the US Congress. "Our divided government limits our ability to deliver for the American people. I am going to fight as hard as I can and build whatever coalitions I need to build to deliver for the South Bronx."

Now let us turn to three organizations started by young Latinos: Voto Latino and Mijente, founded after 2000, and the National Latina Institute for Reproductive Justice, founded in 1994. This will give us a flavor of the ways young Latinos are walking the path of social activism and following the principle of *Sí se puede!* We will then advance to chapter 11, "*El Círculo*: Inclusiveness Across Generations," which portrays the innovative ways young Latinos lead today.

"Our divided government limits our ability to deliver for the American people. I am going to fight as hard as I can and build whatever coalitions I need to build to deliver for the South Bronx."

—Ritchie Torres

Following the Legacy of Latino Activism

AT THE BEGINNING OF the new millennium, young Latinos activists started launching social-change organizations. One of the most successful is Voto Latino, which aims to create a more robust and inclusive democracy. From the grassroots level to the national one, Voto Latino is educating and empowering a new generation of voters. In the past it was predominantly political and social leaders that founded Latino organizations. Voto Latino, on the other hand, has star power and was cofounded by award-winning actress and activist Rosario Dawson, noted for her roles in *Men in Black II*, *Rent*, and *Top Five*.

Another Voto Latino board member was the opening speaker at the monumental Women's March in Washington, DC, in January 2017. America Ferrera is an actress, producer, and feminist who starred in the ABC hit comedy *Ugly Betty*, for which she won a Golden Globe. Ferrera, a civil rights advocate, understands the power of the vote.

These two Latina powerhouses were joined by Wilmer Valderrama, who stars in *NCIS* on CBS and is most recognized for his role as Fez in the Emmy-nominated series *That '70s Show*. Valderrama has worked on immigration and education reform and is the spokesperson for the Congressional Hispanic Caucus Institute's Ready 2 Lead program, which empowers Latino youth. The engagement of young celebrities in Latino advocacy showcases the growing cultural prominence and political power of Latinos today.

Voto Latino uses innovative digital campaigns to capture people's attention, including videos, public service announcements, media campaigns, national action days, and the voter registration app VoterPal. Their ability to build coalitions is evident in their campaign Mi Familia Vota, which brought together more than eighty-seven partners, resulting in 261 million social media impressions and reaching 81 million people across platforms. By October 2020, Voto Latino had registered more than a million new Latinos voters!

The National Latina Institute for Reproductive Justice was founded in 1994 and fights for reproductive health, dignity, and justice at the community, state, and national levels. Anchored in grassroots power, the Latina Institute supports community-based organizations that promote reproductive health, such as the Colorado Organization for Latina Opportunity and Reproductive Rights (COLOR), which worked with a statewide coalition that passed the 2022 Reproductive Health Equity Act. This legislation ensured that every person has the fundamental right to choose or refuse contraception and that every person can choose to continue a pregnancy or to have an abortion.[4] As other states were passing bans on abortion, COLOR stepped to the front lines and ensured that reproductive rights are fundamental rights in Colorado.

Because reproductive rights are a contentious and emotional issue in our country today, the Latina Institute develops national campaigns and conducts research to shift the cultural narrative on reproductive justice. A 2016 study commissioned by the institute and conducted by Lake Research Partners found that 82 percent of Latino registered voters believe a woman should make her own personal decision about abortion. A full 67 percent would give support to a friend or family member choosing to have an abortion.[5] This information sheds light on Latino support of reproductive justice and can be leveraged to engage people.

At the state level, the Latina Institute has networks in Florida, New York, Texas, and Virginia. Nationally, they amplify their work by pushing for policy change in the areas of sexual and reproductive health equity, abortion access and affordability, and securing immigrant women's reproductive health rights.

Mijente (My People) was launched in 2015 as a political home for Latinx and Chicanx activists who seek racial, economic, gender, and climate justice. (*Latinx* is the gender-neutral term used by young Latinos, and *Chicanx* refers to Mexican American activists seeking to secure their historical identity.) Mijente is creating digital activists and connecting people across a wide network that reaches millions who fight for progress. Their online petitions challenge deportation, database surveillance, discriminatory corporate practices, and youth incarceration. They also teach people how to start and manage digital campaigns.

Beyond digital movement building, Mijente engages people at the grassroots level to tackle issues in their communities through local campaigns. In Chicago they joined community activists to stop the creation of a gang database that was 90 percent information on Blacks and Latinos.[6] In Tacoma, Washington, they rallied to close a detention center that had repeated medical emergencies and unsanitary conditions.[7] In Hall County, Georgia, they urged the city council to reopen voting sites in predominately Black and Brown communities.

Mijente is a movement for justice for all people and strives to promote kinships across identities, generations, language, and place. As such, it defines itself as a pro-Black; pro-Indigenous; pro-worker; pro-woman; pro–lesbian, gay, bi, trans, and queer; and pro-migrant. The next chapter identifies this intersectional approach as a key strategy for young Latinos leaders.

Sí Se Puede—Calling a New Generation of Activists

THE LATINO SOCIAL-CHANGE AGENDA is gaining momentum, fueled by immigration, exploding numbers, youthful vigor, and a stronger Latino identity. Established Latino organizations are maturing (many were founded in the 1980s) and now have the capacity and influence to promote a broader social-change agenda. New organizations are emerging that build on this legacy and follow the social activist path forged by previous generations. Antonia Pantoja described this approach: "The role of the leader is the role of advocate. The purpose of leadership is to exercise one's power, knowledge, and access to change the oppressive and destructive situations in society."

This commitment to advocacy is based on the humanistic Latino worldview, which has people's welfare at its heart. Solis underscores this commitment: "I believe there has to be justice. There has to be equal opportunity, fairness, and protection under our laws."

Latino Leadership Principles

Early Latino leaders were on the outskirts of power, pushing open the doors of opportunity. Today, Latino activists might be wearing a suit and have a law degree from Harvard, like Julián Castro, or may have worked as successful executives in corporate America, like Carlos Orta. Janet Murguía and Arturo Vargas lead powerful national organizations. Young Latinos like congressmen Gallego and Torres advocate for change from inside the halls of power.

Yet today's discrepancies, critical issues, and gross inequities necessitate a *Sí se puede* activist form of leadership. Young Latinos are heeding this call. They recognize today's advancements are due to the tireless efforts of the past and they must continue bending the arc of justice toward the equal and just society.

The next chapter puts forth a model for intergenerational leadership based on the strategies and practices young Latinos use today. This model can provide valuable insights for working with young leaders everywhere, and it is applicable to leadership across all communities and sectors.

¡Ahora! Reflection and Application

Consistencia—A Lifelong Commitment

Consistencia is perseverance. Regardless of obstacles or personal sacrifices, the leader will do whatever it takes for as long as it takes to deliver. The leaders in this book (chapter 11 includes young leaders) have made a lifelong commitment to their work and community.

Pick one of the leaders included in this book and do additional research on their leadership journey. Then think about these questions:

How did this leader's early life prepare them for leadership?

What sacrifices have they made to be able to remain a community leader?

How do they engender people's trust?

What inspires you about their commitment and achievements? *Would you follow this leader, and why?*

A Group Activity: Creating a Collective Identity

In previous chapters you noted your identity and shared your family history. Now we will promote the unity that is quintessential for fostering collective civic action. When you are working with others, the following activity can assist you in fostering a collective identity.

List all the ethnic, racial, and national identities and heritages of each of you. On a large piece of paper, draw lines between the connections among you.

What did you learn about one another? What groups are represented? Excluded?

What does this say about identity in the United States today?

How can sharing backgrounds facilitate working together?

Advocating for the *We*

Sí se puede is an activist form of leadership. As the voice for marginalized people, Latino leaders have fought for equity and civil rights. This has been accomplished through building coalitions and partnerships. Successful coalitions are based on mutual benefits and on having a greater impact on critical issues.

Group Activity

Check out the websites for the organizations below—each has decades of successful partnerships. Review their mission, coalition partners, and achievements.

Congressional Hispanic Caucus Institute (chci.org)

League of United Latin American Citizens (lulac.org)

National Association of Latino Elected and Appointed Officials (naleo.org/about-naleo)

UnidosUS (unidosus.org)

Now answer these questions:

How have these partnerships/coalitions strengthened the impact of these organizations?

Since these coalitions have stood the test of time, what has made them successful?

What are the key factors that keep coalitions such as these working together and having a larger scope and impact?

CHAPTER 11

El Círculo: Inclusiveness Across Generations

T HE LATINO *BIENVENIDO* SPIRIT is reflected in the way the culture embraces the circle of life, from the promise of youth to the wisdom of age. Unlike societies in which people retire, Latinos honor their elders, who continue contributing. As a silver-haired octogenarian, when I am asked if I am going to retire, I assert, *"No, no!* I am just getting started. You ain't seen nothing yet!" I plan to follow in the footsteps of the social justice trail blazer activist Dolores Huerta, who is going strong in her nineties!

Just as *mis padres* sacrificed so their children could have a better life, Latinos have an unshakeable commitment to educating, supporting, and including younger generations. We know they are *el futuro*; coming generations will actualize Latino power and potential. Since Latino leaders understood that it would take many centuries to advance, preparing subsequent generations has been an age-old practice.

This approach is even more urgent *ahora!* Youth is a defining characteristic of the Latino community—nearly 6 in 10 are millennials or younger. One-third are under eighteen.[1] Never before has an ethnic group made up so large a share of the youngest Americans. By sheer force of numbers alone, young Latinos will shape the twenty-first century.

This youthful vitality, however, is not just a Latino phenomenon. We are experiencing immense demographic shifts! In the general population, millennials and Gen Zs are the most numerous in history. Projections show that by 2036 they will make up more than half of all eligible voters.[2] At the same time, ten thousand baby boomers retire every day. Advancing the next generations to take the helm of leadership is one of the pressing challenges of our times.

Moreover, young people today face an uncertain future. To address this, many identify as change makers. Change makers utilize an activist form of leadership that aims to uproot systemic oppression. Young people lead with an intersectional, multicultural approach that includes a nonbinary identity and global connectivity. Wired to the internet and social media, they define themselves as digital activists utilizing technology and the media to promote social change and engage millions of people.

Young Latino leaders are on the front lines of social-change activism and are addressing unique issues such as cultural identity, immigration, and continued discrimination. For instance, 35 percent of Latino millennials are immigrants, and fully one-quarter of those under eighteen have at least one unauthorized immigrant parent.[3] These immigrant roots make young Latinos more global and give them a fierce determination to change US policies on immigration.

This chapter puts forth an intergenerational leadership model based on the strategies and practices young Latinos are using today. The young leaders included in this chapter are stoking up the *Sí se puede* tradition established by generations before them. First, let's look at intergenerational leadership and how this approach requires restructuring relationships across different ages into more equitable and respectful practices.

 Since Latino leaders understood that it would take many centuries to advance, preparing subsequent generations has been an age-old practice.

Intergenerational Leadership

INTERGENERATIONAL LEADERSHIP IS SHARING responsibility with people of different ages and integrating into the leadership process the vision, priorities, and methods utilized by distinct generations. A generation is a group of people born within a certain time period whose shared age and life experiences shape a distinct worldview with particular characteristics, preferences, and values.

The concept of "generations," generally accepted today, is a recent invention based on expanding life expectancy, which results in multiple generations existing in the same historical time frame. The first official generation designated by the US census was the baby boomers, those born from 1946 to 1964.[4]

Crafting an intergenerational leadership model requires understanding the key political, economic, and social factors that shape each generation. In this chapter we zero in on millennials and Generation Z, who make up 42 percent of the US population. When you add in our youngest generation, that number jumps to 51 percent![5] A more in-depth view of generational differences is included at the end of this chapter.

Traditional leadership implied a hierarchy in which established and usually older leaders handed down knowledge and doled out rewards. In contrast, intergenerational leadership is based on the principle of the leader as equal, which fosters collaborative relationships and develops each person's capacity.

Equitable relationships cultivate a deep sense of *We* and foster mutual respect and partnerships. Intergenerational leadership invites the unique wisdom and strength of every generation to come together to create a more viable and equitable future.

Latinos are an intergenerational community. Social occasions, fundraisers, political rallies, community events, and family gatherings will include a mélange of ages, from *abuelas* to *niños* (children). Young Latinos were raised in traditionally *We* cultures, so that intergenerational collaboration resonates with their upbringing and worldview. Moreover, Latinos come from large extended families comprising multiple generations and have a tradition of living and working with many ages. (In my *familia*, for example, my sister Rosemary was twenty years older than me and helped buy the family *casa* where I grew up.) Today, 27 percent of young Latinos live in households that are multigenerational, and 14 percent live in three-generational households.[6]

Building an intergenerational leadership force is essential when a group's advancement depends on people power, collaboration, and collective resources. Intergenerational leadership strengthens community capacity, ensures continuity, and builds leadership by the many—the critical mass needed for social change. Hilda Solis notes the Latino intergenerational spirit: "We have to motivate our young people to build upon our legacies. We have to encourage them to reach out and include other people. We need to make sure there is a pathway to follow, and that leadership is passed down generation to generation."

Latinos will transform the future together—each generation supporting the others and tapping into the unique gifts different ages bring. Jamie Margolin underscores this tendency: "Our movements must be intergenerational. . . . We, the youth, are standing on the shoulders of the change makers before us, and we must always acknowledge and respect that."

Intergenerational leadership is sharing responsibility with people of different ages and integrating into the leadership process the vision, priorities, and methods utilized by distinct generations.

An Uncertain Future: Igniting Youth Activism

WHILE WE CANNOT REVIEW all the myriad issues affecting young people's lives, we will explore five that are crippling their futures: college debt, housing insecurity, climate change, job or income challenges, and life-span threats. These impact all young people

but have a greater effect on Latinos because they also must address continued discrimination and lower economic status.

In the past twenty years, the average tuition at private universities jumped
124 percent while in-state tuition at public universities increased by a whop-
ping 179 percent. This means graduating from college leaves students with an
average debt of $28,950.[7] How can young people envision their future when
they are saddled with crippling debt even before they begin their adult lives?

Young people are getting shut out of the housing market, especially in
urban areas. Seventy percent cannot afford to buy a casa.[8] Nearly a third
are rent burdened, meaning 30 percent or more of their income goes to
rent.[9] In 2020 (abetted by the COVID-19 epidemic), 52 percent of all
young adults returned home, becoming the first generation since the Great
Depression to "have to" live with their parents. For young Latinos (eighteen to twenty-nine years old), this number was 58 percent.[10]

In their short lifetimes, millennials and Zs have witnessed one
ecological disaster after another—raging forest fires, catastrophic flooding,
horrendous hurricanes, and suffocating summers. Climate change is
a source of anxiety for 59 percent of young people.[11] This jumped to
83 percent of Gen Z, leading to a term, *eco-anxiety*, related to fears about
the future of the environment.[12]

Millennials have less wealth than earlier generations, despite having the
highest workforce participation and education. Baby boomers controlled
21 percent of the nation's wealth when they were around the same age
as millennials today—that's over four times as much as millennials
own now.[13] Millennials are also burdened with wage stagnation and
job insecurity—a staggering 1 in 4 jobs is currently at risk of being
automated.[14] Additionally, growing income disparity is even more dire for
Latinos. According to the US Federal Reserve, in 2019 White households
owned 85.5 percent of the nation's wealth, Black households owned
4.2 percent, and Hispanics owned 3.1 percent.[15]

Finally, millennials are the first generation to have a shorter life span
than their parents. One out of two is predicted to get cancer.[16] Since 2017,
gun violence is now the leading cause of injury-related deaths among children and young adults.[17] These issues are fueling young people's activism,

urging them to work for a better future—the one they will inherit. In doing so, they follow the tradition of activists who came before them and fought for social change.

César Chávez was only thirty-four when he started advocating for farm workers' rights. A few years later he cofounded the National Farm Workers Association, which later became United Farm Workers.[18] At twenty-eight years old, Martin Luther King Jr. formed the Southern Christian Leadership Conference, which fought to end segregation and to achieve civil rights. In the 1960s, young college students across the nation marched to end the war in Vietnam. In 1963, during the Children's Crusade, a march in Birmingham, Alabama, thousands of youth ages six to sixteen were arrested at a peaceful rally, resulting in national outrage and a civil rights victory.[19]

I began my activist journey at nineteen, when I demonstrated to end segregation at the University of Florida. During my senior year, two African American students were admitted. At twenty-six I joined early feminists demanding equal rights for women. And at thirty-five I was a founder and then executive director of Denver's Mi Casa Resource Center for women.

Likewise, today, Indigenous youth ignited the movement at the Standing Rock Sioux reservation to protect their water and block the Dakota Pipeline. Black Lives Matter—the international movement to stop state-sanctioned violence against Black people—was founded by three young women activists, Patrisse Cullors, Alicia Garza, and Opal Tometi.[20] Undocumented young Latinos pushing for immigrant rights launched United We Dream (UWD). Even though they risked being deported or otherwise separated from their families for taking part in demonstrations, they describe themselves as fearless youth fighting to improve the lives of themselves, their families, and their communities.[21]

Traditionally, young people have been the forerunners carrying the torch for equality and justice! Margolin explains, "Youth leadership is transformational and visionary. Youth must lead because they have always shifted culture towards progress and collective liberation."

Promoting a Cultural Shift— Transforming Social Identity

YES! YOUNG LATINO LEADERS are igniting a new activism. Through technology, they engage larger numbers of people, augmenting leadership by the many. They identify as multicultural and global, accept a whole spectrum of gender identities, and champion LGBTQ rights. Young Latinos today are transforming our social identity.

We are using the term *social identity* here not in the personal sense but in the way a majority might define themselves—something like "national character." Historically, America's social identity centered around a White, Anglo-Saxon, Protestant ethic that defined man's nature as competitive, acquisitive, and individualistic.[22] It also touted White superiority and dominance. The aftermath is a segregated and racist society based on exclusion, conformity, and homogeneity.

Latinos and other young people today are rejecting these tendencies and welcoming an inclusive, diverse, and universal concept of our common humanity. They are constructing a new social identity, which is being championed by the following practices: being multicultural and global, acknowledging gender fluidity and LGBTQ normalcy, sharing personal narratives, and cultivating allies and partners.

A Multicultural and Global Identity

The Black Lives Matter movement brought front and center the urgency for racial reckoning and healing. A new desire to dismantle structural racism, injustice, and inequities exists today. Now is the time to focus resources and energy to heal old wounds, repair the past, and acknowledge the pain and suffering White supremacy has left in its wake.

Yet these conversations and actions are really the fodder for older generations. Most young people are on the other side of this and instead are celebrating their multicultural, mixed, and expansive diversity. Diversity defines them! Half of millennials and Gen Z come from communities of color, and Latinos make up 27 percent of millennials and 35 percent of Gen Z.[23]

Additionally, as we have noted, according to the 2020 census the multicultural population increased 276 percent in the previous decade. The "White and Some Other Race" population grew more than 1,000 percent.[24] This phenomenal identity shift gives Latino and other young leaders the people power to lead the transformation to a diverse multicultural society.

This generation has also grown up with a global mind-set; they communicate and connect across the globe every day! Since half the people in the world are currently under thirty, a new international youth culture is emerging.[25] If you look at young people in the United States, in many parts of South America, in Europe, and even in China, you'll notice they dress in a similar fashion (casual, layered, and gray/blue/brown colors; sneakers and boots). They listen to world music that has an Indigenous and fusion flair; watch the same shows, news, and movies; and use Facebook and WhatsApp to build community. They spark international social movements. This has been birthed by a global consumer culture that markets music, technology, clothes, and food products worldwide, along with technological access and travel.

Moreover, many Latinos have ancient kinship ties to people from twenty-six countries and have immigrant roots which nurture an international identity. Twenty-two percent of Gen Zs and 14 percent of millennials have at least one immigrant parent, bringing the world right to the family dinner table.[26]

These factors have also sparked youth-led international social-change movements and have made younger generations more favorably disposed to working with groups, leaders, and countries beyond their border. For instance, millennials are at least 10 percentage points more in favor of the United Nations than are Gen Xers or boomers.[27] And as we will see, young people understand that issues such as climate change affect us all, especially the generations that will follow.

Young Latino immigrants and migrants are especially keyed into the global impact of many issues that threaten their future. One of United We Dream's guiding principles states, "UWD recognizes that the root causes of migration include imperialism, colonization, violence, persecution, natural disasters, and capitalism and economic globalization that impose poverty and displacement—too often due to policy decisions being made in other countries. To reach true justice, we must push back against global policies that force people to move. We are part of the international community and will stand with all people seeking a better life, peace, and safety."[28] Because of their numbers and their multiracial and multiethnic heritage, young Latinos are lynchpins for fastening together broad, diverse, intergenerational, and international coalitions.

Championing Gender Equity and LGBTQ Rights

As my Gen Z grandson Ishmael explained to me, "Most people in my generation (or at least almost everyone that I know) see gender and sexuality not as something set in stone but as a spectrum." From transgender to cisgender (a person whose sense of identity and gender correspond with their birth sex), there is gender fluidity. This is apparent in the listing of pronouns (He/She/They/Ze) after a person's name and has become so accepted that Merriam-Webster chose the singular *they* for a person with a nonbinary gender as its word of the year in 2019.[29] The growing acceptance of LGBTQ+ rights is one of the great social transformations of our times.

Decades ago, I was talking with my good friend José, who was steadying himself to come out of the closet to his familia. He was nervous and yet hopeful, and I comforted him: "We would never stop loving our children! Familia primera y siempre [first and always]!" And that is exactly what is happening. As a people-centered culture with a bienvenido spirit, Latinos are wired to accept differences, including the spectrum of gender identity. Excluding people from the *comunidad* or familia would be a cultural anathema. (Although in every group there remain religious, conservative, and homophobic factions that are not supportive.)

This has now been validated by the GenForward Survey, which found that Latino millennials were more likely than other ethnicity groups to self-identify as LGBTQ or nonstraight. Twenty-two percent identify as LGBTQ, compared to 14 percent of African Americans, 13 percent of Whites, and 9 percent of Asian Americans.[30] Jamie Margolin, for instance, dedicated her book, *Youth to Power*, "To the queer kids. We are unstoppable." LGBTQ Latinos are shaping political movements.

Cristina Jimenez agrees. "When we look at United We Dream, most of the people have been women or queer. In the context of immigrant youth organizing, LGBTQ+ are front and center in shaping this movement."

And when gay Latinos are on the "inside," they break new ground! Ritchie Torres is the first openly gay Afro-Latino in the US Congress and was the first gay representative on the New York City Council. As a member of the council, he helped to open the first homeless shelter for LGBTQ youth and secured funds for senior centers to serve LGBTQ people.

Torres speaks about his decision to come out publicly about being gay: "It was a question of integrity. I'm asking residents who have been failed by their elected officials to trust me. How can I be trusted if I'm telling lies about something as basic as my sexual identity? Coming out has taught me an ethic of radical authenticity. Not only am I open about my sexuality, but I'm also open about every aspect of my life. . . . My experience as an LGBTQ person has made me far more authentic as an elected official than I otherwise would be."[31]

Young Latinos also serve as allies for the LGBTQ community. Congressman Ruben Gallego is proud of his support. "When I was in the military, I was involved with Voices of Honor [a nationwide effort to repeal the military's 'Don't ask, don't tell' policy]. I've always been supportive of the LGBTQ community and am a member of LGBTQ Equality Caucus in Congress. Having a male, a Latino veteran, does help change people's minds, especially about gender equality. I'm a cultural translator for some Latino men who are still carrying a lot of homophobic feelings."

"Coming out has taught me an ethic of radical authenticity. . . . My experience as an LGBTQ person has made me far more authentic as an elected official than I otherwise would be."

—Ritchie Torres

Being Authentic and Real: Share Your Story

Latinos come from a culture of storytelling grounded in the oral tradition. Storytelling weaves connections and strengthens community—so vital to *We*, people-oriented cultures. In part II, "Preparing to Lead," we studied *personalismo*—the importance of the leader's character and how sharing one's own background builds cultural rapport with people. Young Latinos have broadened this to include personal stories, which engenders a deeper level of trust, unity, and community.

Jimenez emphasizes how vital this was for undocumented youth: "Storytelling played a big role in our work because that allowed people in an organic way to build connections. Young people are seeking to be seen and to belong." Jimenez sees sharing stories as a strategy: "We need to create a sense of belonging and pride that systematically, because of colonization, our people haven't had—to be proud of who we are and where we come from. This can erase feeling that we don't belong or should be whitewashed versus celebrating the multiethnic, multireligious, multiracial richness of our diverse community."

Moreover, the passion and promise a person brings to leadership is often rooted in the narratives of their early lives. Torres's childhood birthed his activism: "I was raised by a single mother who kept our family afloat on a $4.25 minimum wage. I grew up in a housing project full of leaks and lead, with no reliable heat or hot water in the winter. As a product of public housing, public schools, and public hospitals, I had a dream of fighting for my community in the hopes of building a better Bronx."

Likewise, Gallego points to his childhood as a training ground for becoming a leader. "I didn't grow up in the best of circumstances. My mom and dad are immigrants. I have three sisters. My father left when I was young. I became a leader first by being a leader in my family, helping my mom raise my three sisters."

Sharing stories is also a useful tactic to create unity among Latino subgroups. Jimenez realized, "Despite being from different parts of the Latin American diaspora, the belonging comes because of language, music, food, because of the similar stories around how our parents raised us, but also similar stories of migration."

"We need to create a sense of belonging and pride that systematically, because of colonization, our people haven't had—to be proud of who we are and where we come from."
—Cristina Jimenez

Becoming Allies and Partners

Many young people recognize that relationships based on hierarchy and dominance perpetuate inequality. They are seeking instead respect, engagement, mutuality, and partnership. In the past, more experienced, well-positioned people often guided younger ones through mentoring—the mentor taught the behaviors, attitudes, language, rules, and norms that fostered success. They opened doors and networks so their protégés would be accepted by those with access or power. In a society structured around racial inequity and White privilege, however, mentoring implied a hierarchy and an approach in which established, usually older, White male leaders handed down knowledge and bestowed influence. Mentoring was integral to succession planning so that power, wealth, and privilege were retained and passed on to select people. Mentoring groomed White leaders and those in their favor, which perpetuated hierarchy, inequity, racism, and White privilege—the very dynamics young leaders oppose.

Instead, today young people are seeking *allies*, which signifies a relationship with people of many ages based on mutual respect and learning. An ally infers a partnership—a lateral relationship with someone who stands side by side, watches your back, and supports you. *Ally* is also used in social change work to describe someone who is not a member of an underrepresented group but who utilizes their position of power and credibility to challenge inequality and support inclusion.

Allies reach across generations, listen, and are open to new ways of working together. Young people inspire and offer a vision for the future. Older leaders serve as cultural ambassadors, provide historical perspectives, and make connections. Julián Castro speaks to this: "People from different generations need to work together. This way, we can preserve our history, keep the integrity of those who have more experience and a long-term perspective. Young people will understand the sacrifices made in the past. Otherwise, young people may compromise and lose their culture. Only by staying connected across generations can we keep moving forward together."

Cooperation between generations requires older leaders to shake off the belief that they know best or they should be in charge, and it requires young people to develop patience and to learn from those who have come before. Antonia Pantoja, who started ASPIRA, which has now trained seven generations of Puerto Rican youth, had a knack for building circular relationships and encouraging young people to take responsibility. "What do you do about the future?" she asked. "I make the future. You make the future. We make the future together."

Latino leadership is like a relay race where one generation passes the torch to the next—and then the next and the next. Ensuring every generation has a seat at the leadership table supports continuity and ongoing progress.

 "What do you do about the future? I make the future. You make the future. We make the future together."

—Antonia Pantoja

This Is How You Do It! The Circle of Latina Leadership Program

THE CIRCLE OF LATINA Leadership in Denver was an intergenerational leadership initiative that brought together Latinas ranging from age ninety to their early teens. Twenty years later, the young women who completed the program are mature leaders and the voice for Latina empowerment in metro Denver.

In the early 2000s, I invited a group of seasoned Latina leaders to talk about the future of our community. We realized that the mutual support, networking, and the coaching we had received from more established leaders and from each other were foundational to what we had accomplished, and we wanted to play that forward.

Thus was born the Circle of Latina Leadership, a yearlong intergenerational program for emerging leaders in their twenties and thirties. The word ally had not surfaced yet, but the Circle brought together four generations to support each other and to advance Latina progress.

More established leaders guided program participants, connected them with their cultural identity, and assisted them in charting their careers and community contributions. One founder, Lena Archuleta, the first Hispanic principal in the Denver Public Schools, shared her wisdom and experience with Circle women until she passed away at ninety. Lena and a small group of community madrinas (honorary godmothers) stood as reminders of their lifelong commitment to advancing the Latino community. Participants in turn adopted junior high school girls as hermanitas (little sisters), helping them with self-esteem, school success, and cultural identity.

Over 165 emerging leaders completed the program and today run nonprofit organizations, serve on boards of directors, direct government agencies, and advocate for critical issues such as education, women's empowerment, climate change, and reproductive rights. A new generation of Latina leaders has taken the helm!

Strategies for Social Justice

YOUNG LATINOS SIMPLY HAVE a vision for a new world that is multicultural and global and welcomes the wide spectrum of gender identity. Now we look at four leadership strategies that they bring to social-change work: being change makers, understanding intersectionality and systemic oppression, leveraging an insider-outsider approach, and utilizing technology to multiply impact.

The Change Makers

Watch out, because in the last ten minutes, while you were reading this chapter, twenty young Latinos turned eighteen, and they have the critical mass to influence and transform society.[32] To accomplish this, many are assuming the role of change makers—a term utilized by young people who push for large-scale social change and see themselves as capable of creating this. Change makers are described as a force for social evolution who, through innovative thinking, gathering resources, and determination, make change happen.

UWD cofounder Cristina Jimenez realized, "I began to see that young people had the power to influence change and the responsibility to fight for our community. We knew the language. We understood how to navigate different systems. We had access to social media. We also had the courage that young people have and the urgency to act, regardless of the consequences."

Young Latino leaders, due to higher education, comfort with technology, and a global perspective, understand that promoting social justice is a lifetime work. Torres clearly states, "I am on a mission to fight racially concentrated poverty and to be a national champion for the urban poor!"

Jimenez concurs. "What's clear is the work that I do is a lifelong commitment. Regardless of a particular role or title, organization or project or campaign, I want to be a vessel for empowering people, particularly communities of color and Latinos. To let the next folks in. And to make sure that we can live freely, thrive, and have a life with dignity."

In *Youth to Power*, Margolin, the climate activist, claims that young people should be "disrupting the status quo, making your voice heard, challenging problematic authority, changing the culture, changing laws, and yes changing the world."[33] And young people are stepping up: 32 percent of Gen Z and 28 percent of millennials took at least one of four actions (donating money, contacting an elected official, volunteering, or attending a rally) to help address climate change in 2021, compared with 23 percent of Gen X and 21 percent of baby boomers and older adults.[34]

Congressman Gallego, who at forty-two is a spring chicken (considering that the average age of House members is fifty-eight and of senators is sixty-four), urges young people to be bold. "If you're a young leader, at least in politics, you're going to have to break the rules in order for you to lead. And some of that means going against old political structures that do not want to let you in. So being strong and aggressive and taking initiative helps you." Similarly, Congressman Torres states, "Members of my generation, the millennials, and Generation Z have a strong ethic of social justice." Following the activist tradition of young Latinos, the first Gen Z elected to Congress in 2022 is Maxwell Alejandro Frost, an Afro-Latino. He has experienced firsthand the impact of poverty, gun violence, and climate change and campaigned on the promise, "I've dedicated my life to fighting for justice."

Margolin also sees young people as having "fresh energy, insight, and a unique power to create change in our world. The voices of young people are so powerful because we have the moral high ground. We didn't create any of the systems of oppression that hold us and our world down."[35]

"Members of my generation, the millennials, and Generation Z have a strong ethic of social justice."

—Ritchie Torres

Understanding Intersectionality and Systemic Oppression

They stood outside the US Capitol on a cold, wintry day, thousands of miles from the warm climates their families had come from. Despite fear of deportation and being called "aliens," undocumented, and even criminals, the young immigrants stood firm. "Together, we fight for education, economic, racial, gender, reproductive, and environmental justice. We fight to build power within our communities, justice, and dignity for all—regardless of immigration status." This is the rallying cry for United We Dream, the largest immigrant youth–led organization in the United States.

Many undocumented Latino immigrants are on the front lines of social justice work. They know personally how immigration and the growing number of refugees are part of systemic oppression with long,

gnarled roots. The UWD mission states, "We believe in leading with
a multi-ethnic, intersectional path. Climate change, sexism, gender
discrimination, racism, colonialism, economic disparity, gun violence, and
unbridled capitalism are interconnected."[36]

While the immigrant crisis impacts people crossing national borders,
climate change affects everyone on the planet, regardless of borders.
Young Latino leaders understand that climate change and immigration
are intersectional issues. Margolin explains, "Systems of oppression
(capitalism, colonialism, racism, and patriarchy) have led to climate
change; therefore, we must shift our culture away from these systems.
Intersectional movement building is the only way we can achieve
collective liberation . . . and unify communities who wish to join our
struggle for a safe and healthy future."[37]

In past times, people worked on social justice issues in a silo fashion—
movements were segmented. This piecemeal approach limited impact and
scope. Young Latino activists today understand the systemic origins of
injustice and inequality. Torres speaks to this: "Young people increasingly
defined racism as institutional rather than in individual terms. Not simply
as the intent of an individual but the impact of institutional arrangements
on vulnerable communities such as the Latino community. So it's certainly
true that Latinos increasingly view inequality through a systemic lens."

*"We believe in leading a multi-ethnic, intersectional path.
Climate change, sexism, gender discrimination, racism,
colonialism, economic disparity, gun violence, and
unbridled capitalism are interconnected."*

—United We Dream

Leveraging an Insider-Outsider Approach

Young Latino change makers utilize voting and the political process,
but they also make use of movement- and cause-oriented strategies.
Their tactics reflect an insider-outsider approach. Congressman Torres

is a stellar example of promoting issues from inside the halls of the US Congress: "If you are on a mission to fight racially concentrated poverty . . . then you have to be a policy maker on the national stage."

Yet he champions putting pressure on the system. "What distinguishes young Latino leaders is the willingness to play the outside game, to agitate publicly to be creative disruptors of the status quo. I think that has become an essential element of leadership in our present political moment, because we've seen the limitations of the inside game. We've seen that it doesn't work well anymore."

An impressive example of utilizing an insider-outsider strategy was the 2012 executive order by President Obama establishing Deferred Action for Childhood Arrivals—an emotional victory for undocumented young Latinos. DACA meant they would not be deported, could go to college, and could legally get a job. To secure DACA, thousands of undocumented youths rose up, told their stories, and made their plight a cause célèbre that garnered support across the country.[38]

UWD used multiple strategies. Jimenez recounts, "Obama campaigned on being very progressive, and promises to push for immigration reform and the Dream Act. Then he gets into office—and, granted, it's an economic downturn, a total crisis—but he chooses to make health care his priority and not work on immigration. So we rally for Congress to work on immigration reform. Clearly the votes are not there for legislation. When this happens, we regroup and restrategize. People from Latino, civil rights, Black organizations were saying, 'Don't push Obama. He is our friend. Go and push Congress.' But we said, '*We already did that!*'"

Jimenez continues:

> We talk to creative legal minds and immigration experts, who
> advise us to pressure Obama to take an administrative action
> and to stop deportations. That is when we went against some
> civil rights leaders and more conventional or older activists. We
> launched our campaign that included a National Day of Action,
> with rallies, marches, and protest across the nation. We mobilized

thousands of youths, used social media to tell our stories,
brought together allies such as labor leaders and the faith sectors.
Ultimately, this led to the victory of DACA in 2012—the first
major immigration policy in over 25 years!

Torres notes how young activists are redefining an old tradition: "Every
movement requires moderates and radicals. An insider like President
Lyndon Johnson needed an outsider like Dr. Martin Luther King. And
a moderate like Dr. King needed a radical like Malcolm X. And it's the
creative tension between the insider and the outsider game, the creative
tension between moderates and radicals, that creates the conditions for
social transformation."

He continues, "I am an insider, but I need activists on the outside to
create space for me to move the ball forward as much as I can on the
inside. And that gives me leverage. The outside game can expand the
realm of what is politically possible on the inside. I think an older generation might view it as a nuisance. The younger elected officials celebrate the
value of the outside game. Because you wouldn't be sitting in that seat if it
wasn't for the outside game."

 *"It's the creative tension between the insider and the
outsider game, the creative tension between moderates
and radicals, that creates the conditions for social
transformation."*

—Ritchie Torres

Using Technology to Multiply Impact

OK, young Latinos, run to your computers and look up "mimeograph
machines." In the early sixties, this was a coveted tool of community
organizers. We would crank it up and print flyers. Then we would
post them on bulletin boards, speak at meetings, and go door to door

spreading the good news. Making Xerox copies replaced this, but all and all, community organizing was a labor-intensive, on-your-feet process. Technology, especially the internet, social media, and cell phones, has revolutionized social change and movement politics.

Torres explains, "The tools are different. We're living in a time when you're one hashtag away from sparking a social movement on Twitter: #Me too, #I can't breathe, #Black Lives Matter. Millennials and Gen Z are masters at harnessing the power of social media to elevate political causes. Demonstrations that would have taken years to organize can now emerge spontaneously overnight."

Margolin met the three cofounders with whom she planned the national day of mass action, to protest inaction on climate change, on the internet. In less than a year, they virtually organized twenty-five sister cities, from Los Angeles to New York and internationally. The Washington, DC, marchers met with lawmakers to push for the Green New Deal. These actions led to founding Zero Hour, which advocates for climate justice and has partner chapters around the world, including in Australia, Brazil, Colombia, India, and Spain. Utilizing technology, these activists are uniting support for youth-led climate activism globally.

Stephanie Valencia describes herself as a "digital strategist" and is "at the nexus of politics, technology, and leadership." She is a founder of EquisLabs, a virtual organization that tracks online information on Latinos and holds social media platforms accountable on Latino content.[39] The aim is to provide digital and communications support to Latino organizations to massively increase civic participation and power. While Latino leaders have worked on this for generations, the use of technology to grow "Latino media ecosystems" can explode the influence of the growing Latino demographics.

As a long-term community organizer, I am in awe of the larger scope and impact that young Latinos are having through the internet and social media. Jimenez underscores this: "Our generation 'lives' the internet and has access to a much larger number of people. With UWD, for example, we were touching about 5 million people every month. There is a much larger number of people aware of what is happening."

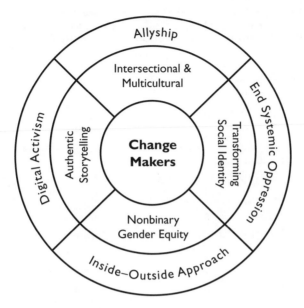

Young Latinos Leadership

Young Latinos are infusing their community with new vision, energy, and drive. They are revitalizing Latino activism and bringing it into a modern context. As Congressman Maxwell Frost advised the Democratic Party, "I think our party shouldn't be afraid of talking about bold, transformational change, things that maybe we won't get tomorrow. It's what we're fighting for. It's the world we (young people) believe in."[40]

¡Ahora! Reflection and Application

Understanding Four Generations

Review these brief descriptions of the four generations living and working together today. Then complete the exercise. This can help generate the understanding and respect needed for intergenerational leadership.

Characteristic	Baby Boomers	Generation X	Millennials	Generation Z
Birth year span	1946–1964	1965–1979	1980–2000	2001–2020
Communication	Face to face; adapting to technology	Technology savvy	Technology wired	Digital natives
Personal orientation	Competitive and team oriented	Self-reliant and skeptical	Confident/ collaborative	Diverse, global, and progressive
Job preference	Job loyalty, status/ symbols	Flexible/informal workplace	Entrepreneurial/ social responsibility	Self-direction and interdependence
Work style	Workaholic	Entrepreneurial/ Flexible	Rewrite the rules; achievement oriented	Innovative and creative
Motivation	Health and wellness	Life–work balance	Family and friends first	Collective action; mutuality

Source: "Generational Differences in the Workplace [Infographic]," Purdue Global, https://www.purdueglobal.edu/education-partnerships/generational-workforce-differences-infographic.

Born in Different Times: Group Exercise

Form groups based on generation and discuss these questions:

What makes your generation unique?

What major global or social events impacted your generation? Events or trends?

What significant contributions has your generation made, or hope to make?

If the group does not include all four generations, people can role-play to represent the views of their parents, grandparents, and older or younger friends and discuss characteristics of the generations these people came from.

Generational groups report back and learn from each other.

What did you learn about the unique characteristics of the four generations?

How has this broadened your understanding of how generations can work together?

What challenges, connecting points, and learning opportunities might hinder generations in working together? What suggestions do you have to address this?

Intergenerational Leadership

Review the dynamics that make intergenerational leadership an imperative today. Why is this particularly crucial for Latinos?

Young Latinos are forging a new social identity that is multicultural, global, and nonbinary.

What is your personal reaction to the identity transformation that is taking place? Do you think this is beneficial?

How will this change transform America's monocultural identity as a White, heterosexual society?

Why is this change fundamental for increasing inclusion and diversity today?

The Change Makers

An uncertain future and generational inequalities are driving young people to be change makers and to work for social justice. While they are building on the Latino tradition of *Sí se puede*, list the ways in which their activism differs from and expands the work of previous generations.

Strategies for Social Justice

How would you describe "Leading with an intersectional approach," built on the understanding that multiple forms of discrimination—racism, sexism, homophobia—combine, overlap, and intersect?

How does intersectionality address systemic and institutionalized racism?

What is the difference between an ally and a mentor? Why are young people seeking allyship and how would this promote partnerships across generations?

Group Activity

As described, an insider-outsider approach has been an effective change strategy. As a group, brainstorm historical examples of this approach (think about the civil rights movement in the 1960s and 1970s). Now note examples of how younger generations are using this strategy to promote change.

Technology has multiplied community organizing and social action. What examples were provided of this? What else have you observed about how technology advances social change?

Does this chapter give you hope for *el futuro*, and if yes, why? Please make this an affirmative statement: "I am hopeful about el futuro because . . ."

CHAPTER 12

Gozar la Vida: Leadership That Celebrates Life!

I TELL FRIENDS THAT I sometimes get on my knees and just thank God I was born Latina, because it is so exciting and so much fun. Latinos introduced the word *fiesta* into our society! In a "we love people" culture where resources have been scarce, it's easy to gather folks together. Everyone brings something (we have to eat anyway), the music starts playing, and . . . ¡Orale! Everyone is having a good time!

My working-class family didn't have *dinero* for vacations, eating out, or entertainment. My parents didn't have hobbies or leisure time. Their good times centered on their children, outings to parks, church events, and family celebrations. Like many other Latina *madres*, however, my mom had a knack for making everyday things fun.

Although my mother worked five days a week in the school lunchroom and Sundays at the church nursery, on Saturday, her day off, she would organize a "housecleaning party." With salsa music blaring, my brothers, my sister, and I would find ourselves washing walls, sweeping the sidewalk, vacuuming, and making everything spick-and-span. Housework was a family affair. My sister Margarita called us the Busy Beaver Club. My mother loved *música*, dancing, and singing. She was a fantastic cook who could s-t-r-e-t-c-h a single chicken to feed a whole tribe. She stayed positive and happy during hard times because her deep-rooted philosophy of *gozar la vida*—to enjoy life—was grounded in her spiritual beliefs.

Mi madre taught me a valuable leadership lesson, which I found again in Rich Castro, a civil rights activist who began his political career as a fiery campus radical and was elected at twenty-five to the Colorado state legislature. During the 1970s, when Hispanic political power was just budding, he became one of Colorado's most significant leaders.[1] Today an elementary school and a city building bear his name. A bust of him sits in the state capitol, and the University of Denver awards the Richard T. Castro Fellowship each year. Yet he was only forty-five when he died of an aneurism. How could he touch so many people in such a fleeting time?

Yes, Rich served ten years in the legislature, was a key ally of Denver mayor Federico Peña, ran a city agency, and contributed to the emergence of countless organizations, but that still doesn't explain the special place he held in people's hearts. Rich was intelligent and always willing to help people, and he lived for his community. He also had a hilarious sense of humor, *corazón*, and *pasión*. He truly loved people and made the hard work of civil rights engaging and fun. The *personalismo* that encourages self-expression was certainly evident in the life of Rich Castro.

Rich often dressed up in a dark suit, with sunglasses and a black fedora hat. He and his coworker Michael Simmons, who headed up Denver's Youth Commission, would entertain *gente* with rocking renditions of songs by the Blues Brothers. Rich also talked a group of high-level leaders into forming the Latino Temptations to sing hits like "Get Ready" and "My Girl." When I asked Rich why he did this, he said, "People have to have a good time if you want them to keep doing the hard work. And they must be able to laugh at you, to see you are not taking yourself too seriously. This way they know you are one of them."

Today when I teach leadership, one of my adages is "Nobody wants to follow an uptight leader or one who stresses people out!" Making work fun is a key dynamic of Latino leadership and one that was first taught to me by my mother and was truly lived by my friend Rich Castro.

"People have to have a good time if you want them to keep doing the hard work. And they must be able to laugh at you, to see you are not taking yourself too seriously. This way they know you are one of them."

—Richard Castro

A Cultural Tradition

THE CULTURAL TRADITION OF *gozar la vida* can be found in the oh-so-good-for-you salsa, the spicy, hot condiment giving food flavor and bringing zing to the palate. Since each batch of salsa is different, it is a good metaphor for Latino diversity. And yes, salsa is also a dance. But remember, *salsa is also a way of life*—the spice, the energy, vitality, and gusto! Salsa is a communal celebration to be shared with *familia* and *amigos*. One bowl with everyone dipping their chips puts a little gusto into life. Salsa reflects the culture's festive nature, so beautifully contained in gozar la vida, enjoyment of life, relationships, work, and community.

Life can be difficult, and like a seesaw has ups and downs. For minorities who have struggled economically and have not always been validated for their contributions, life can be even more trying! For immigrants separated from their families, for migrant workers, or for children starting school not knowing *inglés*, life can be difficult indeed! The feeling of not belonging can be disorienting and defeating. Latinos have faced all of these obstacles, but they are still dancing, singing, celebrating, enjoying their families, and having more fiestas than any other group in America.

The *banda* is blaring, people are conversing at full throttle, waving their hands and making expressive gestures. Everyone is talking at the same time. The noise level is decimals above a nice Anglo cocktail party where people are chatting. Latinos are loud! Bright colors, spicy food, and having fun are relished. Latinos commemorate many occasions by entertaining family and friends. Consumer studies confirm this tendency: Latinos spend more money on food than other groups and tend to grocery shop with a family member, making it a communal experience.[2] And while they are at the store, they might check in with folks, since Latinos also have the highest cell phone usage.[3]

Of course, nothing says celebration like *musica*, which is a revered tradition. The love of music is supported by a Nielsen report that noted Latinos spend more on music than any other group in the United States.[4] And you can find Latinos at the movies, since they attend more movies than any other group at the theater![5] Talk about Latinos enjoying life, family, celebrations, and fiestas!

Gozar la vida fashions a celebratory leadership process. This tradition reaches back to the Indigenous people of the Americas, who had many community celebrations and festivals that honored the change in seasons, rites of passage, and people's special feats and accomplishments. Community celebrations strengthen bonds, bolster collective identity, and create communal memories.

Similarly, the highly sociable Spanish are devoted to their *días de fiestas*—a one-week community celebration where everyone eats, drinks, and dances together. Main streets close as people promenade dressed in red and white, which adds to their sense of camaraderie. Días de fiestas are a community vacation. Everyone is off at the same time and public funds are set aside to pay for bands, parades, fireworks, and entertainment. Bread, sausages, wine, sardines, and coffee are free on special days. Since each town has its días de fiestas, some of the folks attending come from other places. *No importa*—if you are there, you are welcome to share in the food and festivities. (Another antecedent of Latino inclusiveness and the *bienvenido* spirit.)

Like their Indigenous and Spanish ancestors, Latinos will find any excuse for a fiesta: hosting visitors; celebrating births, baptisms, birthdays, anniversaries, Holy Communion days, or *quinceañeras* (when a girl reaches fifteen); getting a new job, moving to a new place, getting a promotion, or retiring. Although Anglos celebrate similar life events, the

Latinos' large extended family, which is more like a tribe, makes fiestas into community celebrations. For hundreds of years, it was the propensity for gozar la vida that shaped the optimistic, hopeful, and festive nature of the culture and its leaders.

Leadership as Celebración

In Celia Cruz's last recording, the venerated salsa diva sang, "Ay, no hay que llorar, porque la vida es un carnival." No need to cry, because life is a carnival. La vida can be difficult, but it is still an amazing and festive journey. Just imagine how this good counsel uplifts people when they are having a crisis, don't have enough money, or are dealing with social inequities.

In a *cultura* that regenerates through fiestas and celebrations, gozar la vida flavors the leadership process with congeniality, so that it includes good times and laughter. Before and after any gathering or meeting, a social window must be opened to allow people to connect and communicate. Like good cooks, Latinos are stirring the gusto into leadership.

Leaders make tasks exciting, meaningful, creating a chance to work with friends and to make new ones. Commemorating group achievements and individual contributions, recognizing anniversaries and birthdays, all are ways to celebrate people. A hard-and-fast rule is to celebrate small and large wins, and always serve food. Young Latino leaders are in sync with this tradition. Maxwell Frost, who served as the national organizing director for March for Our Lives to protest gun violence, uses the power of celebration, "Not just holding protests and registering young people to vote, but bringing in artists, cultural leaders and other influencers to make political engagement appealing to a younger crowd."[6]

In a cultura that regenerates through fiestas and celebrations, gozar la vida flavors the leadership process with congeniality, so that it includes good times and laughter.

Young Latino leaders are in sync with this tradition. Mijente, which was discussed in chapter 10, formed a partnership with Cumbiatón, an intergenerational cultural movement, which uses music as a vessel to heal and uplift oppressed communities. People can download "Yo Perreo Solx," a Spotify playlist for young activists, or attend music venues where they can move to the rhythms of Selena, Shakira, Bad Bunny, Rosalía, and Daddy Yankee as a way to keep walking and dancing on the long road to justice.

Remember the old business adage "You don't need to like someone to work for him"? Well, my answer has always been "Yeah, but wouldn't it be a lot better to like or even love and admire them?" Great Latino leaders care about their people, and in turn, they are loved by their communities. Dora Valdez was once asked about her husband's close relationships with people. "It was very simple," she sighed. "Bernie loved his people. And his people loved him."

The love of socializing, dancing, and sharing food is even evident in many national Latino conferences, which are always headlined by several popular singers or music groups. Lunches might feature a jazz *conjunto* or *mariachi* group. Conferences close with a big fiesta. Many Latino dances are with partners, so people get up close and personal even at business events. Yes! People dance with their leaders. Intergenerational aspects are also evident, since young and old dance together. Conferences still have information, learning opportunities, and workshops, but just as important (and maybe even more) are venues for sharing good times, seeing friends, and strengthening relationships.

Communicating with Carisma and Cariño

Indigenous people pass on values and history through storytelling. The Spanish are loquacious and expressive. Rooted in both cultures, Latinos cherish the oral tradition. Integral to gozar la vida is the ability to *charlar* (converse)—to express feelings, share appreciation, and get up close and personal with people. Latinos are a talk, talk, talking group that loves chatting about ideas, interests, dreams, plans, and people. Being able to converse is part of being *simpático*, a great leadership asset.

Communication is essential in a community that centers on getting things done through people. Leaders assume many communication roles: as translators, storytellers, community scholars, dream makers, consensus builders, cultural brokers, and the voice of the people. Let's look at how leaders leverage their ability to converse in a heartwarming, inspiring, and convincing manner.

Being able to charlar—to make small talk and friendly conversation—is the prelude to any leadership action! A leader must understand the Latino experience and culture and speak the people's language and not use fancy or technical terms. Raul Yzaguirre says, "When I speak to Latinos, if I say a *dicho*, it resonates. Or if I speak a few words in Spanish, and it's genuine and relevant, it establishes a bond. People know I understand where they come from because of my background. I have lived with many of the same issues they have, so I can connect and use this as a springboard. I know the levers that attract Latinos and can get a response from them."

Being able to converse is part of being simpático, a great leadership asset. Communication is essential in a community that centers on getting things done through people.

On a collective level, since the community is still in the identity-formation stage, leaders must traverse the diversity of Latinos, communicating with recent immigrants, grassroots people, youth and elders, as well as educated professionals, and speak to their common elements. They must be able to talk with diverse Latino groups, help them identify commonalities, find consensus, and agree on collective action.

Leaders are storytellers who share the lessons about the courageous deeds that have kept Latinos moving forward and who integrate history into the present. Thus, young people connect to their roots and take pride in their community's accomplishments. Building on the successes of yesterday, leaders help people believe in the possibilities of tomorrow. Latino leaders are thus dream makers, sharing a vision of what could be and pointing the way for collective advancement of culture.

Leaders function as community voices speaking in a strategic, convincing, and culturally appealing manner. They are translators, ensuring that the interests and concerns of the Latino community are represented in mainstream culture and that partnerships are built with mainstream groups. Finally, they serve as "community scholars," reaching out and bringing information and knowledge to people in a way that they can understand and utilize.

As we know, leadership has a community-organizing and social-change orientation. Because of limited resources, leaders can't compensate people with money, special perks, or pork barrel rewards. Community leaders must find other ways to inspire and unify people. Two revered ways they do this is through *carisma* (charisma) and *cariño* (affection).

Con Carisma

Latinos value emotion, self-expression, and spontaneity. They admire charismatic leaders who speak with passion and conviction. Carisma is the ability to convey ideas with influence and persuasion, so people are moved to action and overcome doubts and difficulties. "Carisma," reflects Carlos Orta, "is the ability to use your charm, your wits, and personality to get people to do what you need them to do. Charismatic leaders are positive and likable."

Yzaguirre frames carisma as inspired leadership: "When people are asked to take something on, there is no concrete reward. They have to be motivated, not ordered around. It just won't happen without inspired leadership—being able to encourage folks to take on perhaps an impossible task, against what might seem like insurmountable odds, is the ultimate leadership task."

The fiery and powerful Janet Murguía has a special knack for stirring a crowd. She often starts in the oral tradition, with the story of her parents: "They were two people with very few means, from a small town in México, who worked very hard, sacrificed much, and dedicated themselves to the education of their family and service to their community." Then she speaks to the obstacles they overcame. "In Kansas City in the fifties, when my parents went to the movie theater, they had to sit in a separate section. My father, other Latinos, and persons of color had to use a separate bathroom at the steel plant where he worked." With this story, she has touched people's *corazónes*.

Since carisma can move a crowd to action, people must be assured that the leader is motivated by service to her community and their well-being. By developing conciencia and preparing themselves, leaders temper this special talent and ensure that their carisma is not serving their own agenda.

"Carisma is the ability to use your charm, your wits, and personality to get people to do what you need them to do. Charismatic leaders are positive and likable."

—Carlos Orta

Con Cariño

By expressing affection, or cariño, leaders establish personal relationships, which supports the *We* and the familia focus of Latinos. Cariño is the emotional current connecting people with their leader. In a world where many feel isolated and alienated, expressing cariño is a special contribution Latinos make. Leaders demonstrate how truly caring for people and seeing them as familia holds people together during difficult times and makes the journey more enjoyable.

As a contact culture, Latinos are comfortable with physical closeness, touching, and self-expression. Leaders are expected to relate in this manner and to have close interactions. Many Latinos, for instance, don't shake hands; they give each other *abrazos*—warm hugs. Leaders routinely embrace and kiss people and give them warm abrazos. Traditionally, Latinos kissed each other on both cheeks when greeting each other—a custom that is evident in Spain today.

The warmth and affection Bernie Valdez showed toward people aligns with the concepts put forth by Asociación Española de Personalismo (personalismo.org), which emphasizes the dimensions of feelings and affection. The association promotes the belief that the heart rather than the intellect is the key element in human relationships. They stress the relevance of love.

Love? Now there is a concept that would transform communities and leadership theory! A congenial, charming, charismatic leader that is *muy simpático* and makes followers feel loved is the Latino ideal!

Cariño is the emotional current connecting people with their leader. In a world where many feel isolated and alienated, expressing cariño is a special contribution Latinos make.

Expressing Feeling—Living with Corazón and Pasión

A GREAT WAY TO EXPRESS cariño is by sharing *sentimientos*, or feelings. Emotions and feelings are the joy of life—a way to show love to family and friends. Feelings join people together. The prominence of feelings and passion is one of the distinctions between the Latino culture and the Anglo-Saxon one. Sentimientos influence the way Latino leaders relate to their people, and reflect a different philosophy of life.

Suppressing one's feelings would stifle the flair, gusto, and passion that bring color, vibrancy, and amiability to the culture. Since feelings and emotions are so cherished, I distinctly remember sitting in my college philosophy class when suddenly my mind shattered like falling glass as we studied René Descartes—one of the fathers of modern philosophy (*European* philosophy, that is). I instinctively knew that his renowned quote "I think, therefore I am" was not on point! But how does a nineteen-year-old immigrant from the back hills of Nicaragua validate her belief that "I *feel*, therefore I am" when she is up against seventeenth-century rationalism?

Many years later, I went to España. On the very first *noche* (night), at a fiesta, a dashing Spaniard approached me. After the customary niceties I asked, "What do you think is the main distinction between US culture and the Spanish?"

"Yo siento, ergo soy," he replied, as if he had been waiting all his life for someone to ask this question. The shattered glass became a mirror in which I could see myself clearly. *I feel, therefore I am.*

Descartes saw the mind and body as separate. As an integrative culture, Latinos tend not to compartmentalize but rather to embrace mind, body, and heart (feelings), as well as spirit, as glorious aspects of life. Sentimientos are charged energy and light life's fire—the source of *ganas* (desire)! Feelings spring from the ever-powerful subjective, or right, brain, the source of vision and inspiration. And feelings allow people to gozar la vida and to nurture close relationships!

Cultures that are more intellectually oriented and self-contained may be uncomfortable or think that Latinos are "hot blooded," volatile, or overreacting when they express their feelings. Ideas and opinions may appear emotionally charged. Several studies confirm this tendency: Latinos who respond to surveys are more likely to choose the extreme response categories (*strongly agree, strongly disagree*) than the middle categories, to a greater degree than Euro-Americans.[7]

Sentimientos Are Good for You

Latinos are a touchy-feely culture and they convey this by drawing physically closer and being more likely to touch during a conversation. Something to consider is that expressing sentimientos is actually good for you. Keeping emotions bottled up negatively impacts health, well-being, relationships, and longevity. Emotions are tied to the autonomic nervous system, which controls the heart rate, blood pressure, digestion, respiration, and perspiration.[8] Feelings signal that something is happening that we should attend to. We know our hearts beat faster when we are excited. The challenge for leaders is using this energy to nurture relationships as well as to get results.

Living La *vida Latina* means tapping into the wellspring of our emotions, so we can enjoy better health and lead more fulfilling lives.

Expressing positive *sentimientos* can bring happiness and joy to our lives and to people around us. Daniel Goleman, in his revolutionary book *Emotional Intelligence*, relates that learning to express feelings can have a larger impact on living successfully than our intelligence quotient.[9] People from backgrounds where expressing emotions is not encouraged might find that learning to share feelings is one of the advantages to becoming a Latino by corazón, or affinity. (This process is described in more detail in chapter 13.)

Passion has been described as a powerful and compelling feeling. Antonia Pantoja, a charming, courageous, and charismatic leader, urged people to tap into this energy: "One cannot live a lukewarm life. You have to live with passion!" Leadership experts James M. Kouzes and Barry Z. Posner urge leaders to "encourage the heart," because this will provide the emotional fuel to inspire and motivate.[10] Latino leaders bring this passion to their work—a fire ignited by their love of people, commitment to social justice, and desire to improve life for future generations.

"One cannot live a lukewarm life. You have to live with passion!"

—Antonia Pantoja

Achieving a Cultural Balance

STRATEGIC THINKING, PROBLEM SOLVING, and the ability to analyze and synthesize information are key leadership functions that require objectivity. These actions often necessitate a mental separation from a problem or group. This can sometimes be difficult for Latinos because the culture is feeling- and process-oriented and centers on *We,* or the collective, and not the *I,* or the individual. Closer connections and identification with people can make separating oneself and being objective more challenging.

Another consideration is that many leaders have traveled the path of social activism. Their sense of urgency can be unfamiliar to people who come from the majority or from an affluent group. The many needs and challenges in the Latino community drive its leaders to want action now—*¡ahora!*—not on a more comfortable timeline. The stakes are high! This may lead to the perception that they are too emotional or too pushy and perhaps do not have good manners or know protocol. Latino leaders must learn to step outside of their emotionally centered culture, channel their feelings, and moderate their expressiveness and tone of voice when dealing with the majority culture. They must step out of their collective cultural field.

The leaders interviewed for this *libro* have acquired these skills—all have advanced degrees from prestigious universities. Julián Castro, Anna Cabral, and Janet Murguía have law degrees, which taught them to integrate the analytical, strategic, and problem-solving abilities of mainstream leadership with the passion, feeling, and celebratory tendencies of Latino leadership.

The final chapter proposes that *Latino destino* (our unique contribution) is to build a diverse and humanistic society. Because of our history and evolution as a Mestizo, mixed people, Latino leaders can bring others into the multicultural, global age and create authentic inclusion. We can promote humanistic values that put people first and promote responsibility for the welfare of others.

To accomplish this, leaders must empower the Latino community to reach its potential and invite others to join us in creating a caring and inclusive society. I will suggest ten strategies to further this work. In keeping with our bienvenido spirit, non-Latinos are invited to become Latino by corazón, or affinity. We will look at the acculturation process, which allows everyone to become cultural adaptives and to fully partake in our increasingly diverse society and world.

¡Ahora! Reflection and Application

Communication is essential for all leaders, but it is a lifeline for a culture of oral tradition and for leaders who get things done through people.

Communicating Latino Style

Carisma, cariño, corazón, pasión, and sharing sentimientos generally are not associated with mainstream leadership. Yet for Latinos, this is the bond, the glue, the energy that keeps people together. (Hey non-Spanish speakers, look at all the words you understand! *Felicidades!*—Congratulations!)

> What benefits do you perceive in leaders having an emotional connection with their people? (Let's put this in context of Latino leadership and not demagoguery.)

> Review the roles Latino leaders assume—as translators, storytellers, community scholars, dream makers, consensus builders, cultural brokers, and the voice of the people. Discuss how these roles help leaders connect, communicate with, and bring people together. How do these roles foster collective action?

Experiencing Latino Leadership as Celebration

We learned that Latinos regenerate and keep moving forward by celebrating life. Now it's time to *experience* our festive and optimistic culture. While not many leadership books contain musical suggestions, I would be remiss as a Latina not to include this cultural bastion. I use music and dance in all my programs and presentations as interactive, kinetic, and team-building techniques.

So, sit back, relax, grab a *cafecito*, *aqua fresca*, or *cerveza* and listen to the music below, which embodies the Latino experience.

"Canta y no Llores" (Sing Don't Cry) is a lullaby sung to me by *mis padres* and to many, many *niños*. The message is singing makes you happy and assuages difficulties.

Celia Cruz was hailed as the queen of salsa. Her last song was "La Vida Es un Carnival" (Life Is a Carnival). It was both celebration and a social activism anthem about tackling war, weapons, pollution, and health.

Marc Anthony's song "Vivir Mi Vida" (Live My Life) is full of Latino optimism, joy of living, and overcoming obstacles.

Keep your Latino groove on by listening to Joan Baez's rendition of "De Colores," or Santana's song "Everything Is Coming Our Way." And popular with younger generations is Pitbull's "Don't Stop the Party." Being Latino is a celebration of life!

PART V

Latino *Destino*

OUR MULTICULTURAL NATION IS RAPIDLY emerging. Yet building a truly diverse and equitable society necessitates a new vision of inclusiveness. When the Constitution was written, only White male property owners were allowed to vote. Black men, as slaves, were counted as only three-fifths of a person, and women could not vote until the passage of the Nineteenth Amendment in 1920.[1] Because Hispanics were considered "White," they theoretically could vote, but as we know, they did not have an official US designation until the 1980 census. Birthing our multicultural society requires uprooting this race-based view of our country and embracing a more encompassing and equitable vision of our humanity.

A premise of this book is that Latinos, because of their inherent diversity, demographic prominence, and *bienvenido* spirit can guide our transformation to a multicultural society. I refer to this as Latino *destino*—the unique contribution Latinos will make to the Americas.

As we have learned, Latinos are a culture, not a race, and since culture is learned there is the potential to invite people to partake in the many facets of *Latinidad* (the Latino experience). People who connect to our culture and values can become Latinos by *corazón*, or affinity. Not exclusion, but inclusion. This would turn America's race-based consciousness upside down!

This process is not new to Latinos. Most of us already have extended *familia* that are not Latino by birth and include *amigos* who are not blood related. Our extended familias are elastic and stretch to welcome others. And then, of course, Latinos are the only group that self-identifies, which facilitates the *entrada* into culture because it is not based on race or bloodline. And the bonus is once a person becomes a Latino by corazón, they become a cultural adaptive—a person who can respectfully acknowledge and adopt beneficial behaviors, values, and reference points from different cultures. This is a coveted skill for our multicultural future!

Furthermore, Latino humanistic values emphasize social responsibility, a needed attribute in fashioning a society that embraces not only diversity but also equity, a society that genuinely cares for (and takes care of) its people. Our final chapter, "Latino *Destino*: Building a Diverse and Humane Society," summarizes ten strategies Latinos can use to move us closer to creating this society.

Our journey ends with an intriguing vision put forth by Mexican philosopher José Vasconcelos more than one hundred years ago: la Raza Cósmica—the Cosmic Race. His vision foresaw the mixing of the four major groups of humanity into a new familia that combined the best characteristics of all the races. As we have noted, multicultural identity is proliferating particularly among young people.

This indicates that Vasconcelos's prophesy is happening *Ahora!* Latinos are already the fusion of many cultures and celebrate *de colores*—the radiant rainbow of humanity. Latino destino is to lead the multicultural transformation of our society and to actualize the vision of la Raza Cósmica.

CHAPTER 13

Latino *Destino*: Building a Diverse and Humane Society

S TARTING SCHOOL NOT SPEAKING *inglés* was my first foray into the Anglo world. My teachers seemed cold and distant, had strange rules, and did not hug or touch the children. And the food tasted bland. Before the civil rights movement, America was white bread. I never saw a Latino in any professional position or as a teacher, bus driver, or even a clerk in a nice store. The schools stripped children of color of their cultures and taught the history, norms, and values of the dominant society. Like most children, I wanted to be accepted, and the path to success was assimilation. I learned to read and write inglés and even forgot *mucho español*.

When I became a teenager, there was no Catholic *escuela* (school) on the outskirts of Tampa, where we lived. This did not deter *mi madre* for *un minuto!* She boarded a bus with me in tow and journeyed across town. Humbly, she entreated the mother superior at the Academy of Holy Names to give her daughter a scholarship. The mother superior agreed to half a scholarship. Every Sunday, my mother and I would get up at 5 a.m. to babysit children at church during the five Masses to earn the remaining tuition.

My senior year I found out many of my classmates were going to college. That sounded like a great idea! My parents immigrated here so I could get a good education. But mi madre, with a fifth-grade education, thought high school was *una buena educación*. The University of Florida was only 120 miles away, but to my parents, that was as far as their distant homeland. Seeing my determination, however, my parents, in their loving and humble way, gave me their blessing.

In the early 1960s, being a Latina at a university was a Lone Ranger experience. Well, I knew how to fit in—I had learned it in grade school. I started highlighting my father's French ancestry, denied my fabulous Nicaragüense-ness, my rich Indigenous and Spanish roots, and my immigrant experience. I dressed and acted like the other students and even joined a sorority. I assimilated.

Human beings are group oriented—we want to be part of the tribe. I became accepted, but I had an empty feeling inside. You see, when my *abuela* came to visit, I couldn't talk to her. Many Hispanics in my generation have felt this deep loss.

What's in a name? A person's identity, culture, and family roots. In my generation many teachers could not pronounce Spanish names. Eduardo became Eddie, Jaime became James, and Marisól became Mary. I was called Jeanne because my parents thought an English name would be easier on me (and more American). They were chagrined when, in my twenties, I insisted on being called Juana. Anglicizing a child's name was a common practice. Today, however, García is the sixth-most-common surname in America, with Rodriquez at number nine.[1] Martinez is number ten, making mi abuela Ella Martinez *muy contenta!*

Raul Yzaguirre observes, "The road to success that has been offered is to assimilate, change your name, and lose your accent. All those things hold an empty promise that will result in a hollowing out. *Te quita el corazón*—it rips out your heart."

"The road to success that has been offered is to assimilate,
change your name, and lose your accent. All those things
hold an empty promise that will result in a hollowing out.
Te quita el corazón—it rips out your heart."

—Raul Yzaguirre

Assimilation—Becoming Homogenized

THE ASSIMILATION WOUND IS not just a Latino phenomenon. Immigrants have always struggled with this conflict. If your *familia* has been here for generations, you might not remember, but your European great-grandparents felt this loss as they stepped away from Ellis Island or when they realized their grandchildren did not speak Italian, Russian, or German. Like my *padres*, they wanted their children to learn *inglés* and be successful. But cutting one's ancestral roots can leave a deep psychological scar.

Assimilation melded one people out of the myriad nationalities that came to our shores, integrated our national character, and unified our young country. At the same time, the melting pot set the tone for a country where conformity and homogeneity fed ethnocentricity. This in turn bred cultural insensitivity and a predisposition to impose our values on others. The understanding that all cultures are unique expressions of the human experience was as lost as the languages our grandparents spoke.

As our country becomes Latinized and multicultural, assimilation is no longer an adaptive advantage. Today, people need to acculturate—to be receptive, skillful, and able to adapt to many cultures. Unlike assimilation, in which one's culture, language, and background are discarded, acculturation is an add-on process. Acculturation increases one's cultural repertoire, adaptability, flexibility, and cross-cultural competence.

Pero un momento—wait a minute! Can people who have assimilated choose to acculturate and become cultural adaptive? *Sí!* Yes! I know because this happened to me in my early twenties.

As our country becomes Latinized and multicultural, assimilation is no longer an adaptive advantage. Today, people need to acculturate.

Becoming a Cultural Adaptive

FOR A FEMALE IMMIGRANT from a low-income family to obtain a college degree in the early 1960s was as rare as the tiny quetzal bird that floats in the tropical rain forests. Why was I given the prize of a higher education? What was I supposed to do with my life? During my soul searching, President John F. Kennedy was shot. Kennedy was an inspiration to my generation and revered by Latinos as a charismatic, socially responsible leader who resonated with our values.

Inspired by his call to public service, I told my dear padres, "I'm joining the Peace Corps." *Ay, Dios mío!* If going 120 miles away to college was a cultural storm, going to the other side of the world was a Category 5 hurricane. Telling me I could always come home, mi familia watched as their petrified yet excited youngest daughter boarded a plane for Santiago, Chile.

In my assimilated stupor, I thought I was going to help those backward countries south of the border. Imagine my shock to find that Santiago had an old European flavor, with flowered *avenidas* surrounding stately museums and government buildings. Chile was the second-oldest democracy in the Western Hemisphere, with highly educated citizens. President Eduardo Frei was Hispanic, as were the senators, mayors, presidents of Chilean universities, TV station directors, the heads of its army and navy, and executives of every business. And, of course, their historical figures were Hispanic as well.

Growing up in the good old USA in the 1950s, I had no idea someone of my culture could achieve such high-level leadership. In my childhood, successful people were without exception White, which is still true for most leaders in top positions. I realized then that while the land of opportunity had given many gifts, my history and culture had been stripped like the lost city of the Inca.

Thus began the redemption of my Hispanic soul. I embraced my Latina heritage. This did not diminish the gratitude I had for my adopted homeland. In fact, it enabled me to make a greater contribution. I chose the path of acculturation and became a cultural adaptive. Raul Yzaguirre passionately believes this is essential: "Hispanic success, for both practical and pragmatic reasons, as well as for esthetic, self-fulfilling, self-actualizing reasons, the quality and the meaning of life—for all those reasons—needs to be 'I treasure who I am. I treasure who my parents were, my culture, my language, and I don't have to give any of that up in order to succeed. Indeed, if I keep all those things, it will make me more successful in practical terms as well as in self-fulfilling terms.' Latinos have a unique contribution to make to America. We can't do that if we give up our cultural core—that which makes us who we are."

"Latinos have a unique contribution to make to America. We can't do that if we give up our cultural core—that which makes us who we are."

—Raul Yzaguirre

Bienvenidos: Latinos by Affinity y *Corázon*

YOUNG LATINOS TODAY DO not have to assimilate to be successful. In fact, the Latinization of America implies that adaptation is now a two-way street. Latinos are learning how to be successful in the mainstream culture and at the same time are bringing their cultural assets to enrich America.

For people who are not Latino or multicultural, or for those who assimilated, as I did, there remains the opportunity to acculturate. I am referring to an acculturated person as cultural adaptive—a person who adopts beneficial behaviors, values, and reference points from a variety of cultures.

The Latino culture offers the most user-friendly way to do this because the door is open for a person to become a Latino by *corazón*, or affinity! Let's summarize why becoming a Latino by corazón is the easiest way to become culturally adaptive!

1. Since Latinos come from many nationalities and races, they learn to acclimate to many subgroups. A Latino group (or extended familia) might include a Puerto Rican, a seventh-generation Hispanic from New Mexico, and a newly arrived Venezuelan. In Latino organizations, many nationalities and backgrounds work side by side, so diverse people will be welcomed and find a home.

2. Cultural adaptability was a survival mechanism for Latinos, who learned at an early age how to succeed in a White culture, like I did. Latinos who now work in mainstream organizations can model the benefits of being adept in more than one culture.

3. Latinos are Mestizos—cultural hybrids with a long history of integrating cultures, races, and nationalities. Fusion defines their identity. Latinos can serve as prototypes for becoming multicultural.

4. Inclusiveness and *bienvenido* are cultural treasures ingrained in values such as being hospitable, *simpático*, and generous. This opens the door for people to experience cultural immersion and acclimation.

5. The elastic familia, where close friends become "relatives," is an ancient Latino custom. *Comadres* and *compadres*, *tías* and *tíos*, *madrinas* and *madrinos*, *primos* and *primas* (good friends, honorary aunties and uncles, godparents, and adopted cousins) become family not just by blood ties but also through shared experiences, values, and a history of contributing to others.

I am referring to an acculturated person as cultural adaptive—a person who adopts beneficial behaviors, values, and reference points from a variety of cultures.

By becoming a Latino by corazón, people step out of their cultural conditioning. Jessica Smith served in the Peace Corps in Guatemala. Heather Tang taught in Chile for two years. Janelle Wilkins was an exchange student in Spain. Reid Lawrence was a Hispanic studies major at William and Mary College. They are all Latinos by corazón and actually have a "Hispanic" personality. When speaking español, they wave their hands, talk faster, and are more animated and expressive. Of course, a person doesn't have to go to these lengths; just by reading this book you are immersed in the Latino culture and leadership. *Felicidades!* You are on your way to becoming a Latino by corazón and a cultural adaptive who can form affinities with other groups.

Let's acknowledge that with changing demographics and increasing diversity, many people are already cultural adaptives. Cultural fluidity is a defining characteristic of the millennials and Zs who see themselves as a multicultural generation. They revel in the music, style, slang, and social values of many cultures. They love the variety, excitement, and richness diverse cultures bring.[2]

Likewise, people who grew up in multiethnic neighborhoods, lived in a foreign country, married into a family from a different tradition, learned a foreign language, or served in the Peace Corps have become cultural adaptives.

Regardless of their ethnic or racial antecedents, people can acculturate into diverse cultural modalities. People of color who have mainstreamed can choose to come back to their origins. My own experience in reconnecting to my Latina soul is personal testimony to the power that acculturating brings. The door to partake in the cultural smorgasbord and Latino buffet is open. ¡Bienvenido! Come on in!

Ten Strategies to Actualize Latino Destino

WE HAVE SURMISED THAT Latino destino is building a humanistic and diverse society. Below are ten strategies to further this vision and address key issues. It is important to recognize that several national Latino organizations have missions to specifically address these and can be contacted for additional information and resources.[3]

1. Capitalize on Latino Inclusiveness, Hospitality, and Diversity

Why wouldn't people want to join in? The Latino culture offers community, celebration, hope, and a people-centered vision for the future. We have an international flair and good old-fashioned values. People today are hankering for belonging and meaning. A few generations ago we lived in intact communities and had large extended familias. Latinos can revitalize these traditions. Our hospitality and bienvenido spirit welcome Latinos by corazón to participate in our generous culture.

Furthermore, an inclusive America can heal the divisions that exist today and bring people together to work for a stronger, more representative, and just democracy. Latino destino will weave equity and inclusion into the American fabric.

2. Strengthen Cultural Pride and Unity

A Pew Study on Latino identity found that 7 in 10 Hispanics in the United States (69 percent) believe they come from many different cultures, while only 29 percent believe they share a common culture.[4] A premise of this book is that Latinos are a culture of synthesis. Because of this complexity, leaders need to create opportunities for conversation and dialogue so Latinos can forge a shared identity and recognize cultural connection points. This is particularly crucial for emerging and young leaders.

Janet Murguía urges Latinos to bear this in mind: "There's a sense of connectedness across our ethnic roots, and that connectedness is our strength. We have common bonds and values that we share. We should unify around those, because when we are separated or divided, we are not a strong community." A key function of Latino leaders is to assist people in finding these common bonds, to identify shared history and values, and to take pride in the accomplishments of the past. Chapter 4, "*Conciencia*," noted seven strategies to achieve cultural unity and understanding.

"There's a sense of connectedness across our ethnic roots, and that connectedness is our strength. We have common bonds and values that we share."

—Janet Murguía

3. Connect and Work with Young Latinos

As discussed in chapter 11, young Latino leaders have a vision for a new world that is multicultural and global and welcomes the wide spectrum of gender identity. They are revitalizing Latino activism, infusing new vision and energy, and take pride their Latino identity. Yet because of their sheer numbers, there is a need to reach out to millions of young Latinos, connect them to their culture and history, and provide the skills, training, and experience they need to be successful. As we have seen, young leaders have started organizations that reflect their priorities and operate in a way that aligns with their generation. Digital activism, addressing systemic oppression, and an intersectional approach are driving factors.

Established Latino leaders and organizations must cultivate an intergenerational leadership force that leverages the power of our youth. They must work hand in hand, recognizing their role as allies and partners. Many Latino organizations have youth-serving programs and initiatives. Now is the time to bring Latino millennials and Zs to the table and ensure that these programs reflect their priorities, ways of operating, and leadership practices. Organizations must allocate resources to involve and empower youth as partners in Latino empowerment, including them at all levels and positions.

4. Integrate Immigrants into the Latino Community

Thirty-three percent of US Latino population growth in the last decade was due to immigration. Leaders continue the ongoing work of assisting the newly arrived and helping them become part of their new country. More than 52 percent of young Latinos (ages sixteen to twenty-five) identify themselves first by their family's country of origin, be it México, Cuba, the Dominican Republic, El Salvador, or other Spanish-speaking countries.[5] This is in keeping with the tendency among Latino adults, a majority of whom identify with their national origin as well.[6] This means that immigrants are acculturating and bringing their national identity with them—an asset in our global community and economy.

Yet today there is anti-immigrant sentiment, and Latinos know that any person who "looks" Hispanic can be discriminated against. According to a 2018 Federal Bureau of Investigation report, hate crimes against Latinos rose more than 21 percent in that year.[7] Many Latinos see immigration as one of the civil rights issues of our times, and young leaders have made immigration reform central to their change agenda. Immigration has galvanized and unified Latinos. Leaders must continue reaching out and providing services that bring immigrants into the Latino mainstream and push for a humane immigration policy. This is an area where young Latino immigrants—the Dreamers—have taken the lead.

5. Empower Latino Organizations

"Latino leaders," notes Carlos Orta, "are committed to the cause. They fully engage and bring a passion to their work. The edge we have is that we are not going to waffle." As president of the Hispanic Association on Corporate Responsibility, Orta orchestrated a coalition of fourteen of the largest national Latino organizations. He is describing the long-term commitment leaders have to fortifying strong organizations that represent Latino interests.

Latinos have advanced because national organizations advocated for change. Young Latinos continued this tradition and have formed organizations that tackle issues plaguing their generation such as United we Dream, Mijente, and Voto Latino. The challenge today is to bring the myriad organizations together to work as an united front that focuses squarely on growing Latino representation and leadership. For a community with many needs and limited resources, organizations have the influence and the power to represent Hispanic interests. Growing and supporting our organizations is key to Latino empowerment.

"Latino leaders are committed to the cause. They fully engage and bring a passion to their work. The edge we have is that we are not going to waffle."

—Carlos Orta

6. Galvanize Economic Power and Entrepreneurial Strength

Latinos are entrepreneurial and are the fastest-growing segment of small businesses in the country. As the 2020 census noted, Latinos accounted for 80 percent of new businesses in the past decade, employed more than 3 million people, and contributed approximately $700 billion to the economy annually.[8] These businesses are using the coalition-building model to come together and create local Hispanic chambers of commerce throughout the nation. Julián Castro, who served as US secretary of Housing and Urban Development, underscores the benefit to our country: "I believe that Latinos have a wonderful opportunity to renew the entrepreneurialism spirit of our country." And let's not forget small businesses are the backbone of the US economy.

Because 70 percent of Latinos are working class and wages have stagnated in the face of rising prices and inflation, there is a strong need for leaders to push for a living wage and benefits for all Americans. LULAC was started to protect workers' rights, and Latino organizations that followed were formed to promote equity and justice. Today's growing economic gap beckons Latinos to continue fighting for economic equity and to join with other organizations and communities of color that have a similar agenda.

7. Grow Latino Political Power

If you were on the streets for the 2020 presidential campaign, you would have seen a beehive of Latino activity. The lead-up to Election Day saw massive efforts to reach the Latino community, from candidates, political parties, and community organizations. Registering and getting people to vote is a priority across Latino subgroups and organizations.

Voto Latino has registered more than a million Latinos, and the number of Latino voters in the 2020 election increased by nearly 30 percent over the 2016 presidential election, making them 13 percent of eligible voters, with a record 16.5 million voting.[9] The 2022 midterm elections resulted in fifty-one Latinos in the US Congress—an increase of 168 percent since 2001.[10] The numbers of Hispanic voters in the United States are projected to surpass the numbers of Whites and other non-Hispanics in the coming decade. There is much work to be done to grow political power. The organizations started by young Latino leaders can take the lead, since youth will make up the largest share of the Hispanic electorate.[11] They understand the issues that impact their lives, such as climate change, college debt, immigration, and job security, can only be resolved through voting and the political process.

8. Build Coalitions and Partnerships with Other Groups

We have noted that the Latino leadership principle of social activism and coalition building—*Sì se puede*—is based on the critical mass theory of social change and urges engagement with other organizations and communities. Most Latino organizations—LULAC, UnidosUS, HACR, Latina Institute—are coalitions that bring grassroots and community organizations together to exercise collective power.

Now is the time to expand this model and form coalitions with other groups. Cid Wilson, the president and CEO of the Hispanic Association on Corporate Responsibility, is a premier partnership builder and works with the Black Executive Forum, Catalyst (focused on women's empowerment), and Leadership Education for Asian Pacifics to further their shared agenda—the economic empowerment of women and communities of color. As an Afro-Latino from the Dominican Republic, Cid also serves as a gateway to strengthen partnerships with African American organizations.

While Latino leadership focuses on coalitions and partnerships, lasting coalitions with non-Latino groups have usually been issue oriented and not long term. It would seem natural that Latinos, with their expansive inclusiveness, could form strong coalitions with other communities and thus leverage the power such unity brings. Some believe that because minority groups compete for scarce resources or scramble to form alliances with Whites, they do not naturally coalesce, even though many of their issues are the same. Latino leaders must discern the reasons long-term coalition building has not succeeded, reach out, find common ground, and use their coalition-building skills to bring diverse groups together, particularly with regard to women.

9. Bolster Connections Between Latinas and Women in Other Communities

Women make up more than half of our society. Their political engagement is key to our future well-being as a democracy. Having worked with women for many decades, I understand the difficulties of nurturing organizations that truly represent women's issues from a Latina perspective. The early women's movement of the 1970s and 1980s had a social agenda that included health care, quality education, pay equity, and of course women's advancement. Starting in the 1990s, the mainstream feminist movement took a turn and focused more on individual success and women's issues than on social change. (For White women, this represents their *I* or individualistic cultural orientation.)

Then, with the historic women's march in 2017, which rallied against the Donald Trump presidency, this began to change. Cofounded by a diverse group of women, the march was a coalition of people of color, immigrants, the LGBTQ community, civil rights activists, and others. With the current challenge to women's reproductive rights, many women are speaking out and realizing the urgent need for concerted and collective action.

Latina feminism has always had a social-change agenda that centers on uplifting the familia and the *comunidad*—not just women. Our feminism follows the activism and community stewardship of Latino leadership. Because Latinas and other women of color remain on the front lines fighting for equality, they can reinvigorate the women's movement to be advocates and activist for building the humane and just society.

10. Embrace Latino Destino

The genesis of our multicultural society began long ago, with the conquest and settling of this hemisphere, where many races, cultures, ethnicities, and nations were unwittingly brought together. While we have acknowledged the anguish and near genocide this entailed, the fact is that through this encounter racial and ethnic mixing occurred, and today, five hundred years later, we stand on the threshold of a multicultural transformation.

Latinos are the prototype for this transformation. Our inclusive bienvenido spirit welcomes differences. As an "open enrollment culture," we invite people to come together, embrace a multicultural identity, and honor the many traditions that make up our country. To create this inspiring tomorrow is the essence of Latino destino!

To prepare for this great calling, Latinos must forge a strong identity, cultivate a collective agenda, coalesce our growing numbers, and embrace our destiny as leaders of the multicultural transformation. Latino Destino is calling us! Ahora! Now is the time for Latinos to embrace the unique contribution they will make to humanity!

Alcanzamos! We Will Get There!

WORKING TO REALIZE THESE ten strategies will build a new America—one with inclusiveness and people-centered values as its core. The Latino bienvenido spirit welcomes people to join us in creating this future. Janet Murguía believes we will get there. "Hard work, determination, faith, a good education, and humility helped us get to where we are today, and these are the same values that will allow us to chart our own course and to realize the American dream."

Latinos must forge a strong identity out of our immense diversity, cultivate a collective agenda, coalesce our growing numbers, and embrace our destiny as the leaders of the multicultural transformation that is rising.

¡Ahora! Reflection and Application

Assimilation—Acculturation Continuum

Assimilation is not an adaptive advantage in our multicultural society. Fortunately, people can learn to acculturate and become cultural adaptives. Where would you rate yourself on this continuum?

Assimilation						Acculturation				
− 5	− 4	− 3	− 2	− 1	0	+ 1	+ 2	+ 3	+ 4	+ 5

Associations center on White culture	Many diverse cultural associations
Minimal experience with other cultures	Actively seeks diverse cultural experiences
Desire to fit in, conform, accept White norms	Learns to adapt White culture
Belief that the White way is superior	Cultural flexibility—benefits of diversity
English only	Supports language acquisition/ bilingualism
Accepts White leadership as the norm	Values and applies diverse leadership

Where are you on this continuum and why did you rate yourself in this manner? Discuss your perception with others, especially people not from your own culture and background. Think about ways to take actions that would increase your cultural adaptability.

Bienvenido! Welcome to Latinos by Corazón

Becoming a Latino by corazón is the user-friendly way to become a cultural adaptive. List three reasons you are (or aspire to be) a Latino by corazón, and three benefits derived:

I love the Latino culture because: Benefits:

Uno:

Dos:

Tres:

Note: We are looking for deep cultural benefits such as values or contributions—not food or music.

Ten Strategies to Actualize Latino Destino

Review the ten strategies that are a call to action to work toward and engage others in actualizing Latino destino—the transformation to our multicultural, equitable, and humanistic society.

Pick the top 3 strategies that motivate you. Note that specific populations (such as women, youth, people of color, immigrants, or entrepreneurs) might resonate with you. Now let's design a mini action plan to get you started and keep you going.

First, pick your three strategic areas:

1.

2.

3.

Second, reflect on these questions:

Why is this important and motivational for me?

Who do I know is engaged in this work?

Who could help identifying people?

What organizations could I contact and work with?

Third, complete the mini plan:

Interest area:

How might I contribute?

Three or four activities/steps to get started:

How will I measure success?

La Bendición—la Raza Cósmica

I N THE EARLY TWENTIETH century, a prophetic and far-reaching vision of humankind's future was put forth by the renowned Mexican educator, philosopher, and politician José Vasconcelos. He believed that humanity would evolve into a new familia that combined the best characteristics of all four major racial groups. He envisioned this as la Raza Cósmica—the Cosmic Race. Vasconcelos believed that the confluence of many cultures and races will result in a richer and more radiant genetic stream and enrich humanity.[12]

The genesis of this vision is rooted in our past. In the beginning there was only one race. Genetic anthropology, which combines DNA and physical evidence to reveal the history of human migration and ancestry, documents how people evolved from the same human family. We all emerged from the same primordial spring! Our common ancestry ties us together.

Writing at a time when American imperialism and the belief in White superiority was on the rise, and twenty years before the concept of Germans being a "superior" race, Vasconcelos was summoning a different vision of human evolution, one that encompassed the beauty and the richness of racial and cultural integration.

This was almost four hundred years after the appearance of Our Lady of Guadalupe, but his vision embellishes the prophecy first heard on the rocky hill at Tepeyac. La Raza Cósmica is based on the expansive inclusiveness Guadalupe expressed: "I am your merciful mother, yours and all the people who live united in this land and all the other people of different ancestries."[13]

And remember the Aztec black belt she wore? To the Aztec this symbolized that she was pregnant.[14] Vasconcelos's vision supports the belief that the child Guadalupe was carrying was the Mestizo, the mixed-race progeny of the future—those who would become today's Latinos and tomorrow's multicultural children, a radiant genetic stream that would bring together the richness of humanity.

The concept of la Raza Cósmica offers an enticing future: that of the multicultural family. In 2002, the Hopi Indian elders came forth with a similar prophesy. They believed that in these times a universal tribe would be born, a rainbow people who would represent the iridescent beauty of humanity. They would heal the earth, bring peace and understanding, and undo the damage caused by previous generations. Then the elders said, "The time is now. . . ."[15] Ahora!

The concept of la Raza Cósmica offers an enticing future: that of the multicultural family.

There is a growing understanding today that we are intricately connected and interdependent, moving us closer to accepting the concept of la Raza Cósmica—the cosmic race and universal tribe. The belief that we belong to one human family is the core of Christianity and most of the other world religions. The address to "*Our* father" at the beginning of the Lord's Prayer affirms that people are one spiritual family.

These same sentiments are found in the song "De Colores," which rejoices in the beautiful colors of the birds, the flowers, the rainbows, and yes, our multicolored humanity! The song inspires us to love people and all their many colors.

The emergence of a *de colores* America will be a defining characteristic of the twenty-first century. Because of Latinos' inherent diversity, Latino destino is to build this multicultural society. As we embark on the good work of creating this noble future, we welcome Latinos by corazón into the familia. We walk hand and hand with our young people. We commit to creating a society that cares for all people. We celebrate de colores—the incredible beauty of life's diversity.

The emergence of a de colores America will be a defining characteristic of the twenty-first century. Because of Latinos' inherent diversity, Latino destino is to build this multicultural society.

Notes

Preface

1. Jen Manuel Krogstad, Jeffrey S. Passel, Luis Noe-Bustamante, "Key Facts about US Latinos for National Hispanic Heritage Month, Pew Research Center, September 23, 2022, https://www.pewresearch.org/fact-tank/2022/09/23/key-facts-about-u-s-latinos-for-national-hispanic-heritage-month/.

2. William H. Frey, "The US Will Become 'Minority White' in 2045, Census Projects," Brookings, March 14, 2018, https://www.brookings.edu/blog/the-avenue/2018/03/14/the-us-will-become-minority-white-in-2045-census-projects.

3. Nia-Malika Henderson, "Latino Mayor to Keynote DNC Convention," *Washington Post*, July 31, 2012, http://www.washingtonpost.com/politics/latino-mayor-to-keynote-dnc-convention/2012/07/31/gJQA3fpqNX_story.html.

4. UCLA Latino Policy and Politics Initiative, "Latino Voters Were Decisive in 2020 Presidential Election," UCLA, January 19, 2021, https://newsroom.ucla.edu/releases/latino-vote-analysis-2020-presidential-election.

5. Suzanne Gamboa, "A Class of Newly Elected Latinos in Congress Sets a Record," https://www.nbcnews.com/news/latino/latinos-record-number-elected-congress-midterms-rcna57943.

6. Glenn Kessler, "Do 10,000 Baby Boomers Retire Every Day?," *Washington Post*, December 7, 2021, https://www.washingtonpost.com/news/fact-checker/wp/2014/07/24/do-10000-baby-boomers-retire-every-day.

7. Stef W. Kight and Sara Kehaulani Goo, "A Decades-Long Blue Wave," *Axios*, November 2, 2020, https://www.axios.com/2020/11/02/blue-wave-decades-biden-democrats.

8. Pew Research Center, "Between Two Worlds: How Young Latinos Come of Age in America," updated edition, July 1, 2013, https://www.pewresearch.org/hispanic/2009/12/11/between-two-worlds-how-young-latinos-come-of-age-in-america.

9. The twenty-six countries include Puerto Rico, which is a commonwealth of the United States. Except for Spain, these were conquered by the Spanish and therefore share a common language and culture.

10. Cary Funk and Mark Hugo Lopez, "A Brief Statistical Portrait of US Hispanics," Pew Research Center, June 14, 2022, https://www.pewresearch.org/science/2022/06/14/a-brief-statistical-portrait-of-u-s-hispanics.

11. Tom Peters, Address to National Association of American Architects, Charlotte, North Carolina, May 2002.

12. Juana Bordas, "Latino Leadership: Building a Humanistic and Diverse Society," *Journal of Leadership and Organizational Studies* 8, no. 2 (Fall 2000).

Introduction

1. Martha White, "As White Boomers Retire, Fast-Growing Latino Labor Will Fill Gaps," NBC News, October 1, 2021, https://www.nbcnews.com/business/economy/white-boomers-retire-fast-growing-latino-labor-will-fill-gaps-n1280592.

2. Jerry Porras, "Latinos: The Force Behind Small-Business Growth in America," CNBC, April 18, 2016, https://www.cnbc.com/2016/04/18/latinos-the-force-behind-small-business-growth-in-america.html.

3. Kathy Kantorski, "US Latino GDP Report: Latinos to the Rescue," *Hispanic Executive*, December 11, 2019, https://hispanicexecutive.com/ldc-latino-gdp-report-lattitude-2019.

4. William Scarborough, "What the Data Says about Women in Management between 1980 and 2010," *Harvard Business Review*, February 23, 2018, https://hbr.org/2018/02/what-the-data-says-about-women-in-management-between-1980-and-2010.

5. Jorge Ramos and Ezra E. Fitz, *The Latino Wave: How Hispanics Are Transforming Politics in America* (New York: HarperCollins, 2009).

6. United States Census Bureau, "Hispanic Origin," July 6, 2022, https://www.census.gov/topics/population/hispanic-origin.html.

7. "Scholarship Connects Chicano, Catholic Identities," review of *The Gospel of César Chávez*, ed. Mario T. Garcia, *The Free Library*, http://www.thefreelibrary.com/Scholarship+connects+Chicano,+Catholic+identities.-a0209618503.

8. "Hispanic Population in the United States, by Country of Origin 2019," Statista, September 2020, https://www.statista.com/statistics/234852/us-hispanic-population. Accessed August 31, 2022.

9. Rachel Marks and Merarys Rios-Vargas, "Improvements to the 2020 Census Race and Hispanic Origin Question Designs, Data Processing, and Coding Procedures," United States Census Bureau, August 3, 2021, https://www.census.gov/newsroom/blogs/random-samplings/2021/08/improvements-to-2020-census-race-hispanic-origin-question-designs.html.

10. Mike Schneider, "Census Shows White Decline, Nonwhite Majority among Youngest," ABC News, June 24, 2020, https://abcnews.go.com/US/wireStory/census-shows-white-decline-nonwhite-majority-youngest-71441394.

11. Luis Noe-Bustamante et al., "4. Measuring the Racial Identity of Latinos," Pew Research Center, November 4, 2021, https://www.pewresearch.org/hispanic/2021/11/04/measuring-the-racial-identity-of-latinos.

12. William H. Frey, "The US Will Become 'Minority White' in 2045, Census Projects," Brookings, March 14, 2018, https://www.brookings.edu/blog/the-avenue/2018/03/14/the-us-will-become-minority-white-in-2045-census-projects.

13. United States Census Bureau, "About the Hispanic Population and Its Origin," April 15, 2022, https://www.census.gov/topics/population/hispanic-origin/about.html.

14. Paul Taylor et al., "When Labels Don't Fit: Hispanics and Their Views of Identity," Pew Research Center, April 4, 2012, http://www.pewhispanic.org/2012/04/04/when-labels-dont-fit-hispanics-and-their-views-of-identity.

15. Luis Noe-Bustamante, Lauren Mora, and Mark Hugo Lopez, "About One-in-Four US Hispanics Have Heard of Latinx, but Just 3% Use It," Pew Research Center, August 11, 2020, https://www.pewresearch.org/hispanic/2020/08/11/about-one-in-four-u-s-hispanics-have-heard-of-latinx-but-just-3-use-it.

Part I

1. World Population Review, "Mexico City Population 2022," https://worldpopulationreview.com/world-cities/mexico-city-population. Accessed August 31, 2022.

Chapter 1

1. Octavio Paz, *The Labyrinth of Solitude* (New York: Penguin, 1990).

2. Carlos Fuentes, *The Buried Mirror: Reflections of Spain and the New World* (Boston: Houghton Mifflin, 1992).

3. "Latin American Network Information Center," *Countries in Latin America & the Caribbean*, http://lanic.utexas.edu/subject/countries.

4. Fuentes, *Buried Mirror*.

5. Fuentes, *Buried Mirror*, 56–73.

6. Erin Blakemore, "Who Were the Moors?," *National Geographic*, December 12, 2019, https://www.nationalgeographic.com/history/article/who-were-moors.

7. Trudi Alexy, *The Mezuzah in the Madonna's Foot: Oral Histories Exploring Five Hundred Years in the Paradoxical Relationship of Spain and the Jews* (New York: Simon & Schuster, 1993).

8. Charles C. Mann, *1491: New Revelations of the Americas before Columbus* (New York: Alfred A. Knopf, 2005), 126–27; "Pizarro Executes Last Inca Emperor," History, https://www.history.com/this-day-in-history/pizarro-executes-last-inca-emperor.

9. Jared Diamond, *Guns, Germs, and Steel* (New York: Norton, 2017), 69–74.

10. Diamond, *Guns, Germs, and Steel*, 211–12, 357–58.

11. Jeanette Rodriguez, *Our Lady of Guadalupe* (Austin: University of Texas Press, 1994), 10–13.

12. Antonio Valerian, "Nican Mojpohua: Original Account of Guadalupe," in Franciscan Friars of the Immaculate, *A Handbook on Guadalupe* (Waite Park, MN: Park Press, 1996), part 11, 194. Translated from the Nahuatl.

13. Virgilio P. Elizondo et al., *Los Católicos Hispanos en los Estados Unidos* (New York: Centro Católico de Pastoral para Hispanos del Norte, 1980), 75–79.

14. Mary Farro, *Our Lady of Guadalupe: Empress of the Americas*, Catholic News Agency, December 11, 2018, https://www.catholicnewsagency.com/news/40124/our-lady-of -guadalupe-empress-of-the-americas. Pope Pius XII declared the Virgin of Guadalupe "Queen of México and Empress of the Americas" in 1945 and "Patroness of the Americas" in 1946.

15. José Ignacio Echeagary et al., *Album Conmemorativo del 450 Aniversario de las Apariciones de Nuestra Señora de Guadalupe* (México: Ediciones Buena Nueva, 1981).

16. Jeanette Rodriquez, *Our Lady of Guadalupe: Faith and Empowerment among Mexican- American Women* (Austin: University of Texas Press, 2001), 30.

17. Elizondo et al., *Los Católicos Hispanos*, 75–79.

18. Rodriquez, *Our Lady of Guadalupe*, 29.

19. "Our Lady of Charity: Patroness of Cuba," Catholic Tradition, http://www .catholictradition.org/Mary/lady-charity.htm.

20. Plinio Correa de Oliveira, "Our Lady Aparecida—October 12," Tradition in Action, http://www.traditioninaction.org/SOD/j227sd_OLAparecida_10-12.html.

21. Paz, *Labyrinth of Solitude*.

22. Rodriquez, *Our Lady of Guadalupe*, 31.

23. Ilan Rachum, "Origins and Historical Significance of Día de la Raza," *Revista Europea de Estudios Latinoamericanos y del Caribe* 76 (April 2004): 61.

Chapter 2

1. Raul Yzaguirre, "Liberty and Justice for All: Civil Rights in the Years Ahead," in *Latinos and the Nation's Future*, ed. Henry Cisneros with John Rosales (Houston, TX: Arte Publico Press, 2009), 28–29.

2. Nicholás Kanellos, "The Latino Presence: Some Historical Background," in *Latinos and the Nation's Future*, ed. Henry Cisneros with John Rosales (Houston, TX: Arte Publico Press, 2009, pp. 15–19.

3. Kanellos, "Latino Presence," 21.

4. Joint Economic Committee, *The Economic State of the Latino Community in America*, US Congress, https://www.jec.senate.gov/public/_cache/files/f16b51b0-5f61-43a6 -9428-8835d0ad6a7c/economic-state-of-the-latino-community-in-america-final -errata-10-15-2019.pdf.

5. Paul A. Janson, "Manifest Destiny and Mission in the 21st Century," History News Network, https://hnn.us/articles/534.html.

6. William Earl Weeks, *Building the Continental Empire: American Expansion from the Revolution to the Civil War* (Chicago: Ivan R. Dee, 1996), 61.

7. Stephen L. Hardin, *The Alamo 1836: Santa Anna's Texas Campaign* (Oxford: Osprey Publishing, 2001).

8. Bill Groneman, *Battlefields of Texas* (Plano: Republic of Texas Press, 1998).

9. S. C. Gwynne, *Empire of the Summer Moon* (New York: Scribner, 2010), 162, 164–65, 167.

10. "'The White Man's Burden': Kipling's Hymn to U.S. Imperialism," History Matters, http://historymatters.gmu.edu/d/5478.

11. Coretta Scott King, *The Words of Martin Luther King Jr.* (New York: Newmarket Press, 1983), 67.

12. William H. Frey, "The US Will Become 'Minority White' in 2045, Census Projects," Brookings, March 14, 2018, https://www.brookings.edu/blog/the-avenue/2018/03/14/the-us-will-become-minority-white-in-2045-census-projects.

13. "Former Spanish Colonies of the World," WorldAtlas, https://www.worldatlas.com/articles/former-spanish-colonies.html.

14. Office of the United States Trade Representative, "Western Hemisphere," https://ustr.gov/countries-regions/americas.

15. Ken Roberts, "It's Official: Mexico Is No. 1 US Trade Partner for First Time, Despite Overall US Trade Decline," *Forbes*, February 5, 2020, https://www.forbes.com/sites/kenroberts/2020/02/05/its-official-mexico-is-no-1-us-trade-partner-for-first-time-despite-overall-us-trade-decline.

16. "Spanish Speaking Demographics in the US," Acutrans, October 8, 2019, https://acutrans.com/a-study-spanish-speaking-demographics-in-the-u-s.

17. Mark Hugo Lopez, Jens Manuel Krogstad, and Antonio Flores, "Most Hispanic Parents Speak Spanish to Their Children, but This Is Less the Case in Later Immigrant Generations," Pew Research Center, April 2, 2018, https://www.pewresearch.org/fact-tank/2018/04/02/most-hispanic-parents-speak-spanish-to-their-children-but-this-is-less-the-case-in-later-immigrant-generations.

18. James Lane, "The 10 Most Spoken Languages in the World," *Babbel Magazine*, June 2, 2021, https://www.babbel.com/en/magazine/the-10-most-spoken-languages-in-the-world.

19. Christina Obolenskaya, "Hispanic Buying Power Rising in US, Bolstering Consumer Sectors," *Insider Intelligence*, December 21, 2021, https://www.insiderintelligence.com/content/hispanic-buying-power-rising-us-bolstering-consumer-sectors.

20. Maria Luisa Arredondo, "Latino GDP in US Ranks 8th in World," *Calexico Chronicle*, November 5, 2021, https://calexicochronicle.com/2021/11/05/latino-gdp-in-us-ranks-8th-in-world.

21. Jerry Porras, "This Is a $1.5 Trillion Force in the US Economy," CNBC, April 18, 2016, https://www.cnbc.com/2016/04/18/latinos-the-force-behind-small-business-growth-in-america.html.

22. Kate Cimini, "'Puro Cash': Latinos Are Opening More Small Businesses Than Anyone Else in the US," *USA Today*, May 23, 2020, https://www.usatoday.com/in-depth/news/nation/2020/02/24/latino-small-business-owners-becoming-economic-force-us/4748786002.

23. UCLA Latino Policy and Politics Initiative, "Latino Voters Were Decisive in 2020 Presidential Election," *UCLA Newsroom*, January 19, 2021, https://newsroom.ucla.edu/releases/latino-vote-analysis-2020-presidential-election.

24. Suzanne Gamboa, "A Class of Newly Elected Latinos in Congress Sets a Record," https://www.nbcnews.com/news/latino/latinos-record-number-elected-congress-midterms-rcna57943.

25. Nate Silver and Walt Hickey, "What Is Americans' Favorite Global Cuisine?," *FiveThirtyEight*, July 25, 2014, https://fivethirtyeight.com/features/what-is-americans-favorite-global-cuisine.

26. Anne Stych, "It's a Wrap: Why Tortilla Sales Are on the Rise," *The Business Journals*, August 29, 2018, https://www.bizjournals.com/bizwomen/news/latest-news/2018/08/its-a-wrap-why-tortilla-sales-are-on-the-rise.html.

27. "What's the Most Popular Condiment in America?," Gilly Loco, September 29, 2016, https://gillyloco.com/blogs/loco-living/what-s-the-most-popular-condiment-in-america.

28. Richard Lapchick, "MLB Race and Gender Report Card Shows Progress Still Needed," ESPN, April 18, 2017, https://www.espn.com/mlb/story/_/id/19185242/mlb-race-gender-report-card-shows-progress-needed.

29. Erika Ardila, "The Growth of Latin Music in the US," *Al Dia*, October 7, 2021, https://aldianews.com/en/culture/heritage-and-history/latin-music-growing.

30. Antonio Gueudinot, "7 Latinos Who Have Won Academy Awards," *Hola!*, February 4, 2020, https://www.hola.com/us/celebrities/20211021324849/oscars-latino-historic-wins.

Part II

1. Lao Tzu, *Tao Te Ching*, trans. Gia-Fu Feng and Jane English with Toinette Lippe (New York: Vintage, 1989).

2. James M. Kouzes and Barry Z. Posner, *The Leadership Challenge*, 6th ed. (Hoboken, NJ: John Wiley and Sons, 2017).

3. Stephen R. Covey, *7 Habits of Highly Effective People* (New York: Simon & Schuster, 1989).

4. Lee Bowman and Terrence Deal, *Leading with Soul: An Uncommon Journey of Spirit* (San Francisco: John Wiley & Sons, 2011).

5. Robert K. Greenleaf, *The Servant as Leader* (South Orange, NJ: Greenleaf Center for Servant Leadership, 2008).

Chapter 3

1. National Alliance for Hispanic Health, *Quality Health Services for Hispanics: The Cultural Competency Component*, DHHS Publication No. 99-21 (Washington, DC: Department of Health and Human Services, 2000).

2. Miguel Corona, "Empowering Hispanic Interns through Personalismo," *Intern Matters*, March 4, 2010, http://internmatters.wordpress.com/2010/03/04/empowering-hispanic-interns-through-personalismo.

3. Andrew Hernandez, Alfred Ramirez, and National Community for Latino Leadership, *Reflecting an American Vista: The Character and Impact of Latino Leadership* (Washington, DC: National Community for Latino Leadership, 2001). No longer in print.

4. Rory Foster, "From Personalismo to Confianza: Building Relationships with Latinos," Common Ground International Language Services, January 26, 2009, http://commongroundinternational.com/from-personalismo-to-confianza-building-relationships-with-latinos.

5. Robert K. Greenleaf, *The Servant as Leader* (South Orange, NJ: Greenleaf Center for Servant Leadership, 2008).

6. Nilda Chong, *The Latino Patient: A Cultural Guide for Health Professionals* (Yarmouth, ME: Intercultural Press, 2002), 24–25, 29.

Chapter 4

1. Robert K. Greenleaf, *The Servant as Leader* (South Orange, NJ: Greenleaf Center for Servant Leadership, 2008).

2. Andrew Hernandez, Alfred Ramirez, and National Community for Latino Leadership, *Reflecting an American Vista: The Character and Impact of Latino Leadership* (Washington, DC: National Community for Latino Leadership, 2001), chapter 3, note 3.

3. Rodolfo Corky Gonzales, "I Am Joaquin," *Latin American Studies*, http://www .latinamericanstudies.org/latinos/joaquin.htm.

4. Peggy McIntosh, "*White Privilege and Male Privilege: A Personal Account of Coming to See Correspondences through Work in Women's Studies,*" *Working Paper 189,* Wellesley Centers for Women, Wellesley, MA, 1988, https://www.wcwonline.org/images/pdf/ White_Privilege_and_Male_Privilege_Personal_Account-Peggy_McIntosh.pdf.

5. Paulo Freire, *The Pedagogy of the Oppressed*, trans. Myra Bergman Ramos (New York: Continuum, 2000).

6. E. J. R. David and Annie O. Derthick, *The Psychology of Oppression* (New York: Springer, 2018).

7. California Department of Education, "César E. Chávez Middle School Biography," http://chavez.cde.ca.gov/ModelCurriculum/Teachers/Lessons/Resources/Biographies/ Middle_Level_Biography.aspx.

Chapter 5

1. Stephen R. Covey, *The 7 Habits of Highly Effective People* (New York: Simon & Schuster, 1989).

2. Norma Carr-Ruffino, *Managing Diversity: People Skills for a Multicultural Workplace* (Andover, UK: International Thomson Publishing, 1996), 41–45.

3. Carr-Ruffino, *Managing Diversity*, 42–43.

4. Juana Bordas, *Passion and Power: Finding Personal Purpose*, 2nd ed. (self-published, 2009).

5. Shirley Griggs and Rita Dunn, "Hispanic-American Students and Learning Styles," *Emergency Librarian* 23, no. 2 (November–December 1995).

6. Zev Chafets, "The Post-Hispanic Hispanic Politician," *New York Times Magazine*, May 6, 2010, http://www.nytimes.com/2010/05/09/magazine/09Mayor-t. html?pagewanted=all.

7. United States Census Bureau, "Quickfacts: San Antonio City, Texas," https://www .census.gov/quickfacts/fact/table/sanantoniocitytexas/LND110210. Accessed September 1, 2022.

8. Steven Greenhouse, "As Labor Secretary, Finding Influence in Her Past," *New York Times*, July 5, 2009, https://www.nytimes.com/2009/07/06/us/politics/06solis.html.

9. Robert Rodriquez and Andres Tapia, *Auténtico: The Definitive Guide to Latino Career Success* (Latino Institute Press, 2017), 18, 20, 23, 154, 233.

10. Joseph Jaworski, *Synchronicity: The Inner Path of Leadership*, 2nd ed. (San Francisco: Berrett-Koehler, 2011).

11. Joseph Campbell, *The Hero's Journey: Joseph Campbell on His Life and Work*, centennial ed., ed. Phil Cousineau (Novato, CA: New World Library, 2003).

12. Greenleaf, *Servant as Leader*.

`13. Covey, *7 Habits*.

Part III

1. Norma Carr-Ruffino, *Managing Diversity: People Skills for a Multicultural Workplace* (Andover: International Thomson Publishing, 1996), 32–38.

Chapter 6

1. Nicole Chavez, "Multiracial Population Grew in Almost Every County in the US. It Doesn't Mean Racism Is Over," CNN, August 15, 2021, https://www.cnn.com/2021/08/15/us/census-2020-multiracial-nation/index.html.

2. Personal communication with Leobardo Estrada, whose focus is on ethnic and racial demographic trends, particularly in the Latino population. The US Bureau of the Census has asked Estrada to provide his knowledge on methodologies related to ethnic and racial groups.

3. Centers for Disease Control and Prevention, "Office of Management and Budget (OMB) Directive no. 15: Race and Ethnic Standards for Federal Statistics and Administrative Reporting," May 12, 1977, https://wonder.cdc.gov/wonder/help/populations/bridged-race/Directive15.html.

4. D'Vera Cohn, "Census History: Counting Hispanics," Pew Research Center, March 3, 2010, https://www.pewresearch.org/social-trends/2010/03/03/census-history -counting-hispanics-2.

5. F. James Davis, *Who Is Black? One Nation's Definition* (University Park, PA: Penn State University Press, 2001).

6. United States Census Bureau, "About the Topic of Race," March 1, 2022, https://www .census.gov/topics/population/race/about.html.

7. Karen R. Humes, Nicholas A. Jones, and Roberto R. Ramirez, *Overview of Race and Hispanic Origin: 2010*, 2010 Census Briefs, C2010BR-02, United States Census Bureau, March 2011, https://www.census.gov/content/dam/Census/library/publications/2011/dec/c2010br-02.pdf.

8. Mark Hugo Lopez, Jens Manuel Krogstad, and Jeffrey S. Passel, "Who Is Hispanic?," Pew Research Center, September 23, 2021, https://www.pewresearch.org/fact-tank/2021/09/23/who-is-hispanic.

9. C. E. Ross and J. Mirowsky, "Socially Desirable Responses and Acquiescence in a Cross-Cultural Society," *Journal of Health and Social Behavior* 25 (1984): 189–97.

10. Robert Rodriguez, *Latino Talent* (Hoboken, NJ: John Wiley & Sons, 2008), 39.

11. Yolanda Nava, *It's All in the Frijoles* (New York: Fireside, 2000), 40–42.

12. Cristina Benitez, *Latinization: How Latino Culture Is Transforming the US* (Ithaca, NY: Paramount Marketing, 2007), 28.

13. James M. Kouzes and Barry Z. Posner, *The Leadership Challenge*, 6th ed. (Hoboken, NJ: John Wiley & Sons, 2017).

14. Kevin Dubina, "Hispanics in the Labor Force: 5 Facts," US Department of Labor Blog, September 15, 2021, https://blog.dol.gov/2021/09/15/hispanics-in-the-labor-force-5-facts.

15. US Bureau of Labor Statistics, "Labor Force Participation Rate of Hispanics at 66.1 Percent in 2017," *TED: The Economics Daily*, September 25, 2018, https://www.bls.gov/opub/ted/2018/labor-force-participation-rate-of-hispanics-at-66-point-1-percent-in-2017.htm.

16. Mark Hugo Lopez, Ana Gonzalez-Barrera, and Jens Manuel Krogstad, "Latinos Are More Likely to Believe in the American Dream, but Most Say It Is Hard to Achieve," Pew Research Center, September 11, 2018, https://www.pewresearch.org/fact-tank/2018/09/11/latinos-are-more-likely-to-believe-in-the-american-dream-but-most-say-it-is-hard-to-achieve.

17. Randall B. Lindsay et al., *Cultural Proficiency: A Manual for School Leaders*, 4th ed. (Thousand Oaks, CA: Sage, 2019), 48.

18. Chavez, "Multiracial Population Grew."

Chapter 7

1. Daniel Goleman, *Emotional Intelligence* (New York: Bantam, 1998).

2. *New York Times*/CBS News poll based on telephone interviews conducted with 3,092 adults throughout the United States, July 13 to July 27, 2003. See Simon Romero and Janet Elder, "Hispanics in US Report Optimism," *New York Times*, August 6, 2003, https://www.nytimes.com/2003/08/06/us/hispanics-in-us-report-optimism.html.

3. Mark Hugo Lopez, Jens Manuel Krogstad, and Antonio Flores, "Key Facts About Young Latinos, One of the Nation's Fastest-Growing Populations," Pew Research Center, September 13, 2018, https://www.pewresearch.org/fact-tank/2018/09/13/key-facts-about-young-latinos.

4. Violeta Parra, "Gracias a La Vida," Lyrics, https://www.lyrics.com/lyric/6739728/Violeta+Parra/Gracias+a+la+Vida.

5. "United Farm Workers' Prayer," National Farm Worker Ministry, April 23, 2009, https://nfwm.org/news/united-farm-workers-prayer.

6. "Education of the Heart: César Chávez in His Own Words," United Farm Workers, https://ufw.org/research/history/education-heart-cesar-chavez-words.

7. Federico Peña, "We Are America," speech delivered in Denver, Colorado, May 1, 2006. Unpublished.

8. "156 Thought-Provoking Quotes by César Chávez That Prove Nothing Is Impossible," Famous People, https://quotes.thefamouspeople.com/cesar-chavez-988.php.

9. Yolanda Nava, *It's All in the Frijoles* (Collingdale, PA: Diane Publishing, 2000), 150–52.

10. Robert K. Greenleaf, *The Servant as Leader* (South Orange, NJ: Greenleaf Center for Servant Leadership, 2008).

Chapter 8

1. Robert K. Greenleaf, *The Servant as Leader* (South Orange, NJ: Greenleaf Center for Servant Leadership, 2008).

2. Federico Peña, *"Not Bad for a South Texas Boy": A Story of Perseverance* (self-published, 2021).

3. James MacGregor Burns, *Leadership* (New York: Harper Perennial, 1978).

4. League of United Latin American Citizens, "LULAC History—All for One and One for All," http://lulac.org/about/history.

5. Latino Policy Forum, *An American Agenda from a Latino Perspective*, April 2008, https://www.latinopolicyforum.org/resources/document/C0589015_LatinosUnited _v3_FINAL_VERSION.pdf.

6. Latino Policy Forum, *An American Agenda*.

7. "American GI Forum," National Museum of American History, https:// americanhistory.si.edu/collections/search/object/nmah_1988707.

8. Peter Miller and Carlos Sandoval, dir., "A Class Apart: A Mexican American Civil Rights Story," *American Experience*, Public Broadcasting Service, February 23, 2009.

9. "Hispanics: A People in Motion," Pew Research Center, January 24, 2005, https:// www.pewresearch.org/hispanic/2005/01/24/hispanic-trends.

10. Rodolfo O. de la Garza and Alan Yang, *Are Cubans Conservative?*, research paper presented at the Symposium on Revisiting the Cuban-American Vote, Florida International University, Miami, November 6. 2013, https://cri.fiu.edu/research/ commissioned-reports/are-cubans-conservative.pdf.

11. Jens Manuel Krogstad, Jeffrey S. Passel, and Luis Noe-Bustamante, "Key Facts about US Latinos for National Hispanic Heritage Month," Pew Research Center, September 23, 2022, https://www.pewresearch.org/fact-tank/2022/09/23/key-facts-about-u-s -latinos-for-national-hispanic-heritage-month.

12. "13 WYAS Hispanic Owners Are Among the Most Generous in Providing Employee Benefits," *Latina Style* Business Series, February 23, 2019, https://bs.latinastyle .com/13-wyas-hispanic-owners-are-among-the-most-generous-in-providing -employee-benefits.

13. Peña, *"Not Bad for a South Texas Boy."*

14. William H. Frey, "Less Than Half of US Children under 15 Are White, Census Shows," Brookings, June 24, 2019, https://www.brookings.edu/research/less-than-half-of-us -children-under-15-are-white-census-shows.

Chapter 9

1. "Hispanic Heritage Month 2010: Sept. 15–Oct. 15," US Census Bureau News, Facts for Features, CB10-FF.17, July 15, 2010, https://www.nrcs.usda.gov/Internet/FSE_ DOCUMENTS/nrcs142p2_015178.pdf.

2. Jeanne Batalova, Mary Hanna, and Christopher Levesque, "Frequently Requested Statistics on Immigrants and Immigration in the United States," Migration Policy Institute, February 11, 2021, https://www.migrationpolicy.org/article/frequently -requested-statistics-immigrants-and-immigration-united-states-2020.

3. Wyatt Clarke, Kimberly Turner, and Lina Guzman, "One Quarter of Hispanic Children in the United States Have an Unauthorized Immigrant Parent," National Researcher Center on Hispanic Children & Families, October 4, 2017, https://www .hispanicresearchcenter.org/research-resources/one-quarter-of-hispanic-children -in-the-united-states-have-an-unauthorized-immigrant-parent.

4. Elaine Kamarck and Christine Stenglein, "How Many Undocumented Immigrants Are in the United States and Who Are They?," *Policy 2020*, Brookings, November 12, 2019, https://www.brookings.edu/policy2020/votervital/how-many-undocumented-immigrants-are-in-the-united-states-and-who-are-they.

5. Jean Kayitsinga, "Latino Population Growth: Community Racial-Ethnic Makeup and Socioeconomic Well-Being in the Midwest," Julian Samora Research Institute, https://jsri.msu.edu/publications/nexo/vol-xxv/no-2-spring-2022/latino-population-growth-community-racial-ethnic-makeup-and-socioeconomic-well-b.

6. Jane Lorenzi and Jeanne Batalova, "South American Immigrants in the United States," Migration Policy Institute, February 16, 2022, https://www.migrationpolicy.org/article/south-american-immigrants-united-states.

7. Kathleen Kennedy Townsend, "Renewing the US–Latin American Alliance for Progress, 50 Years Later," *Atlantic*, September 15, 2011, http://www.theatlantic.com/international/archive/2011/09/renewing-the-us-latin-american-alliance-for-progress-50-years-later/245169.

8. Enrica Detragiache and William J. Carrington, "How Extensive Is the Brain Drain?," *Finance and Development* 36, no. 2 (June 1999), https://www.imf.org/external/pubs/ft/fandd/1999/06/carringt.htm#.

9. Lorenzi and Batalova, "South American Immigrants."

10. Abby Budiman, "Key Findings About US Immigrants," Pew Research Center, August 20, 2020, https://www.pewresearch.org/fact-tank/2020/08/20/key-findings-about-u-s-immigrants.

11. Simona Varrella, "Main Reasons for Hispanics for Immigrating to the United States in 2011," Statista, April 2012, http://www.statista.com/statistics/260454/main-reasons-for-hispanics-for-immigrating-to-the-us. Accessed August 31, 2022.

12. According the 2020 census, there are close to 62 million Latino/Hispanics in the United States and 33 percent of these Latinos are immigrants, making the total 20.46 million.

13. "New Data Shows Immigrant-Owned Businesses Employed 8 Million Americans; Immigrants Wield $1.1 Trillion in Spending Power," New American Economy, March 12, 2019, https://www.newamericaneconomy.org/uncategorized/new-data-shows-immigrant-owned-businesses-employed-8-million-americans-immigrants.

14. David Wessel, "The US in 2050 Will Be Very Different Than It Is Today," *US 2050: Research Summary*, Peter G. Peterson Foundation, https://www.pgpf.org/us-2050/research-summary.

15. Mweinschenk, "The Dependency Ratio: Use This Number to Find Good International Investments," Investment U, October 1, 2019, https://investmentu.com/the-dependency-ratio.

16. "Projections Show Increasing Future Immigration Grows the US Competitive Advantage," FWD.us, April 2021, https://www.fwd.us/wp-content/uploads/2021/02/GMU_V7.pdf.

17. Budiman, "Key Findings."

18. United States Census Bureau, "Hispanic Population to Reach 111 Million by 2060," October 9, 2018, https://www.census.gov/library/visualizations/2018/comm/hispanic-projected-pop.html.

19. Budiman, "Key Findings."

20. Safia Samee Ali, "Arrests of Undocumented Immigrants without Criminal Records Spikes 150%: Report," NBC News, May 17, 2017, https://www.nbcnews.com/news/us-news/arrests-undocumented-immigrants-without-criminal-records-spikes-150-report-n761156.

21. "Polling Update: Americans Continue to Resist Negative Messages about Immigrants, but Partisan Differences Continue to Grow," National Immigration Forum, September 18, 2020, https://immigrationforum.org/article/polling-update-americans-continue-to-resist-negative-messages-about-immigrants.

22. League of United Latin American Citizens, "LULAC History—All for One and One for All," http://lulac.org/about/history.

23. "Immigration Court Backlog Now Growing Faster Than Ever, Burying Judges in an Avalanche of Cases," TRAC Immigration, January 18, 2022, https://trac.syr.edu/immigration/reports/675.

24. Rocio Velazquez Kato, "The Illinois Trust Act a Great Step Forward but Still Misunderstood by Some," Latino Policy Forum, May 2, 2018, https://www.latinopolicyforum.org/blog/the-illinois-trust-act-a-great-step-forward-but-still-misunderstood-by-some.

25. "Immigration," Voto Latino, https://votolatino.org/issues/immigration.

26. Ernest Gundling, Terry Hogan, and Karen Cvitkovich, *What Is Global Leadership? 10 Key Behaviors That Define Great Global Leaders* (Boston: Nicholas Brealey, 2011); Walter Link, Thais Corral, and Mark Gerzon, eds., *Leadership Is Global: Co-Creating a More Humane and Sustainable World* (San Bruno, CA: Shinnyo-en Foundation, 2006). The Global Leadership Network website is https://globalleadership.org.

27. Gundling, Hogan, and Cvitkovich, *What Is Global Leadership?*.

28. Gundling, Hogan, and Cvitkovich, *What Is Global Leadership?*.

29. Gundling, Hogan, and Cvitkovich, *What Is Global Leadership?*.

30. Gundling, Hogan, and Cvitkovich, *What Is Global Leadership?*.

31. *Between Two Worlds: How Young Latinos Come of Age in America*, Pew Research Center, July 1, 2013, https://www.pewresearch.org/hispanic/2009/12/11/between-two-worlds-how-young-latinos-come-of-age-in-america.

32. Ana Gonzalez-Barrera, "About 6 Million US Adults Identify as Afro-Latino," Pew Research Center, May 2, 2022, https://www.pewresearch.org/fact-tank/2022/05/02/about-6-million-u-s-adults-identify-as-afro-latino.

33. Kim Parker et al., "Multiracial in America," Pew Research Center, June 11, 2015, https://www.pewresearch.org/social-trends/2015/06/11/multiracial-in-america.

34. "Critical Mass," Changing Minds, http://changingminds.org/disciplines/communication/diffusion/critical_mass.htm.

35. William H. Frey, "Less Than Half of US Children under 15 Are White, Census Shows," Brookings, June 24, 2019, https://www.brookings.edu/research/less-than-half-of-us-children-under-15-are-white-census-shows.

36. Nicholas Jones et al., "2020 Census Illuminates Racial and Ethnic Composition of the Country," United States Census Bureau, August 12, 2021, https://www.census.gov/library/stories/2021/08/improved-race-ethnicity-measures-reveal-united-states-population-much-more-multiracial.html.

Chapter 10

1. Antonia Pantoja, *Memoir of a Visionary: Antonia Pantoja* (Houston, TX: Arte Público Press, 2002), 61.

2. James M. Kouzes and Barry Z. Posner, *The Leadership Challenge*, 6th ed. (Hoboken, NJ: John Wiley & Sons, 2017), 28–33.

3. Latino Policy Forum, *An American Agenda from a Latino Perspective* (Chicago: Latino Policy Forum, 2008), 1, https://www.latinopolicyforum.org/resources/document/C0589015_LatinosUnited_v3_FINAL_VERSION.pdf.

4. Colorado General Assembly, "Reproductive Health Equity Act," HB22-1279, 2022 Regular Session, https://leg.colorado.gov/bills/hb22-1279.

5. "New Polling on Latino/a Attitudes toward Abortion," National Latina Institute for Reproductive Justice, https://www.latinainstitute.org/en/Latinopoll.

6. Rey W., "To: Mayor Lightfoot and Chicago City Council: Chicagoans Say 'No New CPD Gang Database,'" Mijente, https://action.mijente.net/petitions/chicagoans-say-no-new-cpd-gang-database-in-chicago.

7. Megan Y., "To Mayor Strickland & Tacoma City Council: Close the Northwest Detention Center!," Mijente, https://action.mijente.net/petitions/close-the-northwest-detention-center-release-immigrants-on-bond.

Chapter 11

1. Eileen Patten, "The Nation's Latino Population Is Defined by Its Youth," Pew Research Center, April 20, 2016, https://www.pewresearch.org/hispanic/2016/04/20/the-nations-latino-population-is-defined-by-its-youth.

2. Robert Griffin, William H. Frey, and Ruy Teixeira, "America's Electoral Future," Center for American Progress, October 2020, https://www.americanprogress.org/article/americas-electoral-future-3.

3. Wyatt Clarke, Kimberly Turner, and Lina Guzman, "One Quarter of Hispanic Children in the United States Have an Unauthorized Immigrant Parent," National Researcher Center on Hispanic Children & Families, October 4, 2017, https://www.hispanicresearchcenter.org/research-resources/one-quarter-of-hispanic-children-in-the-united-states-have-an-unauthorized-immigrant-parent.

4. America Counts Staff, "2020 Census Will Help Policymakers Prepare for the Incoming Wave of Aging Boomers," United States Census Bureau, December 10, 2019, https://www.census.gov/library/stories/2019/12/by-2030-all-baby-boomers-will-be-age-65-or-older.html.

5. William Frey, "Now, More Than Half of Americans Are Millennials or Younger," Brookings, July 30, 2020, https://www.brookings.edu/blog/the-avenue/2020/07/30/now-more-than-half-of-americans-are-millennials-or-younger.

6. D'Vera Cohn et al., "1. The Demographics of Multigenerational Households," Pew Research Center, March 24, 2022, https://www.pewresearch.org/social-trends/2022/03/24/the-demographics-of-multigenerational-households.

7. Melanie Hanson, "Average Cost of College by Year," Education Data Initiative, January 9, 2022, https://educationdata.org/average-cost-of-college-by-year.

8. Sarah Min, "Average Americans Can't Afford a Home in 70 Percent of the Country," CBS News, March 28, 2019, https://www.cbsnews.com/news/housing-market-2019-americans-cant-afford-a-home-in-70-percent-of-the-country.

9. Sean Veal and Jonathan Spader, "Nearly a Third of American Households Were Cost-Burdened Last Year," Joint Center for Housing Studies, December 7, 2018, https://www.jchs.harvard.edu/blog/more-than-a-third-of-american-households-were-cost-burdened-last-year.

10. Richard Fry, Jeffrey S. Passel, and D'Vera Cohn, "A Majority of Young Adults in the US Live with Their Parents for the First Time since the Great Depression," Pew Research Center, September 4, 2020, https://www.pewresearch.org/fact-tank/2020/09/04/a-majority-of-young-adults-in-the-u-s-live-with-their-parents-for-the-first-time-since-the-great-depression.

11. Caroline Hickman et al., "Climate Anxiety in Children and Young People and Their Beliefs about Government Responses to Climate Change: A Global Survey," *Lancet Planetary Health* 5, no. 12 (December 1, 2021), https://www.thelancet.com/journals/lanplh/article/PIIS2542-5196(21)00278-3/fulltext.

12. Sarah Simon, "Gen Z Is Increasingly Developing Anxiety about Climate Change," *Verywell Health*, April 19, 2021, https://www.verywellhealth.com/gen-z-climate-change-anxiety-survey-5179490.

13. Alicia Adamczyk, "Millennials Own Less Than 5% of All U.S. Wealth," CNBC, October 9, 2020, https://www.cnbc.com/2020/10/09/millennials-own-less-than-5percent-of-all-us-wealth.html.

14. Annie Nova and John W. Schoen, "Automation Threatening 25% of Jobs in the US, Especially the 'Boring and Repetitive' Ones: Brookings Study," CNBC, January 25, 2019, https://www.cnbc.com/2019/01/25/these-workers-face-the-highest-risk-of-losing-their-jobs-to-automation.html.

15. Board of Governors of the Federal Reserve System, "Distribution of Household Wealth in the US since 1989," August 5, 2022, https://www.federalreserve.gov/releases/z1/dataviz/dfa/distribute/chart/#quarter:122;series:Net%20worth;demographic:race;population:all;units:shares;range:1989.3,2020.1.

16. Eric Greenberg with Karl Weber, *Generation We* (Emeryville, CA: Pachatusan, 2008).

17. Tanya Lewis, "Guns Now Kill More Children and Young Adults Than Car Crashes," https://www.scientificamerican.com/article/guns-now-kill-more-children-and-young-adults-than-car-crashes/.

18. United Farm Workers, "The Story of Cesar Chavez," https://ufw.org/research/history/story-cesar-chavez.

19. Alexis Clark, "The Children's Crusade: When the Youth of Birmingham Marched for Justice," History, January 28, 2021, https://www.history.com/news/childrens-crusade-birmingham-civil-rights.

20. Black Lives Matter, "Herstory," https://blacklivesmatter.com/herstory.

21. "Our Spaces," United We Dream Network, https://unitedwedream.org/who-we-are/our-spaces.

22. Juana Bordas, *Salsa, Soul, and Spirit: Leadership for a Multicultural Age*, 2nd ed. (San Francisco: Berrett-Koehler, 2012), chapter 11, note 7.

23. Frey, "Now, More Than Half of Americans."

24. Nicholas Jones et al., "2020 Census Illuminates Racial and Ethnic Composition of the Country," United States Census Bureau, August 12, 2021, https://www.census.gov/library/stories/2021/08/improved-race-ethnicity-measures-reveal-united-states-population-much-more-multiracial.html.

25. Carmen Ang, "Visualizing the World's Population by Age Group," Visual Capitalist, June 16, 2021, https://www.visualcapitalist.com/the-worlds-population-2020-by-age.

26. Kim Parker and Ruth Igielnik, "On the Cusp of Adulthood and Facing an Uncertain Future: What We Know about Gen Z So Far," Pew Research Center, May 14, 2020, https://www.pewresearch.org/social-trends/2020/05/14/on-the-cusp-of-adulthood -and-facing-an-uncertain-future-what-we-know-about-gen-z-so-far-2.

27. Christine Huang and Laura Silver, "US Millennials Tend to Have Favorable Views of Foreign Countries and Institutions—Even as They Age," Pew Research Center, July 8, 2020, https://www.pewresearch.org/fact-tank/2020/07/08/u-s-millennials-tend-to -have-favorable-views-of-foreign-countries-and-institutions-even-as-they-age.

28. "Guiding Principles," United We Dream, https://unitedwedream.org/who-we-are/ guiding-principles.

29. "Pronouns," Washington State University Gender Identity/Expression and Sexual Orientation Resource Center, https://thecenter.wsu.edu/education/pronouns. According to Merriam-Webster, *they* has also been used to refer to one person whose gender identity is nonbinary. Sam Haysom, "Merriam-Webster Unveils Its Word of the Year for 2019," *Mashable*, December 10, 2019, mashable.com/article/merriam- webster-word-of-the-year-2019; Lianne Koliri, "'They' Named as Merriam-Webster Dictionary's Word of the Year," CNN, December 10, 2019, https://www.cnn .com/2019/12/10/americas/merriam-webster-they-word-year-scli-intl.

30. Eric Duran, "Latino Millennials Least Likely to Identify as Heterosexual, Survey Finds," NBC News, July 23, 2018, https://www.nbcnews.com/feature/nbc-out/latino -millennials-least-likely-identify-heterosexual-survey-finds-n893701.

31. Ritchie Torres, "How Ritchie Torres, Openly Gay Council Member from the Bronx, Came to Live a Life of 'Radical Authenticity,'" *I'm from Driftwood*, https:// imfromdriftwood.com/ritchie_torres.

32. Alexia Fernández Campbell and *National Journal*, "Every 30 Seconds, a Latino Reaches Voting Age. You Read That Right," *Atlantic*, August 26, 2015, https://www .theatlantic.com/politics/archive/2015/08/every-30-seconds-a-latino-reaches-voting -age-you-read-that-right/432627.

33. Jamie Margolin, *Youth to Power: Your Voice and How to Use It* (New York: Hachette, 2020).

34. Alec Tyson, Brian Kennedy, and Cary Funk, "Gen Z, Millennials Stand Out for Climate Change Activism, Social Media Engagement with Issue," Pew Research Center, May 26, 2021, https://www.pewresearch.org/science/2021/05/26/gen-z -millennials-stand-out-for-climate-change-activism-social-media-engagement -with-issue.

35. Margolin, *Youth to Power*.

36. "Guiding Principles," United We Dream Network, https://unitedwedream.org/who -we-are/guiding-principles.

37. Margolin, *Youth to Power*.

38. "Deferred Action for Childhood Arrivals (DACA): An Overview," American Immigration Council, September 30, 2021, https://www.americanimmigrationcouncil .org/research/deferred-action-childhood-arrivals-daca-overview.

39. "Stephanie Valencia," Georgetown University Institute of Politics and Public Service, https://politics.georgetown.edu/profile/stephanie-valencia.

40. Blake Hounshell, "He's a 25-Year-Old Gun Control Activist. Now He's Heading to Congress," https://www.nytimes.com/2022/11/22/us/politics/maxwell-frost-congress -florida.htm.

Chapter 12

1. Richard Gould, *The Life and Times of Richard Castro* (Denver: Colorado Historical Society, 2007).

2. CommSense, "8 interesting Stats about US Hispanic Grocery Shopping Habits," http:// commsense.com/2017/12/hispanic-grocery-shopping-habits.

3. eMarketing Editors, "1.5 trillion Spending Power of US Hispanics Has a Caveat," August 21, 2019, *Insider Intelligence*, https://www.emarketer.com/content/1-5-trillion -spending-power-of-us-hispanics-has-a-caveat.

4. Anna Washenko, "Nielsen: Hispanics Spend More on Music Than the Average Listener," *Rain News*, October 13, 2017, https://rainnews.com/nielsen-hispanics -spend-more-on-music-than-the-average-listener.

5. Motion Picture Association of America, *Theme Report 2019*, https://www. motionpictures.org/wp-content/uploads/2020/03/MPA-THEME-2019.pdf.

6. Blake Hounshell, "He's a 25-Year-Old Gun Control Activist. Now He's Heading to Congress," https://www.nytimes.com/2022/11/22/us/politics/maxwell-frost-congress -florida.htm.

7. Norma Carr-Ruffino, *Managing Diversity: People Skills for a Multicultural Workplace* (Andover, UK: International Thomson Publishing, 1996).

8. Tracy Alston, "Why Expressing Emotions Is Beneficial?," Mental Fitness Matters Blog, August 6, 2020, https://tracyalston.com/why-expressing-emotions-is-beneficial.

9. Daniel Goleman, *Emotional Intelligence* (New York: Bantam, 1998).

10. James M. Kouzes and Barry Z. Posner, *The Leadership Challenge*, 6th ed. (Hoboken, NJ: John Wiley & Sons, 2017).

Part V

1. "The Thirteenth Amendment: The Abolition of Slavery," http://law2.umkc.edu/ faculty/projects/ftrials/conlaw/thirteenthamendment.html.

Chapter 13

1. Neelam, "50 Most Common Surnames in the United States," *Gud Story*, July 10, 2021, https://www.gudstory.com/most-common-surnames-in-the-united-states.

2. William H. Frey, "The Nation Is Diversifying Even Faster Than Predicted, According to New Census Data," Brookings, July 1, 2020, https://www.brookings.edu/research/ new-census-data-shows-the-nation-is-diversifying-even-faster-than-predicted.

3. "10 Latino Organizations You Need to Know," *The Latin Way*, September 2, 2022, https://www.nic.lat/10-latino-organizations-you-need-to-know.

4. Paul Taylor et al., "When Labels Don't Fit: Hispanics and Their Views of Identity," Pew Research Center, April 4, 2012, https://www.pewresearch.org/hispanic/2012/04/04/ when-labels-dont-fit-hispanics-and-their-views-of-identity.

5. Taylor et al., "When Labels Don't Fit."

6. "Between Two Worlds: How Young Latinos Come of Age in America," Pew Research Center, July 1, 2013, https://www.pewresearch.org/hispanic/2009/12/11/between-two -worlds-how-young-latinos-come-of-age-in-america.

7. Brad Brooks, "Victims of Anti-Latino Hate Crimes Soar in US: FBI Report," Reuters, November 12, 2019, https://www.reuters.com/article/us-hatecrimes-report -idUSKBN1XM2OQ.

8. Rohit Arora, "Latinos: A Powerful Force Turbocharging Small-Business Growth and Driving $700 Billion into the US Economy," CNBC, September 25, 2018, https://www .cnbc.com/2018/09/25/latinos-are-a-powerful-force-fueling-small-business-growth -in-the-us.html.

9. "Latino Voter Registration Rates Reached an All-Time High in the 2020 Presidential Election," Center for Latin American, Caribbean, and Latino Studies, May 7, 2021, https://clacls.gc.cuny.edu/2021/05/10/latino-voter-registration-rates-reached-an-all -time-high-in-the-2020-presidential-election.

10. Suzanne Gamboa, "A Class of Newly Elected Latinos in Congress Sets a Record," https://www.nbcnews.com/news/latino/latinos-record-number-elected-congress -midterms-rcna57943.

11. "Latino Voter Registration Rates."

12. José Vasconcelos, *La Raza Cósmica* (Mexico: Espasa Calpe Mexicana, SA, 1948), 47–51.

13. Valerian, "Nican Mopohua," 194, note 11.

14. Mary Fong and Rueyling Chuang, eds., *Communicating Ethnic and Cultural Identity* (Lanham, MD: Rowman & Littlefield, 2004), 112.

15. "We Are the Ones We've Been Waiting For: Prophecy Made by Hopi Elders," University of Minnesota, July 23, 2020, https://artistic.umn.edu/we-are-ones-weve -been-waiting-prophecy-made-hopi-elders.

Glossary

Abriendo Caminos (Opening Pathways)—title of the film about Antonia Patoja

abrazos—embraces

abuela—grandmother

abuelos—grandparents

ahora—now, or do it now!

Alemania—Germany

amigos—friends

¡ándale!—go quickly

antepasados—ancestors

aspira—to aspire

a sus órdenes—at your service

¡Ay, Dios *mio!*—Oh my God!

"*Ay, mi hijita, nunca olvides quién eres y de dénde venistes*"—Oh my dearest little daughter, never forget who you are and where you came from

Ay, no hay que llorar, porque la vida es un carnival—No need to cry, because life is a carnival

banda—band

barrio—neighborhood

bendición—blessing

bien educado—well-educated

bienvenido—welcome

bueno—good or OK

¡caramba!—wow!

cariño—affection

carisma—charisma

caudillo—boss

celito lindo—beautiful heaven

charlar—chat

Chicano—American of Mexican descent

chico—kid

!Claro que sí—Yes of course!

comadre—female friend of the family

compadre—male friend of the family

compartir—to participate

comunidad—community

con gotas se llena el valde—the barrel fills up drop by drop

con permiso—with permission

conciencia—conscience, self-awareness

confianza—confidence

conjunto—set

conquistadores—conquerors

consejo—counsel

consistencia—consistency

corazón—heart

cultura, la—the culture

de colores—of many colors

de—of or from

destino—destiny

días de fiestas—days of festivities

dicho—saying

dignidad—dignity

dinero—money

echando flores—giving flowers

el—the (masculine)

El Día de la Raza—the day of the race (new Latino people of the world)

El Golfo de México—the Gulf of Mexico

El Pueblo de Nuestra Señora la Reina de Los Angeles—the Village of Our Lady, the Queen of the Angels of the River Porziuncola

¿Entiende Ud. español?—Do you speak Spanish? (asked formally)

es tu primo—he's your cousin

España—Spain

español—Spanish

esperanza—hope

es la hora—yes, it's the hour or it's time

está en las manos de Dios—it is in the hands of God

estoy—I am (temporary)

familia—family

fe y esperanza—faith and hope

fuerza—force

futuro—future

igualdad—equality, fairness, and justice

fiesta—party

finca—farm

flores—flowers

frijoles—beans

ganas—desire

gente—people

gozar la vida—to savor life

gracias—thank you

gusto—taste or liking

hacienda—estate

hágalo con orgullo—do it with pride

hermanos—brothers; *hermanas*—sisters

hombre de palabra—man of his word

historia—history

identidad—identity

inglés—English

in Lak'ech—You are in me and I am in you (Mayan)

jamón—ham

juntos—union, we are together

la—the (feminine singular)

La Raza Unida—organization whose name means "the united race"

Latinismo—Latinism

lengua—language

libro—book

isla—island

los—the (masc. plural); las (fem. plural)

los que no trabajan no comen—those that don't work don't eat

madrina—godmother

maestro—master

maíz—corn

mande—tell me what you want me to do

más—more

mestizaje—experience of Mestizo mix

Mestizo—mixture of European (predominantly Spanish) and Indian

mi—my

mi casa es su casa—my house is your house

milagro—miracle

mucho—much

mundo—world

música—music

muy contento/a—very happy

niños—children

no importa—it's not important

¡Órale!—Keep it up! Right on! or Way to go!

padres—parents

padrino—godfather

palabras—words

para servirle—to serve you

partera—midwife

pasión—passion

paso a paso—step by step

personalismo—persona

pico de gallo—a diced chunky salsa; literally, "beak of the rooster"

poder—power

por favor—please

primos—cousins

problema—problem

¡Que viva el español!—Long live Spanish!

¿Que es destino?—What is destiny?

¡Que simpatico!—How easygoing!

rancheros—ranchers and Mexican polka music

Raza, la—the race; best defined as "the new Latino people of the world"

Raza Cósmica, la—the cosmic race

respeto—respect

rico—rich

salsa—sauce

sentimentos—feelings

ser—to be (permanent)

ser honesto—to be honest

Si quieres hablar español, oprima el número—If you speak Spanish, press the number

sí se puede—yes, we can

simpático—easy to get along with

solitas—alone (plural)

soy—I am (permanent)

soy como soy—I am the way I am

Suave—smooth

La vida es un carnival—life is a carnival

te quita el corazón—it rips your heart out

tiempo—time

tilma—a traditional Indian poncho

tía abuela—grandmother aunt

tías—aunts

tíos—uncles

trabajar—to work

último, el—the best, the last

un—a

único—unique

unidos—united

unidad—unity

vámonos—let's go

Valle del Sol—Hispanic organization, literally, "valley of the sun"

vaqueros—cowboys

verdad—true

vida—life

vida Latina, la—the Latin life

yo decido—I decide

yo siento, ergo soy—I feel, therefore I am

In Gratitude—*Gracias*

G RACIAS FOR READING THIS book. You honor me, my ancestors, and the thousands of Latinos who are uplifting our community and country every day. Gracias to those who laid the foundation for the incredible forms of leadership that have allowed Latinos to emerge. Gracias to the many people who embrace *de colores*—the magnificent splendor of our diversity. Most of all, thank you to the young leaders who will come after us. They will realize Latino *destino* and create a caring and inclusive society. They will realize the power of latino leadership.

Gratitude is a cherished Latino trait. Thank you to the many, many *gente* (people) who have helped and guided me in my leadership journey, especially *mi familia*. A special gracias to my talented and dedicated *amigos* for reading and making suggestions on the second edition. Their insights, leadership experience, and contributions have enriched these words. A special acknowledgment to Lynette Murphy and Sylvia Puente for their brilliant contributions. To my grandson, Ishmael Harris, gracias for your insights on how young people lead. And to Dr. Linda Olen, whose wisdom and experience helped shape the reflection and application sections.

To Steve Piersanti, the most inspiring editor in the world, and the Berrett-Koehler staff: thank you for your guidance in shaping this work. Gracias for your dedication in publishing books that are creating a world that works for all. I am blessed with an extended familia like this and am forever grateful.

Index

About the Author

JUANA BORDAS LEARNED LEADERSHIP from her immigrant parents, especially her mother, Maria, who cooked food, washed dishes, and scrubbed floors in the school lunchroom so Juana could get a scholarship to a Catholic school. "Their vision for the future, determination, and sacrifice taught me the very essence of servant leadership."

The first in her family to go to college, Juana joined the Peace Corps and worked in the barrios of Santiago, Chile. In the late 1970s, Juana was a founder and executive director of Denver's Mi Casa Resource Center. She was founding president of the National Hispana Leadership Institute, the only program in America to prepare Latinas for national leadership. In 2001, she launched the Circle of Latina Leadership in Denver. For her extensive work with Latinas, she was commended by *Latina Style* magazine for creating "a nation of Latina leaders."

A former faculty member at the Center for Creative Leadership, Juana served as advisor to Harvard's *Journal of Hispanic Policy* and the Kellogg National Fellows Program. She was vice-chair of the Greenleaf

Center for Servant Leadership's board and a trustee of the International Leadership Association.

Juana received an honorary doctorate from Union University in 2009 and the Lifetime Achievement Award from the International Leadership Association in 2019. She is the first Latina honored with this prestigious award, which has been received by Warren Bennis, Robert Greenleaf, James MacGregor Burns, and Margaret Wheatley.

Juana's best-selling book *Salsa, Soul, and Spirit: Leadership for a Multicultural Age* was awarded the 2008 International Latino Book Award for Best Business Book (English). The first edition of *The Power of Latino Leadership* was also awarded this honor in 2013, and the Nautilus Book Award for Best Indigenous Book.

The *Denver Post* and the Colorado Women's Foundation named Juana the 2009 Unique Woman of Colorado. She also is in the Colorado Women's Hall of Fame (www.cogreatwomen.org/project/juana-bordas).

Juana is president of Mestiza Leadership International, a company that focuses on leadership, diversity, and organizational change. MLI's mission is to prepare collaborative and inclusive leaders for our multicultural and global age.

To learn more and to exchange ideas with Juana, contact:
JuanaBordas.com
Friend on Facebook: facebook.com/JuanaBordas
Follow on Twitter: twitter.com/JuanaBordas
Check out Tia Juana_Bordas on TikTok

Dear reader,

Thank you for picking up this book and welcome to the worldwide BK community! You're joining a special group of people who have come together to create positive change in their lives, organizations, and communities.

What's BK all about?

Our mission is to connect people and ideas to create a world that works for all.

Why? Our communities, organizations, and lives get bogged down by old paradigms of self-interest, exclusion, hierarchy, and privilege. But we believe that can change. That's why we seek the leading experts on these challenges—and share their actionable ideas with you.

A welcome gift

To help you get started, we'd like to offer you a **free copy** of one of our bestselling ebooks:

www.bkconnection.com/welcome

When you claim your **free ebook**, you'll also be subscribed to our blog.

Our freshest insights

Access the best new tools and ideas for leaders at all levels on our blog at ideas.bkconnection.com.

Sincerely,

Your friends at Berrett-Koehler